JAMES JOYCE
REMEMBERED

EDITION 2022

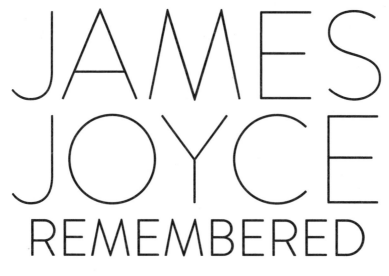

JAMES JOYCE
REMEMBERED

EDITION 2022

C.P. CURRAN

WITH ESSAYS BY
H. CAMPBELL, D. FERRITER, A. FOGARTY,
M. KELLEHER, H. SOLTERER

COLLECTION PRESENTED BY
E. ROCHE & E. FLANAGAN

UCD
PRESS

James Joyce Remembered
Edition 2022

edited by
Helen Solterer
with Alice Ryan

with essays by

Hugh Campbell
Diarmaid Ferriter
Anne Fogarty
Margaret Kelleher
Helen Solterer

the UCD Curran–Laird collection
presented by Eugene Roche and Evelyn Flanagan

A special edition:
with a drawing by Plattenbau Studio

Published by
University College Dublin Press
Preas Choláiste Ollscoile Bhaile Átha Cliath

2022

First published 2022
by University College Dublin Press
UCD Humanities Institute, Room H103, Belfield,
Dublin 4

www.ucdpress.ie

ISBN 978-19-1-0820803

CIP data available from the British Library

Design: Kende Creative | www.kende.ie

Printed in Scotland on acid-free paper by
Bell & Bain Ltd, Glasgow, G46 7UQ, UK

Contents

To my daughter Elizabeth Solterer and to the
memory of my wife Helen

LIBER
CONSTANTINI · CURRAN

PREFACE

Parting from Miss Sarah Purser some years ago on the steps of Mespil House, she broached a fresh subject, for it was still only midnight and she was reluctant to face the empty house. She had been reading O'Flaherty's *Informer* and she failed to recognize in it anything of the Dublin she knew for nearly ninety years. Was it now a city of brothels and pubs? Of course most of the drawing-rooms she had known were closed. They began with her aunt's in Capel Street. There each year the chandeliers were taken down in preparation for the Parliament season and carefully cleaned, crystal by crystal. Of course, she meant Gratton's Parliament. She had known many men of letters and men of action. They were all—even George Moore— quite respectable and her friend Michael Davitt did not frequent pubs. Was the life of Dublin now centred in the Palace Bar? So she gathered from her *Irish Times*. 'But perhaps you do not go there and can't tell me?' She felt chilly and grown old.

I don't know what answer I made but, driving home, my mind turned on the many *Pictures of Dublin* written in the early 1830s, the personal narratives and the later novels from Sheridan Le Fanu and Lever to George Moore and Joyce. Just as the dead kings of France passed into the embalmers' hands and, being eviscerated, their bodies were laid in St. Denis and their noble and ignoble parts divided and distributed throughout the kingdom, so it was with Dublin. The men of letters bend over the dissolving and ever-renewing city; with honey and bitter aloes they stuff their disparate urns. What sarcophagus can hold its volatile spirit? Under which thimble the pea?

In post-war years tales of a turbulent city drew the cross-channel newshawks where also good food and drink were unrationed and talk ran free. The pub crawl was established and—to use a tiresome cliché —a new 'image' of Dublin created. Some old lineaments, however, persisted in the new frame. Presently the newshawks were reinforced by transatlantic expatriates from the prohibition period as well as by serious transatlantic researchers who have made valuable contributions to the study of Irish literature. In the centre of it all there emerged the mythical Joyce. Out of a few pages of his books, out of a few months of his life, out of the preconceptions, as I dare to think, of some of his commentators Joyce in relation to Dublin has been presented in a misleading light. So much of Dublin has been so vividly recreated by the artist that one readily imagines his vignettes to represent the whole. His early contemporaries know they were selective. The artist's omissions were deliberate, not being part of his design. How little, for example, does the Abbey enter into *Ulysses*? The theatre occupied a great share of his mind in his early days. But why should he develop a field already tilled by George Moore, one of his masters, or pursue the theme of his own 'The Day of the Rabblement'?

The pages which follow had their origin in my midnight conversation with Sarah Purser on the steps of Mespil House and in my desire to set down as much as I can accurately remember of Joyce without reference to outside sources. What I have to say has its only value in this independence. There may well be, therefore, inaccuracies, wrong judgements, and certainly the repetition of facts now familiar through other writers.

I have written memories but not memoirs and touched only lightly on the politics of my day. These are now radically and happily outmoded in the Dublin of today. But I have found an autobiographical element unavoidable and have diverged far from my original purpose in attempting to live over again in the climate which Joyce and I once inhabited, and to breathe airs whose currents do not obviously blow through his writing. Count Leopardi, whom I later invoke, thought that a man's pride should not extend beyond his town. I write in vindication of my town and generation and out of 'the attachment', which Edmund Burke approved, 'to the subdivision, the love of the little platoon we belong to'.

Some of this text in one form or another has appeared in *Studies* and *Vogue* and in *A Struggle with Fortune,* as well as in certain broadcasts.[1] My grateful acknowledgement is made for the debt; but most of all I am grateful to Miss Sheila Murphy whose help in every respect has been invaluable, and to Mrs. MacMenamin for the index.

1967

[1] For texts see: C.P. Curran, "James Joyce as Man and Artist," *Irish Times* 14 January 1941; "When James Joyce Lived in Dublin" *Vogue,* 1 May 1947; "Recollections," *Envoy* 5:17 (April 1951); "Memories of University College, Dublin, The Jesuit Tenure, 1883-1908," ed. Michael Tierney, *Struggle with fortune. A Miscellany for the centenary of the Catholic University of Ireland, 1854-1954* (Dublin, 1954); "Joyce's d'Annunzian Mask" *Studies: An Irish Quarterly Review,* 51:202 (Summer, 1962), pp. 308-316.

For broadcasts see: "Texts of talks broadcast by Raidió Eireann on the occasion of Joyce's fifty-sixth birthday. 2 February 1938", National Library of Ireland. *The James Joyce - Paul Léon Papers.* 1930-1940, and "Memories of James Joyce" *Press Conference,* broadcast on RTE, 12 June 1954. RTE Archive

PREFACE

This re-issue of C. P. Curran's *James Joyce Remembered* comes some two generations after he completed it. Readers will discover his text much as it was published then — an artful work of criticism that encompasses his writing over some 30 years. To keep the character of his text as his first public read it, we make only a few, small editorial changes. For example: to translate Ibsen for those of us whose Dano-Norwegian is not up to snuff, to signal passages and identify writers not as familiar today as in the 1960s, and to confirm dates as best we can. This is our way to invite you to discover Curran's understated conversations with Joyce's writing, among others, with Cesare Ripa's iconology, Douglas Hyde's poetry, Jules Michelet's histories.

This updated book also comes 50 years after the Constantine Curran—Helen Laird collection opened to the public at University College's James Joyce Library. Readers will encounter a set of essays that benefit from Anthony F. Tighe's first study of it in his University College Dublin thesis (1997). Seven contributors use the collection to situate Curran's writing on Joyce and his photography in a wider context, here and now, to build on the most recent insights about Joyce & Company, to think with them anew. These essays set into relief the ventures of these creative people, 'at home,' in Dublin, as in other places in Europe, and the wider world they made their own.

H. S.
2022

FOREWORD

Some years ago I read in a philosophic review, the title and date of which I failed to keep in mind, that literature that has magnitude comes out of tensions and that, at their most effective, tensions are produced during a period of transition in a community. Athenian drama, for example, came out of tensions produced by the transition from elementary religious conceptions to philosophical disciplines. Thinking of what used to be called the Irish Revival, this statement came into my mind. One can now see that this literary productiveness—Movement, Revival, Renaissance, or whatever we like to name it, had creators of a literature that has magnitude—William Butler Yeats and James Joyce. Was the community to which they belonged making a transition? From what and to what?

I think it was, and I think that the tensions that gave these particular writers their magnitude came from tensions produced from a transition from the nation to the State. The same transition was made forty years before when Norway, with Ibsen as its dominating figure, passed from the consciousness of the community as a nation into the consciousness of the community as a State. Yeats and Joyce show, as Ibsen showed, their stressful involvement in the political and social drift of their country. On the Irish side there was recognition of Norway's priority of accomplishment: Joyce's tribute to Ibsen is known; Yeats invoked his name in connection with the project for a national theatre. I should place the period of transition in Ireland between the Parnell epoch and the establishment of a national government.

Constantine Curran was an observer of these tensions. His boyhood knew—closely knew, as he came of a Dublin family of Nationalist tradition—the decline of a powerful movement and the rise of an astonishingly constructive one. He passed through the College that was the one most directed towards national affairs, knowing the contemporaries that were to be the personalities and the leaders in the Ireland that was coming into being. He became part of the social and intellectual life of the capital. He entered the office of the Supreme Court, the centre of the administration. All this made him, a man of inquiring mind, an excellent observer of the period I have indicated. And he could evaluate it all the better being a Nationalist Irishman and a good European well read in several languages and familiar with centres on the Continent.

The foremost literary authorities have presented us with a James Joyce formidable in his learning and literary accomplishment and enigmatic in his history. Constantine Curran's book gives us Joyce as a familiar figure. He meets Joyce on his own social and intellectual level: the houses, the teachers, the books that formed one student are part of the other student's daily life. Then the acclaimed European artist is united with the student who remembers the jokes and entertainments of his Dublin days. The title of the book is fitting: James Joyce, a person, is revealed in a person's remembrance.

Fitting, too, is the writing of *James Joyce Remembered*. It flows evenly but with emphases that bring us to attention. It has humour. Indeed, as I read it I have the feeling that I am listening to good talk in a Dublin drawing-room. As he goes on, the talker knowledgeably removes some misstatements that are in the Joyce texts. Was the background to Stephen Dedalus's struggle as ruinous as Joyce makes it out to be? In his own abode, yes. Outside, no. He was not a man of visual perception, the talker reminds us. He is misleading about the appearance of the College he attended: the houses were dignified, and one had style; the classrooms were from a great house. The students were not dependants. They were the European students as from the time of Abelard, with discourse that gives liveliness to pages of *A Portrait of the Artist*. Several were to leave a mark on the formation of a new state, some on the history of their country.

PADRAIC COLUM

June 1967

PLATES

Part One

Joyce at University College

MY first sight of Joyce was in a classroom of No. 87, one of the three houses on Stephen's Green which made up University College. Modest compared with Nos. 85 and 86, it is an agreeable red-brick house of the type characteristic of our Dublin squares, and this classroom was on the first floor with three windows overlooking the Green. The ground floor was then occupied by the editorial office of the *Irish Monthly*, the magazine edited by Father Matt. Russell which published some of the early verse of Oscar Wilde, W. B. Yeats, and Katherine Tynan. The rest of the house was devoted to such of our classes as did not meet in No. 85.

Our entrance was under the leaden lion by Van Nost which surmounted the porch of No. 86. Passing up by a well-worn, stone service staircase hidden away from the finely decorated main staircase of the eighteenth-century mansion, we reached our classroom. This particular morning the class—a First Arts class—was in English literature; the professor was Father Darlington, the Dean of Studies, and his opening words were from Aristotle's *Poetics*. It was the first lecture I attended in the College, and to begin with Aristotle seemed to be very right and proper and filled me with a certain academic conceit. Before the lecture was over my growing conceit was punctured. I thought I knew a good deal about English literature. Had I not, only a few months before, won the gold medal for first place in English at the Intermediate (Senior Grade) examinations? I thought, however, that the poetry shop had closed down when the Intermediate course shut the shutters with Tennyson. I was unaware that the business of literature was still being carried on there and then. The lecturer made some passing allusion to Stephen Phillips who had just published his *Paolo and Francesca*. 'Have any of you gentlemen read *Paolo and Francesca?*' he inquired, and then immediately: 'Have you read it, Mr. Joyce?' A voice behind me replied indifferently: 'Yes.' I looked round and saw my first poet.

I grew familiar with that figure in my next three years in College. In my eyes it did not change much in the next forty: tall, slim, and elegant; an erect yet loose carriage; an uptilted, long, narrow head, and a strong chin that jutted out arrogantly; firm, tight-shut mouth; light-blue eyes which I found could stare with indignant wonder and which were uncommonly like Lord Rosebery's as described by Crewe, 'at times altogether expressionless like the eyes of a bird. They gave an air of inscrutability and sometimes of lack of interest in the surroundings of the moment.' So he looked that morning. My friend Walter Callan of the Irish Bar, who was some years senior to Joyce at College, told me that his attention was first caught by Joyce's careful attire, more studied than the average; Callan was a good judge in such matters since he had it in him to become private secretary to the sartorially elegant George Wyndham when he was Irish Chief Secretary. When Joyce had taken his degree, and as his family circumstances worsened, his appearance grew raffish with a certain stylish defiance. This was the brief 1903-4 period of the white peaked cap, tennis shoes, seedy flannels, and the famous ash- plant. Recklessness was not native to him. He resumed his studied neatness in his visits to Dublin in 1909 and 1912, and when I saw him next, after the First World War, the figure that then stepped from a taxi at our rendezvous on the Pont des Arts (and that I was to see whenever later occasion brought me to Paris) had grown in distinction. The adumbration of a beard tentatively came and went, the hair lay lower, the eyes that had seen and suffered so much were now obscured by powerful lenses, a cane replaced the ashplant and swung in his hand as if casually, disguising but aiding the dimmed vision; the graceful figure and carriage remained the same.

Joyce, a year older than I, had come to the College from Belvedere the year before me. I had unwisely matriculated directly after my Intermediate examination and accordingly joined him as an immature freshman in the First Arts class in 1899. He was already an established figure amongst the students, having come to the College during the Michaelmas term of 1898 to read for his matriculation and he had brought with him from his old fellow-students at Belvedere a reputation as an exceptionally gifted writer. So far as teaching can make a writer, it was at Belvedere that the neophyte learned his art. At Clongowes he was but a lad. Between Clongowes and Belvedere he was sent for a time to the O'Connell Schools, North Richmond Street, but this interlude was short.

It was from Belvedere that Joyce took all his Intermediate examinations. These exams set the standard of secondary education in Ireland, and Joyce's record was good, but not conspicuously above the average of a promising student.[1] The curriculum was a full one, distinguished from modern practice by its breadth. In his examiners' reports I have not observed any references which might be taken to bear specifically on Joyce's essay-writing—the award is what mattered—but I do quote the general criticism of Dr. Henry Evans, an exceptional examiner in English, in Joyce's last year: 'None of the compositions are exceptionally brilliant nor is any one strikingly original: but, in general, they are well thought out and expressed and containing very few cases of either faulty grammar or bad spelling. . . . Most know the figures of Rhetoric correctly.' And apropos this last sentence I cannot forbear quoting the same examiner who in the same grade in the next year examined me and surprisingly found that 'the questions in Historical Grammar with the exception of some confusion as to the use of the terms, syncope, epithesis and metathesis, have been on the whole satisfactorily answered'.

Joyce's experience with his earliest Intermediate texts left an imprint. Between 11 and 13 he was reading of Daedalus in Ovid, and of the much-enduring Ithacan in Lamb's *Adventures of Ulysses*. At that age, too, he read like all of us T. W. Lyster's *English Poetry for Young Students* and I have met none of my contemporaries who does not recall with pleasure that admirable anthology prepared by the librarian of the National Library who as such was later to be our universal counsellor and friend. It is a fair guess that it was his reading of Goldsmith in Lyster that put the schoolboy to work on his earliest set of verses, which were recovered by Padraic Colum and published by him in *Our Friend James Joyce*. Lyster, too, brought Samuel Ferguson's *Mesgedra* to the knowledge of every secondary schoolboy in the land. We knew this poem by heart: none made more use of it than Joyce. *Mesgedra* is a tale out of the Irish heroic period but Ferguson, while preserving its special character, gives it its full topographical and historical setting, so that the poem is girdled by the course of Anna Livia from where

[1] See p. 7 for details of his Intermediate marks.

> The heath, the fern, the honey-fragrant furze
> carpet thy cradling steeps.

until, passing the tumulus of Mesgedra's queen at Clane, near Joyce's school at Clongowes, the

> . . . limpid Liffey fresh from wood and wold,
> Bridgeless and fordless, in the lonely Bay,
> Sank to her rest on sands of stainless gold.

under the headland of Howth. Ferguson like Joyce beds the brown-clear river in memories of Tristram, Isolda, and the St. Lawrences. It is beyond conjecture that *Mesgedra* holds the seed of the most memorable chapter of *Finnegans Wake* and also that Ferguson's Homeric vocabulary in this poem remained in Joyce's memory. Ferguson's epithets, the 'bard-protecting chiefs' (l. 22) and the 'ill- befriending morn' (l. 35), plainly built up the 'bullock-befriending' letter writer in *Ulysses* and the twice-repeated 'bullock-befriending bard'.[2] Maybe, too, 'the soft merchandise' of Emma's hand, yielded to Stephen Dedalus in a round dance, owes a little to Ferguson's 'The song, the dance, the softly yielded hand' (l. 208).

These vestiges of his school reading come to light later, but his immediate quality was quickly apparent in College in a special class for English composition conducted by W. P. Coyne. In this class, open to students of any year, Joyce, a newcomer, heard his essays read as models. My friend James Murnaghan told me of one such occasion when essays by Joyce and himself were read out as examples of how essays should and should not be written. Exception was taken to a sentence of Murnaghan's beginning with 'and', but this should not be taken as evidence that Coyne was simply an academic purist. He has some little place after Dempsey of Belvedere in the story of Joyce's development. A pupil of Father Tom Finlay, he won a Fellowship in the Royal, and although his real work lay in economics, his approach to it had been through mental and moral science and he wrote on both literature and economics in the *Lyceum* and the *Freeman's Journal* until he left the staff of University College to join T. P. Gill in the new Department of Agriculture and Technical Instruction. Matthew Arnold's brother was also on the English Faculty surviving from Newman's day. We looked into his *Manual of English Literature* and used his Clarendon Press edition of Addison,

[2] See *Ulysses*: "Nestor" (*U* 2.431), "Aeolus" (*U* 7.528) and "Oxen of the Sun" (*U* 14.1115). See also "Scylla and Charybdis" (*U* 9.321).

JOYCE'S INTERMEDIATE EXAMINATION MARKS

1894 Preparatory Grade	Latin	English*	French	Italian	Arith.	Euclid	Algebra	Natural Philosophy	Chemistry
Max.	1,200	1,200	700	500	600	600	600	500	500
	700	455	400	211	430	230	130	190	100

1895 Junior Grade	Latin	English*	French	Italian	Arith.	Euclid	Algebra
Max.	1,200	1,200	700	500	600	600	600
	636	540	410	223	250	175	175

1896   Joyce did not enter

1897 Middle Grade	Latin	English*	Commercial French	Italian	Arith.	Euclid	Algebra	Natural Philosophy
Max.	1,200	1,200	500	600	600	600	500	500
	642	457	33	342	340	180	230	175

1898 Senior Grade	Latin	English*	Commercial French	Italian	Arith.	Euclid	Algebra	Natural Philosophy
Max.	1,200	1,200	500	600	600	600	500	500
	560	650	102	205	145	40	20	10

* English as an examination subject included Irish and English history and geography. In each year except 1895 Joyce won a prize for English composition.

7

but apart from the interest his family prestige, he enters little into the picture. In our time he took no part in the day-by-day teaching. Joyce, like myself, may have attended some of the formal public course of lectures—already mentioned—to which Tommy Arnold contributed, but our only real contact with him was at the University Orals over which, as the oldest Fellow, he presided.

The honours classes in English were taken by Father Darlington and later by Father George O'Neill, both Fellows of the Royal. As time went on Joyce's interest in these early morning classes slackened and his attendance grew more and more infrequent. For the Dean he always entertained a kindly regard and wrote to me in that strain upon his death in 1939, but to his teaching he does less than justice in *A Portrait of the Artist as a Young Man*. The Dean may have stooped to assist his pupils over academic fences invisible to Joyce; he may not have had any great capacity for continued abstract thinking; but I think none of us, including Joyce, failed to enjoy in him the quick response of a mind which went half-way out to agree with his student and to provoke and stimulate discussion from the point where agreement ended. An Englishman and a convert to Catholicism, he had an original mind, an alert, practical, and most sympathetic intelligence which made him a close friend of Gerard Manley Hopkins, but he was not, I think, really interested in literature. He was Dean of the College rather than of an English Faculty, but we all relished his unexpected sallies. While I recall his scholastic method of 'nominal and essential definitions' which left its trace on Joyce's writing, I remember better his quainter divagations in Shakespearian criticism.

But it must be confessed that the prescribed texts were not well calculated to retain the attention of a precocious student alive to contemporary literature and allergic to early hours. In their attitude to the old and new in literature, the Royal University authorities differed in no way from their fellows in the other universities in these islands. The matriculation standard was naturally not greatly higher than the final of a secondary school; the reading courses in English literature for the next two years were confined to a very limited number of texts, and the cautious approach of the degree class to the nineteenth century proceeded no further than the Romantic School. Such indispensable fodder was quickly and easily assimilated and it left, at any rate, much time for outside reading. In Joyce's case Byron, Shelley, and Newman had Pater and his off-the-course reading had brought him far along paths untrodden by his fellows.

As a seventeen-year-old student his interest lay in Yeats and Blake and the French Symbolists; Dante lay a couple of years ahead in the curriculum but had already joined Ibsen as one of his gods, with D'Annunzio as their somewhat incongruous thurifer. A few of his books, bought, signed, and dated by Joyce at this period, came later into my possession.[3] They are evidence of the early preoccupation with the theatre which brought him in 1899 to the first performances of the Irish Literary Theatre and in 1900 to the paper he read to the Literary and Historical Society of the College on 'Drama and Life' and his *Fortnightly Review* article on 'Ibsen's New Drama'.

This article written on *When We Dead Awaken* is the earliest published piece of Joyce's prose. Its appearance in the *Fortnightly* made something of a sensation in the College and enormously enhanced the prestige of its eighteen-year-old author. Mainly expository, by reason of its subject, it stands as the confession of the writer's admiration of the Scandinavian dramatist whose intransigent qualities he sought to make his own. Written when he was preparing his paper on 'Drama and Life', we may infer that the article contains not merely identical opinions but perhaps actual passages from the unpublished address. This is evident enough from the touching letter he wrote to Ibsen a year later when he heard that the *Fortnightly* article, coming under Ibsen's notice, had pleased the old man. In that letter Joyce referred to the College debating society where he had vindicated Ibsen's rightful position in the history of the drama and had drawn attention to his 'lofty impersonal power' as well as to his other claims. 'I have', he wrote, 'sounded your name defiantly through the college where it was either unknown or known faintly and darkly.' And he continues:

But we always keep the dearest things to ourselves. I did not tell them what bound me closest to you. I did not say how what I could discern dimly of your life was my pride to see, how your battles inspired me . . . how your wilful resolution to wrest the secret from life gave me heart, and how in your absolute indifference to public canons of art, friends and shibboleths you walked in the light of your inward heroism.

Joyce had been elected to the committee of the Literary and Historical Society in 1899, and his paper 'Drama and Life' was read to the Society on 20 January 1900. In that season, 1899-1900, Arthur Clery was auditor. He was devoted to the stage. He had, indeed,

[3] D'Annunzio: *La Gloria* (Milan, 1899). Signed on the cover and fly-leaf and dated 'September 1900' by Joyce. *Sogno d'un Tramonto d'Autumno* (Milan, 1899). Signed and dated 'September 1900' by Joyce. *La Gioconda* (Milan, 1900). Signed and dated 'May 1900' by Joyce. Hauptmann: *The Coming of Peace* (London, 1900), trans. Janet Achurch and C. E. Wheeler. Signed and dated 'February 1900' by Joyce. *Handle, A Dream Poem* (London, n.d.), trans. William Archer. Signed on the cover and fly-leaf and dated 'August 1900' by Joyce. Ibsen: *Little Eyolf* (London, 1897), trans. William Archer. Signed and dated '1900' by Joyce. *The Wild Duck* [I cannot now trace details of this]. Maeterlinck: *Alladine and Palomides, Interior, The Death of Tintagile* (London, 1899), 1 vol., authorized translation. Signed and dated '1899' by Joyce. *Pelleas and Melisanda, The Sightless* (London, n.d.), trans. Laurence Alma Tadema. Signed and dated '1899' by Joyce. Verlaine: *Les Poètes maudits* (Paris, 1900). Initialled 'J. A. J.' and dated '1902'.

made mention of Ibsen before Joyce in an address to the Society on the contemporary theatre—a few months after Joyce entered College and before any of the Irish Literary Theatre's performances. To read papers to the Society was a distinction, to take part in debates was the right of all members—and a right at times stormily exercised—but the reading of a paper was a matter of invitation rarely extended to any but the more senior. That this invitation should have been issued to Joyce in the term following the performance of *The Countess Cathleen* and before his *Fortnightly* article appeared, was a clear and friendly recognition of his minority stand and of the general desire to hear him on a subject he had made peculiarly his own.

For reasons one may only guess at, 'Drama and Life' was not published in Joyce's lifetime. Like *Stephen Hero* he may have thought it a 'schoolboy production', and a text lay dormant in his brother's diary until 1959.[4] In that long interval little of its first reading survived in the memory of those who heard it. To my regret I was not one of them, and my inquiries amongst those who were present bore little fruit. Now I set down what I learned then, although the diary text has seen the light of day. It seems to me worthwhile to reproduce what I have written unaltered, together with my own early speculations, if only to recapture the reactions of Joyce's first audience.

John Marcus O'Sullivan, who spoke to the paper, remembered neither the address nor even that he himself had taken any part in the proceedings. James Murnaghan told me that the paper began with the words 'As Paracelsus says' and passed on to some reference to the *Götterdammerung,* whereupon he professed to finding himself without any further comprehension of its meaning. He found, to his wonder, John O'Sullivan speaking to the paper but, recovering from his surprise, assumed that John O'Sullivan, being a student of philosophy, could appropriately speak as a party to this sort of esoteric conspiracy. But Murnaghan, to my mind, is a bad judge in this matter. His orderly intelligence, disciplined in the classics, revolted from the obscure and sought—in this case vainly— to reduce difficult things to words of one syllable. In general, civilized life ended for him with the eighteenth century. When not Greek, he was Mozartian: Wagner and the moderns passed him by. He was quite unlikely to go along with Joyce in the speaker's dispraise of 'the bland blatancy of Corneille, the starchglaze of Trapassi's godliness, the Pumblechookian woodenness of Calderon'. The committee of the Literary and Historical had invited George Moore to preside at this

[4] This text is in Mason and Ellmann, *The Critical Writings of James Joyce* (London, 1959).

meeting, but when Moore—an unready public speaker—declined the honour, William Magennis took the chair, as later at Joyce's paper on Mangan. He admired, he told me, both performances, but of the first occasion could only remember Joyce thanking him for his attendance. He said that it was not the first service he had rendered him, since it was he who had recommended him for his Intermediate Senior Grade prize in composition. Eugene Sheehy's account to me, brief as it is, alone gives a reasonable outline. Not yet a student of the College, but knowing Joyce at Belvedere, he went to hear his friend and he followed the paper with understanding. There may conceivably have been, he said, some abstract aesthetics, but his recollection is of a debunking of romanticism and a vindication of Ibsen and the truthful handling of reality. What left the strongest impression on his memory was what he thought a most remarkable display by Joyce in his reply to the speakers. When the speakers closed at ten o'clock he rose; he had taken no notes, but taking up the speakers (W. P. Coyne, Arthur Clery, Hugh Kennedy, James J. McDonald, and the others) one by one, he dealt with each point made against him. One of his retorts referred to Hugh Kennedy as 'sheltering under the aegis of a Greek quotation'. The medicals in the back row of the Physics Theatre applauded rapturously, and breaking up at the end he remembers Seamus Clandillon clapping Joyce on the back, saying, 'You were magnificent, Joyce, but quite mad.' Eugene Sheehy, later circuit court judge, told me this before he wrote his *May it Please the Court* which gives a lively and reliable account of Joyce's early days. I have deliberately retained his account to me as supplementing his own writing.

As I have mentioned, Arthur Clery was the auditor on this particular occasion. He appears in the text of *Stephen Hero* as Whelan, the orator of the College, and Joyce quotes him, I should think with exact truth, as confessing that he had been listening to the discourse of angels without knowing the language they spoke. To establish a special relation between Stephen and McCann, Skeffington (McCann) is introduced as the auditor of the Society. In fact, he had been the auditor three years earlier. Other happenings are brought a year forward in order to emphasize Stephen's maturity. William Magennis, the Professor of Mental and Moral Science, was, as I have said, in the chair, and not W. P. Coyne. But of more material interest is the difference in the actual subject of the paper. Though, as Eugene Sheehy says, there may have been some aesthetics in it, it is certain that the main subject was a vindication of Ibsen and his place in contemporary European drama. The whole discussion on aesthetics, the 'applied Aquinas' which occupies twelve pages of *Stephen Hero,* had, I believe, no place at all in this paper. I am satisfied of this not merely by reason of Joyce's absorption at this date with Ibsen but because the title of his address was not altered, as Stephen says it was, from 'Drama and Life' to 'Art and Life'—a change which would have been necessary if aesthetics were its main subject and also because Joyce's elaboration of his 'applied Aquinas' aesthetics was, I dare to say, a matter of later date. His monologues on this topic, begun on pages 76-80 (of the New Directions edition, 1944) before the delivery of his address, are continued later to Cranly on pages 212 and 213. These monologues were heard (but much later—from 1903 onwards) by more than one of Joyce's friends. His brother, Stanislaus, was the chief, J. F. Byrne (Cranly) was another, and I myself in the autumn of 1903 and the beginning of 1904 was a third. Their subjects, the cone-shaped image of art, its disposition into the lyric, epic, and dramatic, the definition of these kinds, the Thomist constituents of beauty, were set forth to me, as no doubt to others, succinctly and dogmatically at times and places I well remember as belonging to a period three years after his 'Drama and Life'. Cavendish Row and the slopes up Rutland Square are indissolubly associated in my mind with such discourse—conversations they can hardly be called, their sententiousness betrays the written word. They were ideas derived from St. Thomas and extended to literature, theories which he had already set down on paper when drafting the text of *Stephen Hero* in or about 1903. They were the 'flag-practices', the trying-out on friendly ears of a book in progress. A little—his special use of the term 'literature' and the definition of beauty—appeared, somewhat earlier, in his paper on Mangan.

I was fortunate enough to be present at the reading of this paper to the Literary and Historical. It was read on the evening of 1 February 1902, a coincidence with his birthday, 2 February 1882, which, if not actually designed by him, would not have escaped his attention. The meeting was held as usual in the old Physics Theatre, a large, octagonal room lit from its end bay by tall, ogival windows against which the benches rose as in an amphitheatre, crowded in the daytime with joint classes of medical and arts students, and filled on Saturday evenings by the members of the Literary and Historical and its camp-followers. On such occasions the guest chairman, auditor, and officers of the Society had their places at the long demonstration table facing the rising tiers and the reader of the paper stood to its left. Joyce's delivery is clear in my memory. He spoke in a withdrawn, impersonal way; his clear enunciation, staccato, even metallic at times; his voice impassive and very deliberate as if coming from some cold and distant oracle. In Joyce's account of Mr. Duffy, in 'A Painful Case' (*Dubliners*), 'Sometimes he caught himself listening to the sound of his own voice. ... he heard the strange impersonal voice which he recognized as his own, insisting on the soul's incurable loneliness.' This passage reminds me strongly of Joyce's manner both in speech and his recitatives of Yeats at the piano. The voice could be singularly musical, rising and passing away in quotation or at will into characteristic aerial harmonies. It lent itself with grace to the elaborate rhythms of the prose into whose complicated web he had so studiously woven his own meditation on the quiet city of the arts and Mangan's relation to the highest knowledge and to those 'laws which do not take holiday because men and times forget them'.

Except for a quotation from 'A Swabian Popular Song', the text was printed in full in the May 1902 issue of *St. Stephen's*, the College magazine, and it has since had a wider public. Professor Hackett, who was on the editorial staff of *St. Stephen's* at the relevant date, has written on this topic.[5] He recalls that in order to print Joyce's complete text, printers had to change type in its closing paragraphs, and also omit this quotation, which he believes came from this poem 'A Swabian Popular Song' and probably from the end of its first verse. He quotes the lines in his article. Other lines like:

> They would not yield their souls the thrall
> Of gold, nor sell the glory of their lays

might, I think, also have attracted Joyce's attention. Gorman mentions that he set this poem to music. I never heard him sing it nor heard it referred to in Dublin, but Stanislaus Joyce says that his brother made settings for some of Mangan's as well as Yeats's poems, when living in Glengariff Parade. This would have been in 1901 or 1902.

These later readers are in a more favourable position to debate the paper than its first audience. That audience was not wholly dedicated to letters and Joyce's aesthetics were obscure enough even to those who most willingly gave themselves up to his silvery incantation. His submerged or explicit references to gods and half-gods, Bruno, Word-

[5] James Meenan (ed.), *The Centenary History of the Literary and Historical Society, U.C.D., 1855-1955* (Tralee, n.d.).

sworth, Baudelaire, Shakespeare, Verlaine, Novalis, Shelley, Whitman, Poe, Blake, Swedenborg, Dowland, Moore, Walsh, Leopardi, Dante, Ibsen, may have had something of undergraduate parade, but they were certainly not made in self-protection nor, in any case, would they have provided any shield against the philistines.

This close-packed paper, prose-poem, or manifesto, will repay close study. It has the interest of its nominal subject but in conception and execution it is in a very high degree spiritual, self-revealing and prophetic. It drew its central theme from a sentence or two of Yeats and John Mitchel. Yeats wrote that Ferguson restored to our hills and rivers their epic interest, and that the nation found in Davis a battle-cry, as in Mangan its cry of despair.[6] In his edition of Mangan, Mitchel wrote: 'Like Ireland's, Mangan's gaze was ever backward with vain and feeble complaint for vanished years. ... It was easy to perceive that his being was all drowned in the blackest despair.'

The paper owed much also to Lionel Johnson who had been writing on Mangan in 1898 and more elaborately in 1900. He found in him, as Joyce did, a drifting will too ready to dwell in the valley of the shadow, haunted by memories, keening an Ireland desolate and derelict. Also, something of it was conceived in Pater's manner of an imaginary portrait; but if a second 'Nameless One' enters by way of self-portraiture, the mask is resolutely set aside in the closing passages to disclose a serene and stronger spirit.

I hardly think any one of us students present was then aware of the parallel which existed between Joyce's father and Mangan's. In an autobiographic fragment Mangan makes frequent mention of his father's irascible temper, his recklessness, and the misery it entailed on his family. His mother bore with admirable fortitude the whims of her street-angel, house-devil of a husband who, Mangan wrote, seemed to think that all feelings 'with regard to family connections and the obligations imposed by them were totally beneath his notice. ... As a last resource he looked to the wretched members of his family for that help which he should rather have been able to extend to them. My father and mother meant well by me but they did not understand me. They held me by chains of iron.'[7]

Mangan spoke of this deplorable parent of his as a 'boa-constrictor'. In *Finnegans Wake* (London, 1939, p. 180) Joyce wrote of his own as a 'Boer-constructor' what time Shem the Penman was still a lexical student. His first audience no doubt missed the parallel, but they did not fail to pick up his allusion to Mangan as lamenting

[6] *Dublin University Review*, November 1886.
[7] D. J. O'Donoghue, *Life and Writings of Mangan* (Dublin, 1897), pp. 3,10,13, 64. For Lionel Johnson on Mangan see his Introduction to Mangan's poems in the Stopford Brooke-Rolleston *Treasury of Irish Poetry* (London, 1900) and his address to the National Literary Society in May '1898'.

no deeper loss to his country than the loss of plaids and interlaced ornament. This topical, now obscure, allusion pointed to Edward Martyn's Maeve whose exacting love required her pattern of Celtic youth to equal 'the rare and delicate perfection' of Celtic ornament. It pointed also, and more immediately, to the new evangel of national dress preached in saffron kilt and plaid to the Literary and Historical just a fortnight before by Fournier d'Albe, an assistant lecturer in physics at the College of Science—better known to us as the inventor of the particoloured, druidical Pan-Celts.

The paper disconcerted some later speakers by ignoring the politics of '48 and Mangan's share in the movement, which they had come prepared to debate. But there was enough to prick them on to battle. Joyce's tapestry presented them with no obscure allegory: the challenges were deliberate and obvious, but they were thrown down as self-evident truths and with a seeming indifference. Remote as from Sinai, but without its cloudy tumult, the lightning stabbed. It was not enough scornfully to dismiss the *Nation* poets as departing half-gods and in the teeth of the history books to qualify Mangan, the greatest of them and the friend of John Mitchel, as 'little of a patriot'. But presented first as one whose natural habitat is in the regions of ideal beauty, Mangan becomes, in Joyce's final view, the last justification of a narrow and hysterical nationalism, the passive inheritor of a tradition of griefs and failures and empty menaces, of a sterile and treacherous order, enemy of life, which would establish upon the future an intimate and far more cruel tyranny than the past of his race had known. For Mangan, a lover of death, Caitlin ni Houlihan is a queen, but for Joyce an abject queen upon whom also death is coming. Another voice, however, the voice of the speaker, is heard singing, faintly now but not to be always so; the future is with this strong spirit who will cast down with violence the high tradition of Mangan's race, its love of sorrow and despair, one who like Dante will take to its centre the life that surrounds it and fling it abroad again amid planetary music and who like Ibsen will sing of earth's joyous fullness *det dejlige vidunderlige jordliv det gaadefulde jordliv.*[8] These were barbed, provocatory thrusts and I recall, by reason of their incongruity, two impassioned speakers impaled by them. The first was John E. Kennedy, a callow fledgling some three months in the College, whose reading at that time had travelled not far beyond *Alice in Wonderland.* Dashing first into the fray, what he wanted to know and insisted on knowing behind all Mr. Joyce's pretentious talk

[8] 'the beautiful, miraculous earth-life – the inscrutable earth-life', Henrik Ibsen, *When We Dead Awaken* (London, 1900), Act Three, translation William Archer, known to Joyce. To compare with the literary translation of Anne-Marie Stanton-Ife in Henrik Ibsen, *The Master Builder and Other Plays* (London, 2014), p. 293.

was whether Mangan was a drunkard or an opium-eater. He pressed his question with all the patriotic urgency at his command. At this stage Tom Kettle—perhaps on some indication from the auditor, Bob Kinahan—thought it well to get the debate running on saner and more courteous lines, but of his complimentary speech I remember nothing. But I do remember that speaker who followed him. Louis Walsh was one of the three or four recognized spokesmen of the Gaelic League, vehement and full of fire. Outraged by Joyce's assault on our nationality and traditions he let loose in the cause of the Gaelic gospel what Tim Healy, speaking of William O'Brien, called the untameable squadrons of his irrelevant eloquence. Louis's accent belonged to the Derry border which for Doric harshness can compare only with west Cork whose speech is as stones rattling from an upturned cart. Coming so soon after Joyce's silvery utterance, Louis reminded me less of a crusader in glittering mail than of a scared hen indignantly rising to no great heights on clattering wings across the farmyard.

This paper on Mangan is not mentioned by name in the surviving fragment of *Stephen Hero*, but its material, I imagine, bulks larger than 'Drama and Life' in that composite text. Its definitions of literature and beauty have been already referred to. There is as well, as I have mentioned, the more personal reference to the poet who alone is capable of absorbing in himself the life that surrounds him and of flinging it abroad amid planetary music. And there is again the 'eloquent and arrogant peroration' *(Stephen Hero,* p. 80). Whether 'Mangan' or the earlier 'Drama and Life' was the 'first of my explosives' *(S.H.,* p. 81) is immaterial. One need not be misled by Stephen's indignation; Joyce regarded him with more ironical eyes. Was his fate, after all, so dreadful or the explosive reckoned so deadly? The fowler had spread his nets and caught the unwary. His other hearers stood free and approved the performance. How else explain the note of the meeting sent by the Society's secretary to the *Freeman's Journal* to appear in its columns on Monday 3 February? It reported categorically that it was 'the best paper ever read before the Society'. This student opinion was re-echoed in the next issue of *St. Stephen's,* which described the paper as 'reaching an unusual height of eloquence' and 'displaying exceptional qualities of thought and style'. Glancing at the two speakers I have mentioned, the same writer, William Dawson, tartly commented on 'the philistinism of young Ulster' and on 'the ignorance which had a field day for the nonce'. Furthermore, the editor and staff saw to it that the 'explosive' should have its fullest detonation at the earliest moment. Ibsen, too, in early days had written of the 'torpedoes' he had placed under the 'Ark'. Joyce's explosives echoed these. The editor printed the address in his next issue, a few months after 'The Day of the Rabblement' had been declined.

St. Stephen's, in which I, too, had a later hand, was a light-hearted students' paper with just sufficient ballast to give it weight outside College circles. Its publication coincided with the days when an old University grievance was being agitated, and many alternate schemes put forward. These were the subject of continual reference in its columns. The magazine was published within the College, and subject to ordinary college discipline; and since it was so sanctioned by the authorities and guaranteed by them against financial loss, its most casual observations might not unfairly be regarded by outsiders as evidence of more than student opinion. In those sensitive days and in hostile quarters the opinion of any contributor might easily be turned to other and not always relevant purpose. Circumstances of time and place must enter, therefore, into any judgement of its editorial conduct; and they enter here into the rejection of 'The Day of the Rabblement' and of Skeffington's article on the position of women.

Dated 15 October 1901, 'The Day of the Rabblement' was prompted by the approaching performances of the Yeats-Moore *Diarmuid and Gránia* and of Hyde's *Casadh an t-Súgáin*. It shows the young writer parting company with the Irish Literary Theatre on the issue of national drama. A short article, trenchant in criticism, imperious in manner, it is none the less, for a manifesto, occasionally oblique and allusively obscure. The relevancy of one or two passages still escapes me. I do not yet, for example, understand what precisely underlies the topical reference, 'today when the highest form of art [meaning, I suppose, drama] has been just preserved by desperate sacrifices', nor can I identify the occasion of Yeats's recent association with a platform from which even self-respect should have urged him to refrain. It certainly coincided with the moment when Yeats stood closest to the Gaelic League, when the Irish Literary Theatre was about to stage its first play in Irish, and when Yeats was writing to Lady Gregory that its organ *Beltaine* 'should be a Gaelic propaganda paper this time'. It was at this date I first heard Yeats address a meeting—at a Gaelic League *sgoruidheacht* in the Gresham Hotel. Velvet-coated, with black, flowing tie and a black lock of hair falling over his forehead, he leant forward from his great height, snapping back again like an uncoiled spring, as he told us that he looked forward to the day when his own books would be unread in an Ireland that had become Irish-speaking. We applauded the self- sacrificing gesture. Did any of all this really earn, except in one young man's eyes, the reproach of a lost self-respect?

Joyce's paper began with the now familiar reference to the Nolan —an allusion which Joyce found irresistible.[9] In the same opening sentence he takes from D'Annunzio's *Le Vergini delle Rocce* Leonardo da Vinci's epigraph concerning the necessary isolation of the artist, and in later passages he refers to both D'Annunzio and Bruno. I propose to return in a later chapter to these first traces of D'Annunzio's influence as well as to the unexpected mention of the Danish novelist, Jens Peter Jacobsen. These allusions were more than literary flourishes. In his expression of pure disillusionment, however, the ardent young student left no one in doubt as to where his quarrel with the Irish Literary Theatre lay. At the start, its promoters seemed to him allies of the contemporary European movement. Ibsen, D'Annunzio, Hauptmann, and Maeterlinck: these names with Yeats's own held for Joyce the promise of the future. *Beltaine* held out this promise; its first number began with the word 'Norway' and references to Ibsen and the new drama filled its pages. When Yeats wrote that the new Irish Theatre would do its best to give Ireland a hardy, national character by opening its door to the four winds of the world instead of leaving the east door alone open, he was setting out a programme that Joyce would have welcomed. But supplementary statements were more disquieting and the programme of the Theatre in its third year went no way towards redeeming its promise. No winds blew from Scandinavia or the Continent. Inspiration was sought only from a western province, and the impatient idealist set down in 'The Day of the Rabblement' his sense of an unworthy surrender to the popular will. Rightly or wrongly he found its root in Yeats's treacherous instinct for adaptability and in the poet's 'floating will'. His reproach seems now surprising; Joyce's hawk-eye had found, I think, this latter phrase and the threatened capitulation of the poet in one of our college texts for that year. In Corneille's *Cinna* the suspicious Emilie rebukes her lover for his *esprit flottant* and like Joyce bids him:

> Va, sers la tyrannie
> *Abandonne ton âme à son lâche génie.*

He would also remember that Lionel Johnson had found in Mangan a 'floating will'.

[9] *Spaccio della Bestia Trionfante*, registered by the Nolan, is Giordano Bruno's title to his treatise on ethics. Yeats's article 'Ireland and the Arts', written for the *United Irishman* in 1901 and republished in his *Ideas of Good and Evil* (London, 1903), sets out his position at this date.

Joyce's standpoint was too well known in the College for his protest to shock the editorial staff of *St. Stephen's*, nor had his *de haut en bas* treatment of the promoters of the Theatre anything in it to offend them. The Theatre had already been under their fire from a diametrically opposite point. They might disagree with both, but left to themselves they would, I am certain, have found the essay useful material for further controversial copy. It was, however, denied publication at the instance of the college authorities. On my very much later inquiry I was told by John Marcus O'Sullivan, a member of the editorial staff whose recollection was clear, that the rejection turned on a single point—the reference to D'Annunzio's *Il Fuoco*. This novel, with much else of D'Annunzio, stood in the Roman Index. Unreserved commendation was inconsistent with the position of the responsible head of college teaching and Joyce's article was accordingly returned to him. I never heard that there was any suggestion of its revision by the writer. That would have been a fruitless endeavour even if the editor knew then—as is known now—what D'Annunzio meant to Joyce at that stage of his growth.

The other instance of college censorship occurred later when Frank Skeffington, then the college Registrar, submitted an article on co-education in the university. Inasmuch as it was written by the Registrar it might appear to lend some semi-official authority on a point of college management. This article was also returned, whereupon both incongruously were issued together in pamphlet form.

My memory of these college years between 1899 and 1902 holds pictures which differ from Joyce's presentation of college life in *Stephen Hero* and the *Portrait of the Artist*. The divergencies do not subtract from the essential character of the central figure. Little or nothing that the writer says is without its element of truth in fact or in the poetic imagination. The space between is the no-man's-land of art, but it is always well to remember that Joyce did what he could to destroy the MS. of *Stephen Hero* and looked with 'disagreeable surprise' upon the survival and ultimate publication of its fragments. These texts have made everyone familiar with the picture of the artist-student absorbed in the aesthetics of literature, jealous of his independence, scornful of his fellows, standing on his defence, arrogantly aloof. He moves with an occasional companion against a frieze of figures, outlined with sharp realism and chosen to represent what he, using Ibsen's word, would always refer to as the 'trolls'—forces threatening his integrity. These selected figures serve the art-

The B.A. degree class of 1902 with its professors.
UCD Library Special Collections CUR P 4

Joyce in 1904 [sic 1902] in the Curran family's garden
UCD Library Special Collections CUR P 1

ist's purpose in accentuating his isolation and maturity. They existed in truth and in fact but they should not be accepted as the authentic background of college life nor as a film of complete actuality. After all, he himself wrote, 'It must not be supposed that the university lacked an intelligent centre.'

Joyce lived a withdrawn life. Reserve, as he said, was always a light penance to Stephen Dedalus, though Joyce's detachment was more than reserve. No artist is without egoism, but the ineradicable egoism with which he endowed Stephen was evident enough to re- pel or keep at a distance some—and not the least reasonable—of his class-mates. Reticence makes few friends amongst youth. Joyce had listened to Flaubert's advice, *'Fais-toi une cuirasse secrète composée de poésie et d'orgueil,'* which was D'Annunzio's also. He buttressed his instinct for self-preservation with what he called a breakwater of order built up against the sordid tides of life without and within. He schooled himself to silence, and this breakwater was rarely breached. He easily assumed a mask—that common end-of- the-century stage property—and it was rarely dropped.

Looking back, I see nothing of Stephen's 'shivering society' but young men going their ways: sometimes together, a few alone, and amongst them Joyce—peculiarly isolated. I see nowhere hostility to him except in the rough-and-tumble of debate. Joyce's furrow was narrow and deep, but there were other minds amongst his fellows quite as active as his own. I have written of some of them elsewhere. I found them, then as now, quite allergic to 'trolls'. Their beliefs were as conscientiously held as Joyce's and as freely arrived at, and no more open than his to any unworthy capitulations. They were students of philosophy, law, science, classics, and economics. Mallarmé and Rimbaud were names not wholly unknown to them, but their principal studies and interests were quite different from Joyce's preoccupations. He was self-centred and centripetal; they were, in the manner of all students, gregarious. In the college societies, on the steps of the National Library, wherever they met they plunged into debate. Night after night when the Library had closed they would continue their interminable discussions, swinging backwards and forwards between their lodgings, loath to separate, unwilling to conclude anything.

In short, they lived as all students since Abelard or Duns Scotus have lived. But Joyce stood aside from such debate; his conclusions were already arrived at, *in petto*. They recognized his distinction, accepted his aloofness from discussion, and retained his friendship or goodwill. Some of his school friends—notably Richard and Eugene Sheehy—were in this group and here there was no question of distance. With them he gave free play to his sense of the burlesque, introducing it with gravest aplomb in the most incongruous circumstances. At their hospitable house in Belvedere Place, in the good Dublin fashion of those years, the carpet would be taken up of a Sunday evening and the night went in music, dancing, and impromptus. Joyce was a very welcome visitor there and he lent himself with great gusto to the improvised charades. He travestied indifferently Ovid, Shakespeare, and street-singers. Eugene Sheehy has already, like myself, recorded his playing of the queen mother in *Hamlet,* distraught and rocking herself with grief at the sight of Willie Fallon (another of his Belvedere schoolfellows) as the mad Ophelia, strewing the floor with cauliflowers. Eugene Sheehy might also have mentioned, because he took part in it, that unusual papal conclave dated very near the beginning of the century at which Joyce, as Rampolla, instructed his aged fellow-cardinals in the proper electoral procedure, meticulously and very clearly spelling out his name to them, R-A-M-P-O-L-L-A, for their better guidance in voting. Charades had lost none of their popularity in the theatre- loving town and, indeed, for the next few years they raged from house to house. At the Morrows' house in Effra Road the half-hanging of Bulmer Hobson as General Munro, or some such Ulster United man, nearly ended in disaster, and further out at Dun Emer I have painful recollections of myself as Master Builder Solness falling down the front of the house through rose bushes and thorns past the window of the drawing-room where the audience were, while Kitty McCormack sang of harps in the air.

Joyce brought this sort of play-acting into one at least of his college classes. Abandoning his English lectures, he was a fairly regular attender at Professor Cadic's French class which was held at a not unreasonably early hour. Cadic, a Breton of no great academic distinction, was a good, conscientious, and kindly teacher who loved but imperfectly understood the fantastic ways of Irish students. At any rate he forgave them everything if their antics were conducted in French; as once, for example, when George Clancy (who later as Mayor of Limerick was murdered by the Black and Tans) sat opposite Joyce in class. Cadic knew they were good friends and was all the more surprised when Joyce, on that day, took great umbrage at some invented remark of Clancy. With great dignity Joyce elaborated a point of honour which Clancy rudely brushed aside. Joyce's punctilio sharpened. Clancy's rudeness got near the *mot de Cambronne*. Cadic vainly tried the role of peacemaker, but blood alone could wipe out the insult and the cartel was coldly drawn up by Joyce for the meeting in the Phoenix Park. The whole class had to intervene before insulted and insulter shook hands across the table and Racine or Boileau was resumed—but not however until they had solemnly in turn advanced to the head of the table to kiss on both cheeks their 'Papa Cadic'.

Cadic, if no great scholar, was a patriotic Frenchman and something of an elocutionist. Each year in his class, for the sake of some newcomer or apropos Du Guesclin or Joan of Arc, one of us would revive the memories of the *année terrible* and would seem to remember that our dear master had played an honourable though youthful part in its sad happenings. Did he not also share in the defence of the sacred soil of the *patrie*? Cadic would then admit that from all the schools in his *département* he, a child, had won the highest award for elocution, and when the war came he had been sent out by the administration to all its platforms reciting verses in aid of the war charities. Ladies tore off their bracelets and heaped jewels upon him. Could he, by chance, remember such admirable verse? Well, perhaps he could, and so Racine was again set aside while our dear Papa recited his ode once more, moving his audience to a profound emotion and to unnumbered tears.

Sometimes, again, the grateful class would be persuaded to hand up French essays. To me, essay-writing in any language, was always an odious *corvée*, a thing to be evaded; one essay in French I remember for the same reason as I remember certain passages from Joyce's paper on Mangan. By this time the class had been enlarged and was held on certain occasions in the Aula Maxima; and the theme prescribed for it had been 'Bells'. I contented myself with fabricating a pseudo-French version of Schiller's *Lied von der Glocke* and escaped worse disaster. Cadic sorrowfully passed over such attempts, but he read out Joyce's essay which seemed to me to be a piece of pure lyricism. Its musical onomatopoeia must have been remarkable to sound still in my not very retentive ears. From little country *clochers* bells tintinnabulated in Joyce's prose or solemn bourdons reverberated and died away in distant harmonies. Reborn, their echoes vibrate in his later pages.

Harmonies were innate in Joyce, and so word-catching was second nature. Ben Jonson was one of his quarries. But an early example of his interest in a new scientific vocabulary dated from his 1899— 1900 Physics class. Physics, or Natural Philosophy as it was called then, was an obligatory subject in his matriculation and First Arts examinations and Joyce accordingly attended Professor Stewart's lectures in the Physics Theatre. Stewart was fond of underscoring his demonstrations with quotations from Gilbert and Sullivan. This appears in *Portrait of the Artist,* but with it also his elliptical and ellipsoidal distinction which becomes the object of Moynihan's (i.e. Bob Kinahan's) ribaldry. More curious, perhaps, is his reference to platinoid and its recent discovery by F. W. Martino. Felix Hackett reminds me that this verbal loot of Joyce goes back to this class where we were students together. He also points out to me that Joyce mixes up the separate vocabularies appropriate to a lecture on electricity and a lecture on dynamics, which the meticulous Stewart would never have done.

Joyce, I imagine, found his Italian class the most sympathetic and rewarding of any. *Stephen Hero* represents himself as choosing Italian as an optional subject, partly to read Dante, and partly to escape the crush at French and German lectures. In fact, the degree in modern literature for which Joyce was reading required English and two foreign languages, and he had already been working at Italian and French for at least six years before entering University College. The seven or eight of us around Cadic's table at the French class made no great crush; in the German class I had Bob Kinahan as the sole companion of my first year, and later I was alone with *Faust* or *Die Braut von Messina,* or brooding, not for the last time, on the use of the Chorus in Greek tragedy. Eugene Sheehy has described Joyce in Father Ghezzi's Italian class—the pair constituted the entire class—and he complained to me that he made nothing of it because Joyce and Ghezzi spent the whole time discussing philosophy in an Italian too esoteric or too fluent for him. Yet Joyce's truly optional subjects, pursued at home or in the National Library, were Danish and German. When I, as a student, was entering into closer relations with him, he had read much of Ibsen in Danish, and he quotes Ibsen in Danish in his Mangan paper. To what extent he spoke the language I do not know, but liking to direct my attention to the poetical element in Ibsen, he would repeat verses like *Agnes, min dejlige Sommerfugl* from *Brand.* At the same time, attracted by Hauptmann, he was interesting himself in German, translating for another exercise *Michael Kramer* and *Vor Sonnenaufgang*. All this, I should think, would be about 1902.

It is rarely possible to pinpoint the moment when friendly acquaintance, at least as between man and man, passes into friendship. But it was in the academic year 1901 that my accidental student acquaintance with Joyce was established on a more friendly footing. Up till then he was a figure whose appearance at class I looked for and relished. My friends were then, for the most part, outside my literature classes. One was a philosopher, one a physicist, the others were heading towards law and medicine. But as the curriculum grew more specialized in the degree classes, Joyce and I saw more of each other, and our reading helped to better acquaintance. Mine was routine, enlarged by the National Library and the secondhand bookshops. In this routine of the advancing years at university the procession of the English classics filed by, accompanied by their linkmen and torchboys—they also in their appropriate hierarchies and place. On the heels of Coleridge and Matthew Arnold came Bradley on Shakespearian tragedy and something of W. P. Ker, much of Saintsbury and a little, and that little too much, of Dowden; in their train followed the painstaking biographers of the *English Men of Letters*. It was still the age of the Romantics in poetry and of character- diviners in criticism. In criticism Coleridge was our closest study and made the deepest impression. He ruled the critical roost—but Saintsbury fluttered more extensively. Saintsbury bobbed up everywhere, both in French and in English. His baroque style, his zest, his blind spots, his chaotic, sometimes wrong-headed, enthusiasms, his contagious delight in a magical verse: all were attractive compared with Bradley's profundities or Dowden's idolatrous character-dowsing. My memory still fondly dwells on Saintsbury, that industrious man who fixed his professorial chair on so many perches. We met him on both our English and our French courses, 'very nearly' (as he characteristically wrote of Tom Moore), 'very nearly if not quite on the top of two trees which if not quite cedars of Lebanon are more than mere grass of Parnassus'. It was, therefore, with a peculiar pleasure I found Joyce in 1922 requesting Miss Weaver to send Saintsbury a copy of *Ulysses,* writing, 'I am old fashioned enough to admire him though he may not return the compliment. He is quite capable of flinging the tome back through your window.'

These were the critics who received corrective consideration at the hands of our Aristotelian and scholastic lecturers. Much of their class-work commentary was necessarily routine work but now and then it was stimulating. It did not occur to me then, nor does it now, that it was obscurantist or thought-repressive. On the contrary, discussion was invited and carried on *à l'outrance*. However, I do not recall any general treatment of aesthetics in the English class, apart from Coleridge and Aristotle. I myself had more roving aesthetic debate when reading Goethe and Schiller with George O'Neill, my German professor. His taste was narrow and more rigorous than mine, but his judgements were acute and well based. In the French class there was good linguistic teaching, but little or no literary argument. Curious, and significant of nineteenth-century taste, there was no Racine. Alongside the periwigged classics, Corneille, Molière, Boileau, Fénelon, Voltaire, we read our Lanson, Taine, the rigid Brunetière, and again Saintsbury, making what we could of these intelligent, contradictory authorities. In any case, dredge as I may in memory, I cannot find Joyce sharing in any of these critical exercises. Assiduous in Italian, he followed the French class mainly for the sake of the language, but his attendance at the English class was, I have already said, perfunctory. However, it was sufficient to leave with him an impression of Father Darlington that affected both his matter and his method. He heard more 'applied Aquinas' from him than from anyone else in those days. He appreciated his quality and, holding his memory in respect, wrote to me kindly upon the death of his well-intentioned teacher.

Lightly as was this routine of college reading observed by Joyce, its track can be followed in his early writings; 'the ragged book written by a Portuguese', which taught the young artist 'what little he knew of the laws of Latin verse', was the familiar *Prosody* by Alvarez used in our Latin class. In its Dublin edition this ingenious composition of a Portugese Jesuit who died in 1582, having been Rector of colleges in Coimbra, Evora, and Lisbon, must have been the last relic in our schools of late Renaissance, classical teaching, and one may still admire the dexterity of its Latin mnemonic lines and the accuracy and brevity of its rules. *Hamlet* belonged to our Second Arts year, 1901, with Sidney, Spenser, Bacon, and Milton; and in the same year Joyce was reading for his Italian examination Petrarch and Dante, Castiglione's *Courtier*, Leopardi, and the *Oreste* of Alfieri, which Stephen Dedalus read with Father Artifone, in its wretched Italian binding, along with 'the dingy chronicle of Machiavelli'.

Such courses are the reasonable, methodical approach to the quiet city of the arts, but students have turbulent minds not always or even ordinarily content with their conditioned serenity. We preferred the free pastures of the National Library, and what the second-hand bookshops offered. The book-barrows too, like Johnson's *Dictionary*, provided fine, confused feeding. In those days the second-hand bookshops, i.e. Webb's, Neale's, Massey's, and Clohessy's, were well stocked. Bennett's, the auctioneers on Ormond Quay, held monthly book sales and their overflow, drifting down the river, silted up on the book-carts in Aston's Row, where Pat McGrath, Clohessy, and Perdissart presided at their twopenny table d'hôte while 'Clicky' Walsh, the runner, hovered about, knowing his clients' taste and purse, ready to fetch out from his pocket a special *bonne bouche*. Pat McGrath was a dealer of quite different calibre, and I would not have his name forgotten. Lame and frail, he was a most loved personality in this Row, with a special store in his living quarters near by in Temple Bar, to which he would welcome various students. He had no mean knowledge even of eighteenth-century Irish literature.

Whither on Saturday afternoons flocked the booklovers: M'Clintock Dix, Séamus O Casaide, and D. J. O'Donoghue; our seniors, John O'Leary and Count Plunkett; an odd professor or two like Dowden, and later Osborn Bergin and H. O. White, with their generation of Arthur Griffith, Padraic Colum, Seumas O'Sullivan, Henderson of the Abbey, and O'Leary Curtis. Dowden found there Shelley's *Address to the Irish People*, and Professor Bergin and I had a long-standing, never-won, bet to equal that rare performance. The poet Seumas O'Sullivan was master in this art. He had special divination in his prehensile fingers, which led them, without looking, and without breaking off his talk, to some eighteenth-century curios. His jaunts to London were paid for by selling on one side of the Charing Cross Road what he bought on the other. On the book-carts of Aston's Row Stephen Dedalus found his dingy texts, but also *The Tables of the Law*. It was possible for the impecunious student—and there was none other—substantially to supplement his college ration.

This cheap market introduced an engaging element of chance into one's reading, and encouraged promiscuous adventure. In my own case, I was at that time reading perhaps as much in French as in English. The sober brown wrapper and clinging pages of the *Revue des deux mondes,* unchanged since the days of Buloz, were in the National Library and held for me its serials: Fogazzaro's *Il Santo* or Bourget's *L'Étape*. I could get on the carts for myself the issue of *Cosmopolis* that held Mallarmé's *Un Coup de dés jamais n'abolira le hasard,* and I can trace the beginning of one line of reading to an early purchase there of Maxime du Camp's two-volume *Souvenirs littéraires* which set me off on the Second Empire and its antecedents and led me on to Verlaine, the Parnassians, and the Symbolists. It was at this point, I imagine, that Joyce and I began to compare notes or, more precisely, it was now that Joyce found another receptive ear and an auditor who would lend him his meek attention. A year later another link was added when I was looking forward to my first journey abroad and to a fairly extensive tour in Italy. This prospect, together with my growing interest in the arts, plunged me into Italian history and my casual reading, taking a more definite direction, became wider and even more superficial. Anything that concerned Italy I read eagerly. As a schoolboy, drawn as he should be to the champions of popular liberty, I had read *Rienzi* and *Romola* and to these were early added all the Italian novels of Marion Crawford on the shelves of the municipal libraries. Now came, in international spate, the travel literature of Hare, W. D. Howells, and Maurice Hewlett; of Gautier, Taine, and Michelet; of W. W. Story, Hawthorne, and more Crawford. All these with much Pater and Ruskin, and the histories of John Addington Symonds, Sismondi, and Villari were gluttonously consumed. With more difficulty I stumbled with translation and text through Dante and a little of the courtly poets and more of Leopardi and Carducci, and borne on by a newborn Franciscan enthusiasm, I one day landed up via Ozanam's *Poètes franciscains en Italie au XIIIᵉ siècle* on Jacopone da Todi. The stranger figure of Joachim di Flora and of the apocryphal *Eternal Gospel* I had come on by way of history as Joyce had by way of Yeats's *Tables of the Law.*

Amongst my new contacts with Joyce I remember particularly Jacopone and Dante. Joyce was probably amused at my flounderings in those Elysian fields and bog-lands, and I was glad to seize on any lifelines he threw out. I might add the name of a third writer to whom at this time I was devoted: Huysmans's *œuvre* was as familiar to me as to Joyce. His *La Cathédrale* was before the public for two or three years and his survey of religious art and symbolism was read at the time by anyone who, like Edward Martyn, was interested in liturgical reform and was not unduly shocked by the violence of Huysmans's attack on *bondieuserie*. When Joyce came back from

Paris in 1903 he wrote him down as an obvious comedian, who had wearied his audience, and as a writer without form. But whatever he may have thought of Durtal's spiritual pilgrimage or of Huysmans's elaboration of a schematic, recondite symbolism, I think Huysmans entered a little way into the writing both of *Stephen Hero* and *Portrait of the Artist*, if it was no more than by his manner of dogmatic, professorial exposition.

Huysmans's symbolism of colours fitted in, too, with the Rimbaud sonnet, *Voyelles*, which Joyce would repeat to me. Imitating Rimbaud and *A Rebours*, we would push these *fin-de-siècle* fancies, as I imagine students were doing in every university town, to the correspondence of colours with the sounds of musical instruments and with the sense of taste, compiling, for example, monochrome meals, tables d'hôte in black puddings and caviare, black sole with Guinness and black coffee. But if he did repeat Rimbaud's sonnet it was not because he was given to reciting verse. Unlike the other young writers of my experience he had not the habit of speaking his own verse or rapturously reciting Yeats or Swinburne or Verlaine. Singing was his release and, unlike other students, his talk was not of his reading. For the rest of us literature was largely matter for criticism, an affair of contrasts and tendencies. For Joyce it had absolute value, it was a world of integral beauty.

So far, therefore, as I recall them, his references to books were fragmentary and only by way of illustration or—most often—by way of reference to something in which I myself was interested. Ibsen, the truth-compeller, the heroic intransigent, was by this time above controversy. At no time did I hear Joyce discuss him as a social reformer—such propaganda was to him inadmissible—and he was first to direct me away from such journalistic criticism to the poetry and symbolism of *Peer Gynt*, *Brand*, and *The Master Builder*. Flaubert frequently cropped up in our talk; it was Joyce who made me read *La Légende de Saint Julien l'Hospitalier*, that ingenious piece of literary *vitrail*, most probably because he was aware of my interest in stained glass and knew from my reading of Huysmans that I was as keen to see the church of St. Severin in Paris as I was to see Notre-Dame. But he himself, as an apprentice craftsman, was more interested in the fatuous doings of Bouvard and Pecuchet, in Flaubert's collection of 'cases', and in what Elizabeth Bowen calls 'the exquisite compilation of a *cliché* dictionary for additions to which one strained one's ears at gatherings'. He was already collecting 'epiphanies'. Of the French poets I can remember him quoting much from Verlaine and something of Baudelaire, de Nerval, and Heredia, but nothing except an odd line from Mallarmé, and nothing except the sonnet from Rimbaud whose work, though it is diametrically opposed in its origin, in certain other ways has a curious resemblance to Joyce's writing.

Amongst English writers, Pater—the deep-freeze of so much end- of-the-century prose—was studied by all budding stylists, but George Meredith was more widely read and discussed. Prejudiced in his favour by his liberal sentiments, we students were not deterred by his quick plunges from the spring-board of fact into fancy. We took his mannered allusiveness and headlong cataracts of imagery and simile in good part and as a challenge. The introductory chapter of *Diana of the Crossways* was accepted as the touchstone of an emancipated intelligence. I still look with some amusement at my copies of *The Egoist* and *The Tragi-Comedians* of which one belonged to Frank Skeffington and where almost every line is underscored or marked by his impulsive, exclamatory pencil. Pater, I am pretty sure, had followed the 'silver-veined' Newman in Joyce's pre-Ibsen school-days and may have taught him to poise an adverb. He lifted his eyebrows when I said I found Meredith in *Stephen Hero*. When I suggested that some of the sentences in that MS. were as involved and obscure as Meredith's own, he wondered at my obtuseness. Joyce's opinion of Meredith at this time appears in his review of Douglas Jerrold's study in the *English Men of Letters* series:

No one can deny to Mr. Meredith an occasional power of direct compelling speech . . .[but he is lacking in] the lyrical impulse, which, it seems, has been often taken from the wise and given unto the foolish.. .. These novels have, for the part most, no value as epical ait. . . . But they have a distinct value as philosophical essays . . .[10]

Of Henry James, who was new to me, he spoke admiringly, and in connexion with the same draft of *Stephen Hero* turned me to *The Portrait of a Lady*.

One need not attach more significance to such names occurring in casual talk than their circumstances warrant. None of them had anything like the importance that Ibsen, D'Annunzio, Blake, and Yeats had for Joyce at this time. Yeats's verse we all knew, admired, and recited, but Joyce's admiration was less limited and extended

[10] *Daily Express* (Dublin), 11 December 1902.

to *The Tables of the Law* and *The Adoration of the Magi*—tales which left most of us cold. Their apparatus of magic seemed to us flimsy tools for one who sought to restore Irish letters, and to be but the distillation of the magic which aureoled and bedevilled Yeats's early path before the artist sloughed off artifice and stood out in his own light. Joyce praised these inventions to me in terms I found hard to reconcile with his stronger admiration for Ibsen's uncompromising search for truth in the conflict of 'average lives'. He found in them, no doubt, as in Blake and Maeterlinck, the breaking up of a 'sterile and treacherous order' and the same perception of 'far-reaching conflicts independent of his actors' that he found in Ibsen's drama. The influence of Arthur Symons was hardly less. He was then playing a part in criticism comparable with Ezra Pound's in later years and he influenced writers greater than himself—amongst them Joyce, to whom he was encouragingly kind. His *Symbolist Movement in Literature* (published in 1899) was dedicated to W. B. Yeats. It introduced most of us to the movement abroad. It was ardently read and it supplied much ammunition to *Beltaine* and *Samhain* and the manifestoes of the Irish Literary Theatre. A single quotation from it fairly represents both his own point of view and the direction of Joyce's mind:

Symbolism ... comes to us now ... offering us the only escape from our many imprisonments. . . . And it is on the lines of that spiritualizing of the word, that perfecting of form in its capacity for allusion and suggestion, that confidence in the eternal correspondence between the visible and the invisible universe . . . that literature must now prove, if it is in any sense to move forward.

Whether thanks to Symons or not, Joyce had acquaintance with Baudelaire, Verlaine, and the Symbolists in his earliest college years. He was talking of them, anyway, in 1900, and his copy of Verlaine's *Les Poètes maudits* is dated 1902 by him. He may have bought it in Dublin or during his first visit to Paris in that year, but it may, just as well, represent an older interest in these poets—Rimbaud, Mallarmé, Villiers de l'Isle Adam, and Verlaine himself—of whose writings it is an anthology with comments. It contains Rimbaud's *Le Bâteau ivre* as well as his *Voyelles* and that other sonnet *Oraison du soir,* 'savamment et froidement outre', as Verlaine qualifies it, for which Joyce furnishes cold and equally deliberate parallels.

Verlaine was a special favourite of his, but to find an immediate
influence of these other Symbolists on Joyce's work would be to an-
ticipate many years' experiment. To ignore it at any time is more
unreasonable. *'Que veut dire symbolisme,'* asks Remy de Gourmont
... *anti-naturalisme ... tendance à ne prendre dans la vie que le détail
caractéristique, à ne prêter attention qu'à l'acte par lequel un homme se
distingue d'un autre homme.'* Does not this point again to the 'epiphanies'? Correspondences, beginning with those that were the subject
of Baudelaire's sonnet, always fascinated Joyce and riveted his attention and when Baudelaire speaks of *confuses paroles*

> Comme de longs échos qui de loin se confondent
> Dans une ténébreuse et profonde unité
> Vaste comme la nuit et comme la clarté.

he is not only bridging the space between Romantics and Symbolists
by way of Mallarmé and Rimbaud but he is also pointing towards
Joyce's last experiments. Rimbaud's verbal alchemy and Mallarmé's
use of words 'that take light from mutual reflection' remaking 'out of
many vocables ... an entire word, new, unknown to the language ...'
are at no great remove from *Finnegans Wake*. Baudelaire may hold our
attention a moment longer to recall him in *Le Cygne* crossing Paris,
his memory invaded with thoughts of a Trojan river which in its poor
cracked mirror reflects the sorrows of the exiled Andromache. And the
poet sees in his path a swan dragging its fair plumage in the city mud,
convulsively lifting neck and head as it strains like Daedalus, *l'homme
d'Ovide*, to the ironic skies as if reproaching God.
Like symbolism, theosophy was in the air in the nineties. As a schoolboy reading W. T. Stead's *Review of Reviews* in my father's house I was
dimly aware of the ambiguous figure of Madame Blavatsky. Later, in
the pages of the *Lyceum* (the early University College publication), I
read more of the cloudy origins of theosophy and its hierophants and
heard something of the Hermetic Society, which, grouped about A.E.,
existed for some time in Dublin as a theosophic centre until, wearied
of schisms and charlatans, it settled down as a discussion group attentive to A.E. In early days at the National Library I ran across A.
P. Sinnett's *Esoteric Buddhism* but neither it nor its Irish echoes made
any lodgement in my hospitable mind. Joyce also had turned over its
pages and, if I was repelled by the condescendingly pretentious claims
of theosophy and in general by the pantheist's surrender of free will, I

cannot imagine that Joyce was much more seriously influenced, even though its vocabulary enters a little into his early writing. What Père Maréchal calls its refusal to recognize the sovereign liberty of the creative act would be sufficient in the long run to repel Joyce.

Tom Kettle excepted, Joyce was the first of my University College intimates to make the acquaintance of A.E. and W. B. Yeats. His seeking out of the two poets recalls the youthful Rimbaud's quest for his two *voyants*. Years afterwards, A.E. told me of that first meeting and I set down his account of it from a note I made at that time. It is an oft-told story—Yeats had written his side of it and Stanislaus Joyce another—but I give it as A.E. told it to me. The meeting, I imagine, would have been in 1902. A.E. said that one night, on arriving home to his house in Coulson Avenue about half past eleven, a good-looking young man called on him and asked him if he was Mr. George Russell. The youth apologized for calling at so late an hour and said he had been waiting for an hour and a half at the corner of the street for his return. A.E. brought him into his room and sat with his legs curled up under him, a pipe hanging from the side of his mouth, while Joyce explained that he had a difficulty in stating precisely what he wished to speak to him of. A.E. said he would do the talking until the reason emerged. But after some time and after another inquiry Joyce was still reluctant to speak. A.E. said he would then have to proceed in Socratic fashion and said that like Gaul he was divided into three parts: economics, poetry, and painting. Had Mr. Joyce called to discuss anything connected with economics? Joyce emphatically said 'No'. They came to poetry, and Joyce admitted he was seeking a new avatar and had hoped to find him in A.E. but on seeing him he had instantly made up his mind that he was not the man.

They spoke of Yeats and after some praise Joyce said that Yeats had now gone over to the rabble. When he left, A.E. wrote to Yeats that what he had long threatened him with had come true; that the new generation was knocking at the door. Joyce afterwards called on Yeats who reported back to A.E. that when he had praised some of Joyce's poems Joyce said he cared no more for his criticism than for that of the man in the street. Joyce said, 'What does it matter? In a little time, both of us, perhaps, will be forgotten.' Yeats entered on a subtle and elaborate defence of his development to the effect that while a young man might exclusively dedicate himself to beauty and consider that alone, he may, as he progresses, devote himself with propriety to experiment. Joyce flew out at this as showing how Yeats had deteriorated and finally he left the room with a parting shot: 'I come too late to influence you; you are too old.' Neither Yeats nor A.E. would be averse to shaping a tale to an effective climax, but for as long as I knew him Joyce invariably spoke in the most friendly and respectful terms of Yeats, and I am still unwilling to accept these words as *ipsissima verba*. Joyce was uniformly courteous and to those he disliked or who disappointed him he was coldly formal. It is inconceivable to me that as a young man he would have waited upon his senior, sought his opinion unasked on his verses, and then turned him and his criticism down in such arrogant terms.

A good deal has been said of Joyce's youthful arrogance. Some things that he admired and most things that he rejected were admired or rejected by him in the teeth of his fellows. He was curt or, if you wish, arrogant, in the defiant proclamation or defence of these opinions. He was not so in behaviour or social conduct. He was aloof, wary, dogmatic in statement, and mistrustful. He was scornful of the opposition he anticipated and he was peremptory in his reply. To that extent, and to that extent only, he was arrogant. Youthful shyness, self-consciousness, arrogance, pose or enigmatic mask—one may interminably debate these points for what they are and draw supporting arguments from his writing without very definite conclusion. One may draw *post scriptum* argument from Rimbaud but get no further than to find the characteristic expression at a certain stage of a certain type of mind. Stephen Dedalus confesses to throwing up defence works in the busy construction of the enigma of a manner. That enigmatic manner was very evident in Joyce in these student years.

Rickword has written of the precocious Rimbaud as arrogant, diffident, timid, perverse, self-conscious, incapable of that momentary surrender of one's egoism necessary to social intercourse. Another critic has written

True, there is something enigmatic about [Rimbaud's] *persona* . . . something in the last resort aloof, something never entirely communicated. This oracular quality is mysterious and therefore confusing. But, as with all such temperaments, with all persons whom we call *reserved,* the mystery lies less in the substance than in the manner.[11]

This latter quotation seems to me exactly appropriate to the present instance and indeed corresponds with what I have written. But it need not be carried further. Neither Joyce's early self-consciousness nor his undeniable egoism were serious barriers to social intercourse. Even when most marked they would break down in a gust of sudden laughter and occasionally, in congenial company, in sustained bouts of hilarious drollery.

Joyce was not naturally a good 'mixer', but he was not anti-social. He was difficult but not uncompaniable. At no time, then or in later years, do I remember him in company taking part in any general discussion. For anything approaching serious talk he preferred the company of one to many, and even then you had to meet him on his own ground. You were reduced to the docile recipient of his earlier meditation, sententiously delivered. Many found his trick of recondite allusion affected. He certainly used it to evade reply. He did not debate. Question was turned aside by dark or gnomic answer. He himself said he offered the gift of certitude and loved the enigmatic. But to the healthy-minded student the proffer of certitude is a challenge and the unriddling of enigmas a pastime. It was the doubling of these parts which gave his speech an air of arrogance and it made for isolation in the student body, but not hostility. It faded out on closer acquaintance and indeed wholly disappeared in later years. But the cryptic answer, the reticence on deep issues, which always seemed to me his dominant characteristic, never disappeared. He was ready enough to enter into explanation of his attitude towards many things, but irony, wry humour, grotesquerie, courteous evasion, or silence—each in turn was enlisted to build up an impregnable defence against intrusion on the inner sanctuary. *Ibo singulariter donec transeam.*

Compared with the rest of us Joyce's reading was unusual. A great share of our reading was, as I have suggested, extra-curricular but it was on the whole bent towards our college studies. Joyce's was directed to his own single purpose. His familiarity with contemporary European literature was greater than that any of us could pretend to—again with the exception of Tom Kettle. He read Blake closely in the Ellis-Yeats edition. As a word-catcher, but not as a word-catcher only, he studied the Elizabethans and Jacobeans. His reading was selective and purposeful and, far from being that dangerous animal, *homo unius libri,* he chewed the cud of his favourites rather than devoured many. He was diligent in following up clues and the modish allusions to more esoteric writers in Yeats and the French Symbolists. His extraordinary memory and natural acuteness did the rest in the way of preserving for use immediately, or after a great space of years, what came his way. So far as I could see, between 1899 and 1904 he was not a notably assiduous reader in the National Library, but his reading hours may well have been my class hours. He was, of course, an *habitué* and had his favourite table; it was his base, a sort of poste restante, but he was not nailed to it: he did not keep regular hours as those of us who did three-hour seances. It may have been otherwise with him at the Bibliothèque Ste Geneviève in the winter of 1902, but in the years I speak of he seemed to me to spend rather less time in the National Library than in roaming, again like Rimbaud, 'with hypnotized steps through the streets of his little town, his *beaux yeux d'azur noyés dans l'extase*'. Neither did he frequent the book-barrows, though we met there occasionally. His circumstances did not permit him to accumulate many books, but if he was neither bookworm nor borrower nor book-collector he was quick to claim his property when he found it and he knew where to look for it. He says as much in *Portrait of the Artist:* 'The lore which he was believed to pass his days brooding upon . . . was only a garner of slender sentences from Aristotle's *Poetics* and psychology' and a synopsis of St. Thomas.

Balzac wrote three novels out of a summary of Swedenborg, winning thereby some credit as a mystic. It would not be just to say that Joyce's scholasticism had as insecure a foundation. It would be untrue, for the natural bent of his mind was towards the realism of Aristotle and Aquinas, but this does not imply that amount of recondite reading which some commentators, to whom the tradition of scholarship is unknown, attribute to him. To these anything that touches the medieval is strange, wonderful, and smacks of murky superstition. Though Joyce's attendance at the English classes in University College was infrequent, the garner of slender sentences to which he refers is the same harvesting of Aristotelian definitions which his class-mates meekly gathered into their own memory or notebooks from Father Darlington's lectures. As to Aquinas, I must also mention Boedder's *Natural Theology*, the textbook used in the class of religious doctrine open to all students. He had a page or two on Thomistic aesthetics starting out with *pulchra enim dicuntur ea quae visa placent*. Rickaby's *General Metaphysics* was read in the philosophy classes. Joyce could not but have seen it in the hands of his friends who were reading philosophy including, for example, J. F. Byrne (Cranly), who sat at the same table with him in the National Library and at least in the first week of the term would have opened its pages. Rickaby, between pages 148 and 151, holds the marrow of Joyce's aesthetics. It is Rickaby who quotes from St. Thomas well nigh all that Joyce uses touching the good and the beautiful which by its mere contemplation sets the appetite at rest. He discusses its unity, or *integritas,* its harmony of parts or, *consonantia,* and its clear lustre, or *claritas*; commonplaces, it may be said. But for me an intriguing detail is that Rickaby illustrates part of his argument by a sudden unlikely reference to a barn, just as Joyce, in his talk with Lynch, suddenly invokes the basket on the head of a passing butcher's boy.

These Stoneyhurst manuals would have escaped the attention of no intelligent student in the College; Joyce could have got what he wanted from them in half an hour. He could as easily have garnered further fodder from the two or three pages of De Wulf's *Introduction à la philosophie néo-scolastique,* in which one finds a clear enough outline of the plan utilized by Joyce's 'applied Aquinas'. There, as in the other textbooks I have mentioned, he would have found the enjoyment of aesthetic pleasure to reside formally in disinterested contemplation and its perception to be of the intellectual order. He would have found not merely Aquinas's three requisites for beauty, ending with the radiant *'resplendentia formae',* but also more than the seed of Joyce's 'epiphanies'. The *claritas pulchri* on which Stephen Dedalus broods is defined as having in view that 'property of things in virtue of which the objective elements of their beauty—order, harmony, proportion—reveal themselves clearly to the intelligence and so elicit its prolonged easy contemplation'. Joyce's epiphanies have a wider range, but their source lies between Aquinas and Flaubert.[12]

Whatever, for a season, his reading may have been in the Bibliothèque Ste Geneviève, Joyce did not follow any of the philosophy courses in University College, and there is no record of his attendance at any meeting of the Academy of St. Thomas, a discussion group meeting irregularly to read papers and debate (mainly from a neo-scholastic standpoint) any philosophic theme. Such papers, in Joyce's period, ranged from Epictetus to Bacon and the neo-Kantians. His acquaintance with St. Thomas derived, I am satisfied, not from such meetings and certainly not from any formal study of philosophy, scholastic or otherwise, in the College. It would have begun in the sodality and advanced classes for religious instruction in Belvedere. A similar sodality and class were open to all students in University College; their general instruction followed the scholastic pattern, and the authorites read or cited were, as I have said, lying

[12] My quotations are from Dr. Coffey's translation published in 1907, but De Wulf's *Introduction* was published in 1904 and it incorporates material from his earlier studies in the aesthetics of St. Thomas published in 1896.

at hand about the College. But the same principles, *ad mentem divi S. Thomae*, his vocabulary and definitions made part of the general atmosphere of college discussions and entered into basic criticism in the literature classes. Joyce had much the same experience of it in English and Italian as I had in German and English. Speaking for myself, a great deal of my German reading was accompanied by the friendliest wrangles across the table with my professor, with whom I occasionally agreed, and in which Aristotle, Aquinas, Baumgarten, and Scherer were the acolytes of Lessing, Schiller, and Goethe. Joyce's scholastic definitions are sprinkled through some reviews he was writing for the *Daily Express* in the winter of 1902; later I was listening to them in monologues on aesthetics which remain in my memory as much from the manner of their exposition as from the matter. The dry, staccato delivery of these *pronunciamientos* was appropriate to their scholasticism, and their didactic certitude squared with the hard core of his mind. What held my attention then was the seeming difference between their sharp concreteness and his devotion to Ibsen and the Symbolists and, in particular, to Verlaine and Yeats: Verlaine strongly influenced the verse he was writing at this time. But our talks were rarely on this aesthetic level; they went with casual meetings as we crossed town together to the north side and ran mostly on the theatre or music, and chance topics.

It seems curious to me now, when I think of Joyce's perambulations of the city and our later absorbing interest in everything that pertained to it, that nothing of its history or aspect cropped up in our conversation. It is not fair to say that the visual arts at no time existed for Joyce. He recognized their existence and their right to prevail with other people, whose interest in them he watched with friendly eyes. But at no time did he seem to me to take a disinterested pleasure in painting, sculpture, or architecture. The growing infirmity of his sight would explain this indifference in his later years, but the same unawareness seemed to me to exist in his early years when his eyesight, though weak, was not yet gravely impaired. There were family portraits in his father's house, which after many vicissitudes hung in his own Paris apartment side by side with later portraits, and with two of Jack Yeats's canvases—one of the Liffey at Leixlip, the other showing the river with one of Guinness's barges. He cared for these for their associations. He took a polite interest in the work of his painter acquaintances and in the protean changes which art underwent in the new century, but he showed no youthful inclination of his own in these directions. All my student friends were devoted to the theatre; some of them shared an equal interest in painting or music. But I never once saw Joyce in the National Gallery or at any picture exhibition or heard him make any comment on Dublin painting or architecture. In the matter of painting I can however, recall one slight instance. Before any of his work had been seen in Dublin, I entertained from reproductions a liking for Puvis de Chavannes. I must have mentioned him to Joyce, who surprised me a little later by praising his touching *Pauvre Pêcheur,* which I did not know. Joyce was at pains to fetch me out a volume on Puvis in the National Library to show me its reproduction. I had spoken of his murals in the Pantheon and Sorbonne and when Joyce returned in the spring of 1903 after a six months stay in Paris I asked him what he thought of them. He passed the Pantheon, I suppose, every day in that six months, yet he had never gone in to see them. The incident is trivial but it betrays a certain indifference to painting, and shows still more the characteristic interest he took in his friends' tastes.

Similarly in regard to architecture. He knew the streets of Dublin by heart and his memory was a map of the town. But his interest in its buildings, as in pictures, was for their associations. On this point I have the advantage of a note kindly given me by Mr. J. J. O'Neill, a former Librarian of University College, who, at the period with which I deal, was a member of T. W. Lyster's staff in the National Library and had for a colleague Mr. Seán T. O'Kelly, later to be the distinguished President of Ireland. I transcribe the note as follows:

My outstanding recollection of James Joyce is meeting him in the Capel Street Municipal Library in company with Seán T. O'Kelly on the occasion of a lecture by John Kells Ingram. Lyster was in the chair and I clearly remember Ingram advising his audience to read the newspapers that were opposed to their political beliefs, as this would lead to the working man thinking for himself and not blindly following the programme of the politicians. After the lecture, Joyce, Seán T. and myself walked along Britain Street (now Parnell Street) and when we arrived at the junction of Dominick Street I pointed out the house where Leonard McNally lived. Joyce did not show much interest in McNally as a political personage but when I mentioned he was also a dramatist and had written one poem that had attained a certain popularity, he enquired the name of the poem, and when told it was 'The Lass of Richmond Hill' Joyce said 'Richmond Hill, that is in Rathmines'. I said, 'as far as I know it is not the Richmond

Hill in Dublin or London but it is a place in Yorkshire.' Joyce seemed disappointed and said he would look it up. A few days later, I met him in Molesworth Street and he informed me I was correct in my location of McNally's poem. Later after the lecture I showed Joyce Sir Samuel Ferguson's house in North Great George's Street and Parnell's House in Temple Street. He appeared much interested and spoke for a considerable time on both Ferguson and Parnell.

In those days there was a Dublin antiquary named Edward Evans, author of a formidable little work entitled *Dublin Almanacs and Directories*. He also occasionally contributed articles of historical interest to the *Irish Builder*. Evans and I became very friendly and we frequently took walks in the evenings through the city streets when he would point out houses that had been at one time the residences of celebrated literary and historic characters. Indeed it was from this source that I laid the foundation of my knowledge of old Dublin which afterwards I was able to pass on to another Irish writer, W. J. Lawrence, the historian of the Irish stage.

Joyce in those days lived in St. Peter's road, Cabra, and was frequently seen in the company of Oliver Gogarty. I met them one autumn night and walked up the Cabra Road, listening to Joyce and Gogarty discussing Shelley. I think that Dowden's *Life* was the book they had in mind. Curiously enough, that afternoon I heard Lyster praise an essay on Shelley that had been published by the Browning Society and Joyce said he would like to read the essay. (It was wholly like Lyster that he should also have forced this essay on my attention when reading in the Library.) A few days later I gave him the book in the Library. Joyce told me to continue my study of the topography and history of Dublin as I appeared to have gained a large amount of information on the subject. I showed him Lady Morgan's house in Kildare Street and the Emmet house in Molesworth Street on another occasion.

This was in 1904, years before the Georgian Society began its study of Dublin architecture and before our eighteenth century became a fashion. But it is none the less singular that, in one who so assiduously paced the stones of Dublin, so little of its most characteristic aspect enters into his writing. Its life was an unfailing stimulus, its skies and the furniture of its streets reflected his mood but the graceful untenanted shell gave him no special pleasure.

Music, on the other hand, was an abiding passion. It was a heritage from both sides of his family. His mother as well as his father was a singer, and also a pianist. It may be because his home was at this time so full of song that to his regret he neglected any formal study of music. He was content to play the piano by ear and, except for a few singing lessons, made no other systematic study. A group of us, college friends, went regularly to the orchestral concerts which Esposito established and maintained over all this decade, to our inestimable gain. Joyce went to none of these. Singing and the opera sufficed for him and he could spend an indefinite time singing at the piano bending with uplifted hands over the keyboard. So I remember him at the piano in the Aula Maxima of the College on a day which marked a stage in our growing intimacy, as it was then that he told me of the death of his younger brother, George, to whom he was deeply attached, and whom his family and teachers regarded as of equal literary promise with himself. He was fifteen when he died. Joyce sang to me two of Yeats's songs, 'Who Will Go Drive With Fergus Now' and Aleel's song from *The Countess Cathleen,* 'Impetuous Heart, Be Still, Be Still', to which he had set music of his own. His brother had asked him to sing them to him as, in his last illness, he lay in an adjoining room. Yeats's 'Had I the Heavens' Embroidered Cloths' was another song to which he had at this time put music. All three he sang in simple recitative modulated with a few supporting chords, singing or chanting in the manner of Florence Farr with her psaltery whom Yeats had introduced to our stage. Others, new to me, were written by Henry VIII and Queen Elizabeth: 'Pastime with Good Company', 'I Love and Shall Until I Die', and 'Ah, the Sighs that Come from the Heart', songs which he probably found in Hullah's *Miscellany*, and the old ballad 'Turpin Hero'. Some of these he would sing on Sunday evenings at the Sheehys' with a variety of others, which I set down as I remember: Yeats's 'Down by the Salley Gardens', 'When First I Saw Your Face', 'Spanish Ladies', 'The Croppy Boy', 'I Arise from Dreams of Thee', 'The Man that Broke the Bank at Monte Carlo', 'Blarney Castle', 'When McCarthy Took the Flure at Enniscorthy', and 'Molly I Can't Say You're Honest'. His sisters recalled to me another, their favourite—'In Her Simplicity'. Rightly or wrongly they laughingly spoke of a sad ballad, 'The Lass of Aughrim', which, they said, Joyce was perpetually singing at home.[13] He purported to know thirty-five verses of it but they could recall only a few lines:

> The rain falls on my heavy hair
> And the dew wets my skin,

[13] But see Mr. Donagh MacDonagh's article in *Hibernia*, June 1967.

If you be the Lord Gregory
Open and let me in.
A dialogue proceeds with the man's
What was my last gift to you?
and the girl's reply:
My babe lies cold in my arms,
Lord Gregory, let me in.

These are a few of the songs out of his great and varied store—some of his own acquiring, more coming from the inexhaustible stock which was his father's, but all very much part of himself. Not many that I heard him sing at that date were from Italian opera. There was Balfe or an odd Gounod or Arthur Sullivan. That may possibly have been because he did not want to obtrude Italian upon his audience. At any rate, his familiarity with Italian opera, through his father's knowledge of it, was nothing like the extensive knowledge that his later residence abroad brought him. But at that time his acquaintance with the Dublin music-hall and with the repertoire of the entertainers who ran one-man shows was prodigious. I find in letters passing between us in 1937 that his interest in Ashcroft, Wheatley, Val Vousden the elder, Percy French, and their peers was still unquenched, and that I could ransack the music shops for them and the *libretti* of old Dublin pantomimes without satiating it. This appetite was independent of their special value to him as raw material. His father had a quite exceptional familiarity with all this vernacular undergrowth of song as well as an old love for the Italian opera. In the 1900s, Mozart and Balfe excepted, Wagner was beginning to oust the older school from our stage. One rarely heard of Donizetti, Bellini, and Rossini, except on the concert platforms. But they lived on in the memory of the older generation and Joyce had knowledge of the singers through his father, whom in other letters he mentioned to me as listening with his friend, James Gunn, one of the two proprietors of the Gaiety, at the back of the darkened theatre when Tietjens and Trebelli were rehearsing.

His early singing, as I remember it, was that of a light tenor, exact and pure in pitch and tone, and particularly notable for its clear articulation. He held the words in equal respect with the music. But absorbed as he was in literature, it never then entered my mind that he entertained the possibility of a career as a singer nor indeed would I have thought that the volume of his voice, then practically untrained, would have allowed it.

Up to 1902 I knew little or nothing of Joyce's family circumstances or of his financial conditions, which were then becoming ever more straitened. Many of us students were living with our families and in my case a monthly allowance that could be reckoned in shillings was ample to provide me with tram fare, theatre and concert entertainment, and additions to my growing library. My friends may have been in better or worse case. Those who lived in lodgings diligently compared with each other the value they got from their landladies. Otherwise I do not remember any talk of money. We lived alike as poor students, very conscious of our high status as such, but we seemed to do all we wanted to do with no iron necessity compelling us to the contrary. Our futures lay before us, not very closely considered but on the whole clearly enough outlined. Without any thought on the matter I assumed that it was not otherwise with Joyce. His ambitions and his capacity lay obviously in literature. Whether they were to be fulfilled by solitary effort or through journalism never came up for discussion. But in October 1902, when we both took our degree, it was plain enough that Joyce was at a loose end and in difficult circumstances. His determination to live for letters was no less and he surprised us by entering his name as a student of the Medical School in Cecilia Street. He told me in all seeming seriousness that he proposed to make a fortune as a doctor in a few years in order to devote the rest of his life to literature. I could hardly imagine him giving such extended credit to the medieval tag, *dat Galenus opes,* yet when with equal abruptness he left Dublin immediately afterwards he presented himself in Paris at the Collège de Médicine, as if the first step was in deliberate preparation for the second. I cannot conceive either to be other than his first desperate resolve to be quit of his domestic entanglements and to live, however precariously, free from otherwise inescapable burdens.

Recalled after six months of great hardship by his mother's fatal illness, he turned to singing as to teaching for his bare support. Both were temporary expedients only. If he had meditated music as his profession, a serious artist like himself would have taken up its study with complete thoroughness. As it was, he counted amongst his friends a half-dozen who had easy access to the concert platform and so he made it a temporary objective. The usual preliminary, then as now, was to win distinction at the Feis Ceoil. Joyce had, as I recall it, one or two exploratory interviews with Signor Palmieri of the Irish Academy of Music. Palmieri was himself a Feis prize-winner in that year, 1904, for his oratorio, *The Exodus*, with a libretto by Thomas MacDonagh. He approached Joyce, but after the event, with an unaccepted offer of training based on a percentage of his future earnings. In fact it was Vincent O'Brien, Count John Mc-Cormack's first singing master and lifelong friend, who did all he could to prepare him for the competition. The test pieces were the recitative, 'Whom God Loveth He Chastiseth', and the aria, 'Come Ye Children' (from Sir Arthur Sullivan), an Irish air by Moffatt, 'A Long Farewell', and a short sight-reading test. Vincent O'Brien found himself with an unusual pupil and sorrowfully lamented to me that Joyce's discussion of the message conveyed in the recitative took largely from the time which should have been given to music. I was present at the competition in May at the Antient Concert Rooms. Joyce sang the recitative and aria magnificently, and in voice and artistry was clearly superior to his rivals. But, the sight-reading test being handed to him, he studied it for a moment and then laid it down on the piano and abruptly left the platform. Accordingly, he missed the gold medal. My wife, who was then unknown to me, was also present. She knew Joyce only by appearance but not quite as he appeared on this occasion—an angelic chorister in a butterfly tie and the whitest of linen. An old lady behind her exclaimed, 'Oh, what a nice boy', and shared our general disappointment when Joyce's failure to attempt the sight-reading test debarred him from the highest award. Luigi Denza, famous as the composer of 'Funiculi, Funicula', was the adjudicator, and in his report to the Feis Ceoil Committee it was significant that he made no reference to the first or second prize-winner, but added, 'I would recommend the tenor who obtained the bronze medal to persevere in studying seriously.' John McCormack had won the gold medal in the preceding year. Eugene Sheehy told me that, as youngsters, Joyce and one of his brothers amused themselves occasionally by singing outside houses on the Howth Road. It was a pastime not unknown to others. The lovable Eugene Collins, a witty raconteur, fine singer, and able solicitor, played pranks of that sort in his early days, with a banjo at English holiday resorts, but he folded up when he spotted an Irish judge in his audience. My wife similarly told that once, being asked to a party at George Moore's, she put a shawl over her party frock, and sang ballads of her own collection outside his house in Ely Place. It was in the early days of the folk-song fashion. George hated itinerant musicians, but she sang touchingly, and a friend within recognized the then unfamiliar air, 'I Know My Love', and sent George down to give the singer her sixpence. Helen returned it to him when she appeared a little later in the drawing-room without her shawl.

Not all Joyce's concert engagements were much more remunerative, useful though they were to him at that time. The programme of one concert where he appears with some of his friends to whom I have alluded, can still be seen. Others were more like the one which Joseph Holloway mentions in his diary, less profitable in sterling than to literature. The concert was supposed to be in aid of our Irish industrial movement and was held in the Antient Concert Rooms. Holloway tartly comments on its slack management and its noisy stewards. Eileen Reidy, the accompanist, left early—for good reason; her improvised substitute proved incompetent. Joyce was one of the irritated company of artists and, when his accompanist broke down, he sat down himself at the piano, and strummed his own accompaniment to 'In Her Simplicity' and 'The Croppy Boy'. Out of these tears 'A Mother' in *Dubliners* was born.

A few brief notes from me to Joyce, dating from this period, survive in the Cornell University Library, and have only recently come under my notice. They had faded from my memory apart from the circumstances of their origin, and I read them now after half a century not so much for their intrinsic interest, which is only personal, as wondering at their odyssey from Dublin to Trieste and to Ithaca, N.Y., and as illustrating how tenacious Joyce was of any trifle that touched his affairs. The first dates from the weeks before the Dublin Feis Ceoil of 1904, and relates to collections of Irish airs made by Patrick Weston Joyce, M.R.I.A., one of them including some translations from the Irish by Mangan. One I was apparently lending or giving to Joyce. The note runs:

Four Courts, Dublin.

Friday May 1904.

I am sorry I was so long in locating your musical namesake but hope I am not too late. I will be around the bookshops on the Quays tomorrow about 1.30 if you chance to be there. Else I will see you in the Antient Concert Rooms next week.

C.P.C

Gimme something for *St. Stephen's*.

The next followed immediately upon the Feis competition:

My dear Joyce,

I know you deserve a good scolding most, but failing that I don't know whether to offer you my congratulations or sympathy. It is simply scandalous that you let the first prize be thrown away, for your singing particularly of the oratorio business was throat, chest and head above the rest of the rabblement. I hope the inclusion in the list will mean that you sing at the concert on Saturday night, to take your place of honour as Dublin's Prime Platform Favourite. . .

A third—dated July 1904—removes any misconception that might derive from an article by Oliver Gogarty in *Intimations* (1950). It concerns a piano hired for Joyce's musical training.

My dear Joyce,   11.7.04.

Herewith enclosed you will find Apollo's hire, and will pardon on its reception my clumsiness and delay in sending it on. Don't let its acceptance stand between you and your sleep of nights. It will cost me no more than a little self-restraint in passing bookshops. This is in all honesty.

Sincerely yours,
C. Curran

The fourth of these Cornell letters has nothing to do with music and its circumstances had passed completely from my recollection. It relates to some early draft of 'The Holy Office' sent me in answer to my demands for copy for *St. Stephen's*, which I was then editing. An adjective in the first sentence gives the clue and I am now, sixty years after, tickled and exhilarated at finding myself so spontaneously and peremptorily rejecting the proposed contribution. It has, at any rate, some interest in showing that both parties to the transaction took the rejection lightly to heart. The letter runs:

6, Cumberland Place, N.C.R.
8.8.4.

My dear Joyce,

You were very safe in granting me the freedom of the press for the appended unholy thing. I feel quite imperial in my enthusiastic rejection of it. Even if the finances of the paper could stand the strain of a libelaction, the inevitable rhymes are too unpleasant for a family magazine—

so *transeat ad inferos.*

But I must have something—say, the same from a merely literary point of view or some satirical Limericks or anything unmarketable from any reason but one, that you have by you.

Sincerely yours,
C. Curran

I had long wondered why Joyce had never sent me his 'Holy Office' upon his departure for Pola. He had been at pains to have copies delivered to many of my acquaintances, the undeserving targets of his verse. I am now satisfied that it was a courteous omission. He knew I had read it without satisfaction. I may add that my use of the word 'imperial' is a repetition of a nickname he used add to my Christian name: Constantine. The fifth and last of these Cornell letters, dated 1917, finds its place on a later page.

2

Later Days in Dublin

JOYCE had returned from Paris in the spring of 1903. His mother's death in the following August was a calamity, leading very shortly to the breaking-up of the family. The summer of 1904 was a struggle to keep body and soul together with a little teaching, a little reviewing, and the occasional publication of a poem or a story. It was then I read a considerable part of the text of *Stephen Hero*. The pages he had already written came to me in a bulky wad of manuscript in June 1904. Other parts he gave me in separate sections as he wrote them and before he left Dublin that autumn with the unfinished work. I had not long before entered the service of the Supreme Court, and was living in my father's house a little higher up on the North Circular Road from where Joyce had been living at Cabra. But Joyce's house, at 7 St. Peter's Terrace, Cabra, was presently sold, and Joyce went to live on the other side of the town in lodgings at 60 Shelbourne Road and for a few weeks in the Martello Tower at Sandycove. I can date the arrival of the first section from his covering letter to me, which is amongst the few of that date which have survived.

> [No address]
>
> Dear Curran,
>
> The Accountant-General would not like me at present—black eye, sprained wrist, sprained ankle, cut chin, cut hand. I enclose eloquent note from 'Saturday Review'. For one role at least I seem unfit—that of man of honour. However, I will not groan through the post. Here is the marvellous novel delivered upon you by my twenty-third sister. An amiable creditor waited on me at breakfast yesterday for the return of fourpence which he had 'lent' me. If you are too busy to read the novel now, no harm. But as soon as you have read it send me word to meet you on some

altitude where we can utter our souls unmolested. The 'Titania' people paid me in nods and becks and wreathed smiles. The Celbridge concert fell through. Nok sagt!

Yours heroically,

23 June 1904 Stephen Daedalus.

The next instalment came, I believe, in July and was announced in the following manner:

The Rain,
Friday.

Dear Curran,

Invaluable: A thousand feudal thanks: I have finished the awful chapter—102 pages—and Russell [A. E.] has the book now. I shall send you the chapter in a week. I am writing a series of epicteti—ten—for a paper. I have written one. I call the series 'Dubliners' to betray the soul of that hemiplegia or paralysis which many consider a city. Look out for an edition de luxe of all my limericks instantly. More anon.

S.D.

We met here and there to discuss his MS.; sometimes our rendez-vous was at the North Bull. We now met there occasionally, joined by Frank Skeffington who cut singular figures in the water, and by Vincent O'Brien, a powerful swimmer, who once passed almost out of our sight in the westering sun, making a lonely trek to the North Wall lighthouse. Most often we met in some cafe, Bewley's in Westmoreland Street was our favourite, but I recall no higher 'altitude' than Blacquiere Bridge over the Royal Canal at Phibsboro' where once I found him waiting, stretched along the parapet in the pose of the Elgin Marbles Theseus, with no other resemblance to the Greek than appears in the photograph I took of him at that time in the garden of our house. This photograph may well have been taken that particular day.

I greatly regret that, notwithstanding these meetings, my recollection of the text of *Stephen Hero* is imprecise and largely unhelpful. It is to me all the more surprising because its reading revealed to me for the first time in any clear or connected fashion the spiritual strain which Joyce was enduring and the sordid circumstances into which his life had, for the moment, passed. Our earlier talks, as I have attempted to show, had been the not exceptional converse of students who cared about literature. By reason of his own reserve, by reason also of my own lack, not of sympathy but of divination, and certainly from my own reluctance to force confidences, I had little idea of the true extent and harshness of the situation which was hidden under his wry humour. The reading of his manuscript was therefore an experience as painful as it was engrossing. Much of our earlier talk was, I am now satisfied, in the nature of the 'flag- practices' on his friends that he has himself described. I think his loan to me of the MS. was otherwise and that it was almost as much by way of an *apologia pro vita sua* as an experiment in criticism. He knew perfectly well that I was wholly removed from his standpoint on religious matters, and that we differed equally on other issues which were vehemently agitated in the Dublin of our day. He knew also that, case-hardened though I was in letters, I was certain to be shocked at the manner of his more intimate avowals or accounts such as that of Isobel's death. Debate over such areas was accepted as futile and I was content to take the loan as a mark of friendship with a very minor role as critic or script-reader attached. This makes it all the more difficult for me to understand how little I can recall of the details of the text or where it began and ended. Memory, Sir Edward Coke said, is *infida et labilis*. My regret, however, is the less acute and my literary conscience the more lightly burdened since we know that Joyce regarded the work as a schoolboy production and, as he thought, destroyed it.

My visual memory of the MS. is of a clearly written script with remarkably few corrections or interlineations. The pages were, I would say, of the same size as my autograph copies of two poems from *Chamber Music,* that is to say 9¼ × 7¼ in., but had I not seen the photostat reproductions in Professor Theodore Spencer's edition I should have thought of them as holding a few more lines. At any rate, the text was neat and easily legible and, since I had no reason to assume it was a fair copy, it was evidence of a fluent and definitive transfer of the writer's thoughts to his page. This does not imply that he had not made separate fragmentary notations of moods, ideas, and persons, which he wove into his writing. He did; that was his habit, and I think the manner of this in-weaving contributes some obscurity here and there to the comparatively apprentice writing.

I believe I read all the text written before he left Dublin in 1904, but my recollection of it is insecure. It is an untrustworthy composite doubly and trebly overlaid with my acquaintance with familiar places and people and later talk about them, with my knowledge of happenings as they actually occurred, and with the recurrence of episodes in *Portrait of the Artist,* where they are more abruptly and sharply delineated. Some image or characterization sticks in my mind to indicate a lost passage. The North Bull episode in *Portrait of the Artist* was certainly in one section I read, treated with the same imagery of cloud and water, and closing with the figure of the girl gazing out to sea. Such another chapter-ending was 'interminable wastes of bogland, interminable servitude of mind'; I disputed the servitude. It points me to another lost passage describing a journey through the Irish midlands—perhaps to Mullingar—when Stephen looks out from the railway carriage upon a dreary landscape, telegraph wires along the line rising and falling. I can recall also a correction I made in a topographical slip which placed Smithfield east and not west of Church Street. This points to the now missing chapter where Stephen goes to confession in the Capuchin Church. The visit is casually alluded to later in the existing text: 'The church of the Capuchins whither he had once carried the disgraceful burden of his sins' *(Stephen Hero*, p. 177). In passing, I may mention that the author, whether deliberately or not, did not remove the confusion he makes on the same page between the convent of the Capuchins in Church Street and the Franciscan library on Merchants Quay. I was reading at that time in that unfrequented library, not indeed the writings of Joachim di Flora, but the Wadding Papers.

Such fragments dredged from the past are not very helpful, nor can I hope that my more general recollections of the impression then made on me by the reading of the MS. are of any more consequence. They are evidence not so much of the real character of the text as of my own reactions at the moment. It seemed to me then anything but a schoolboy production—rather, a mature work; it impressed me by its formidable, sustained effort, its mass, its copious detail, and by the quality of the writing. At the same time it made difficult reading. There were long and involved sentences and paragraphs with elaborate rhythms and deliberate cadences—rhythms and cadences which I admired in themselves and as reflecting the writer's moods. When I repeated them, he heard the repetition with pleasure; still there was much in them that was quite obscure. These obscurities possibly occurred most frequently in early pages with their reveries on distant happenings. That is again mere conjecture, but these are the kind of passages I have in mind:

It was not part of his life to undertake an extensive alteration of society but he felt the need to express himself such an urgent need, such a real need, that he was determined no conventions of a society, however plausibly mingling pity with its tyranny, should be allowed to stand in his way, and though a taste for elegance and detail unfitted him for the part of demagogue, from his general attitude he might have been supposed not unjustly an ally of the collectivist politicians, who are often very seriously upbraided by opponents who believe in Jehovahs, and decalogues and judgments with sacrificing the reality to an abstraction.

How could he be guilty of such foolishness, of such cynical subordination of the actual to the abstract, if he honestly believed that an institution is to be accounted valuable in proportion to its nearness to some actual human need or energy and that the epithet 'vivisective' should be applied to the modern spirit as distinguished from the ancient or category-burdened spirit.[14]

It seems to me there were many such overloaded sentences which held up an already slow-moving narrative, and this slow motion permitted much accumulation of detail. I have already said that I found myself thinking of George Meredith when reading the MS. This was not, of course, that I saw anything in his writing of Meredith's glitter or his fantastic wit. But Meredith stood to us in those days as the wholly novel example of the intellectual novelist into whose introspective and riddling story-telling one had to mine for treasure. Meredith's stylized obscurity, his *boutades* at the expense of the English character and the conventions of English society, and what long afterwards I have seen characterized in him as 'oracular allusiveness' all seemed to me to have some equivalent in what I was reading of Joyce. Anyway, Joyce did not seem to think so, and it was then he mentioned Henry James's *Portrait of a Lady* where indeed there is some resemblance to Joyce's endeavour to render, though with less detachment, an inner life in conflict with circumstance. I found much hard going in his involution of the inner and outer action—if action is the right word—and James has not escaped the same charge of obscurity.

In mentioning Henry James I do not suggest that Joyce regarded him as his model but rather that, if anyone had to be dragged in, he would think him a stronger candidate than Meredith and a writer at least equally worth his consideration. If literary influences are to be sought out, I am now much more ready to be persuaded that in these

[14] *Stephen Hero*, pp. 147 and 204.

years D'Annunzio played a greater part than is generally recognized. Stanislaus Joyce said this clearly enough in his article in *Letteratura* (Florence, 1941),[15] where he also shows his brother, in Trieste, a lonely defender of D'Annunzio's right to use his own life and the lives of those around him as material for his art without regard to private feeling or public opinion. When Joyce was writing in Dublin I knew nothing of his attraction to D'Annunzio beyond his reference to *Il Fuoco* in 'The Day of the Rabblement' and the fact that he had been to see Duse in a D'Annunzio repertoire in London; myself, I knew little or nothing of D'Annunzio at first hand and what I knew repelled me. But the early influence of *Le Vergini delle Rocce* now seems to me unquestionable— as I hope to set out on a later page. It affected his general attitude more than his style. But, even now, on reading it I am impressed with certain resemblances between it and my memory of *Stephen Hero:* its elaboration of trailing sentences, its learned allusiveness, its alliance of landscape and figure, its diffused lyricism, its deeply felt sensuous impressions, the preoccupied apartness of the central character, and what Henry James distinguishes as its rare notations of excited sensibility. Arthur Symons describes D'Annunzio's novels as states of mind and *Le Vergini delle Rocce* in particular as a shadowy poem in which ghosts wander as if seen in a great mirror, their souls wasted away by dreams. This corresponds in some measure to the moods of reverie I recall in *Stephen Hero*, but *Stephen Hero* was a progression through states of mind and reaction from circumstance while Claudio in *Le Vergini delle Rocce* revolves about a static, half-symbolical situation. Stylistic resemblances exist. They do not touch, for example, the method of Joyce's realism. There is nothing in D'Annunzio's dialogue, sparse and sudden though it be, that essentially resembles Joyce's abrupt transitions into passages of realistic, caricatural interchange. One may dally at other points with faint surmise—on the recurrence, for example, of certain metaphors and motifs: water and the whirring of hawks' wings or the contrast between the monstrous landscapes of rocky Corace and the flat, interminable bog-lands seen by Stephen. To such speculation there is no end, but I shall return later to the more significant resemblances between the discourses which make the prelude to D'Annunzio's novel and Joyce's manifestoes.

I do not appear to have been alone at this time in finding some of the MS. obscure. John Eglinton has put on record his own opinion of the MS., arrived at when Joyce offered it or part of it for publication in *Dana*. 'Joyce observed me silently as I read and when

[15] Translated into English as *Recollections of James Joyce* (New York, 1950).

I handed it back to him with the timid observation that I did not care to publish what was to myself incomprehensible he replaced it silently in his pocket.'[16] Stanislaus Joyce mentions a similar rejection of a shorter MS. by Fred Ryan, the assistant editor of *Dana*. I do not know whether this offer refers to the whole MS. as it then existed or to some epitome or episode—Joyce later called it an introductory chapter—or whether indeed incomprehension was his only ground for refusal. I can imagine many acceptable reasons for the editor of even this aggressive magazine of independent thought declining the whole or a part. But assuredly, if it was the whole MS. as I knew it, the author could not have replaced it in his pocket. I still think, however, that any obscurity was only occasional and would yield easily to revision. There was certainly nothing obscure in a section I read one summer's afternoon on a Dublin hillside to three or four of my intimates who were also Joyce's fellow-students. It was the account of his interview with the President of the College in regard to Ibsen and 'Drama and Life'.[17] My friends listened eagerly to the narrative, appreciated its characterization and all its points, but they wondered if such narrowly localized matter could interest a larger public.

Conspicuous in a few passages of the MS. were the coldly deliberate transgressions of 'the limits of decency' to which Joyce refers in the surviving text and the recurring tirades and railings against Church, State, and nation and the other 'trolls' who were spreading the nets of convention about the feet of the aspiring artist. These manifestoes had the effect, as I have said, of interrupting the slow course of his narrative, but I did not read them with any great concern for their literary effect. I read them, as I read the more painful account of his domestic circumstances, with interest as a personal revelation. As objective criticism of the Ireland of 1904 they seemed to me to have little validity. They were quite divorced from the Ireland I knew; they were contrary to my own experience and based on trivial or imagined occurrences. Yeats had already in 1899 written of the intellectual excitement which followed the lull in political life after the Parnell split and of premonitions of things about to happen. When Joyce was writing in 1903-4 these things were in fact happening and all sorts of converging lines were carrying from disparate, newly tapped sources unsuspected energies which in that very decade founded a new school in literature and in the next established a new State. Nothing seemed to me more inept than to qualify the focus of this activity as a hemiplegia or paralysis, however much one

[16] John Eglinton, *Irish Literary Portraits* (London, 1935).

[17] I may note that the interview with Father Delany took place much later than McCann-Skeffington's auditorship of the Literary and Historical and was not in the College garden but in the President's room and that the President did with characteristic care and courtesy accept, read, and return the Ibsen plays which Joyce lent him after the interview.

might quarrel with its exuberances or fanaticisms. That Joyce thought fit to call it so is the measure of his ardour and youthful impatience. But any discussion with him of such arbitrary assertions was futile; denial or attempted rebuttal was met only with some oblique, humorous, unanswerable retort. The poet was his own lawgiver, jealous and imperious, and had given his allegiance to an ideal which had nothing to do with forms of government. As Stephen Hero 'he acknowledged to himself in honest egoism that he could not take to heart the distress of a nation, the soul of which was antipathetic to his own, so bitterly as the indignity of a bad line of verse. ... He wished to express his nature freely and fully for the benefit of a society which he would enrich.' Now his other allegiances to family and religion were deeper and already pledged. For sufficiently intelligible reasons his 'independence of soul could brook very few subjections' to the first. But it seemed to me that to forsake Catholicism for some merely apprehended invasion of his conscience, or even for some feared circumscription of his literary integrity, was strangely precipitate. In 1904 we were much more accustomed to see these tragic conflicts of faith turn on issues of rationalism or modernism. Stephen Hero's fever-fit of revolt had succeeded the fever-fit of holiness and Joyce as Stephen Hero 'desired for himself the life of an artist... he feared that the Church would obstruct his desire'. In this 'mood of indignation', which Joyce himself finds 'not guiltless of a certain superficiality', Stephen found Catholicism to stand in the way of full and free self-expression and 'forthwith he removed it' *(Stephen Hero*, pp. III, 146-7, 204).

Repudiating the claims of family and country, Stephen also repudiates the Church and any discipline that might fetter his imperious will 'to walk nobly on the surface of the earth, to express oneself without pretence, to acknowledge one's own humanity'. All this— so far as it reflected Joyce's attitude—seemed to me, as I have said, precipitate, a burning of bridges before one came to them, but

> ... mind has mountains; cliffs of fall
> Frightful, sheer, no-man-fathomed. Hold them cheap
> May who ne'er hung there.

I did not hold them cheap, but my relations with Joyce were not close enough to warrant more than sympathy, and I am not aware that anyone at any time found him willing to open up his mind on the fundamental issues involved.

It was Stephen's confessional exposures that held my first attention in the MS. and then his harsh characterization, not stopping short of caricature, of our college life and acquaintances. Humour or comic drive was notably absent. There were escapes from bitterness into reverie but the narrative remained deadly serious. Hectic ardours and emotions were recollected not in tranquillity but with morose delectation, such being the icy temper to which the writer had schooled himself to master his *Sturm und Drang*. Equally characteristic were the abrupt transitions into realistic dialogue, spatchcocked into the passages of reverie or aesthetics. That these dialogues, as has been suggested, took up a larger proportion of *Stephen Hero* than of *Portrait of the Artist*, I am not prepared to admit. This is not my recollection. I found the introspective passages difficult and the prevailing gloom monotonous and oppressive. Under this weight the sudden voices from without came, as I remember them, as a relief in a cloudy narrative, denser I think in the early pages where the mood of recollection would naturally be most dominant. These spurts of realistic dialogue contributed an immediacy to the writing which never ceased to be poignantly intimate and they carried conviction by reason of their abruptness. The sudden shifting of planes is more evident in the finished *Portrait of the Artist* and more dexterously contrived—being, indeed, its most obvious technical device.

A friend of mine from those days found, one wet night, a drunken man lying in the roadway, and, as a Good Samaritan, he took him to the safety of the sidewalk and asked him where he lived. 'I live in the Poddle', said the drunk (the Poddle being one of Dublin's underground rivers). 'You can't live in the Poddle', my friend protested; 'the Poddle's a river.' 'I live in the Poddle', the drunk insisted, 'I live in the Poddle. It's not history we're talking.' Neither is *Stephen Hero* history. But there is enough actuality in the setting of this self- portrait of a young man 'affronting his destiny' to make misreading easy and commentators have been so misled.

Prosper Merimée called art *une déformation à propos*. In *Stephen Hero* time is, in general, foreshortened, events are telescoped, and characters are distorted or brought into a relationship momentarily and historically incorrect. The purpose is simple: to concentrate the theme in order to isolate the hero and to exaggerate—superfluously —his maturity. When he came to reconsider his early text, Joyce was himself aware of inappropriate distortion, something that needed more than the rearrangement of his material. His revision is not a matter of compression—though he was faced with the task of pruning an autobiographical novel which, half-way towards completion, had already extended to 150,000 words. In the ferment of his 'schoolboy production' we must paradoxically recognize its cold savour and also the ebullition of what the author himself, writing in the fell clutch of circumstance, had sufficient detachment to acknowledge as 'ingenuous arrogance' and 'the affectation of more brutality than was in his nature'. He can mock at Stephen's fine words, fine oaths. With similar admissions in his later text, his fellow-students may well refuse to accept Stephen's picture of college life as having anything more than a very partial, subjective validity. For this refusal, must they stand rebuked as being merely 'solicitous to cherish in every way and to advance in person the honour of Alma Mater'. Is not their own honour also engaged?

How then does Stephen's picture of University College compare with prosaic reality? Not otherwise than his picture of his home. The atmosphere is already heavy with decay, heavy with threats to his integrity. Bodeful, it is filled with stale odours of authority and decrepitude. The very houses drip. Like the young Flaubert he has *tout jeune un presentiment complet de la vie. C'était comme une odeur de cuisine nauséabonde qui s'échappe par un soupirail. On n'a pas besoin d'en avoir mangé pour savoir qu'elle est à faire vomir.'* And, as he finds a north-side, eighteenth-century street 'the very incarnation of Irish paralysis', so at the outset we find the College, even in its external appearance, forced to conform to his worst apprehension. The building is gloomy and throws an anticipatory shadow over Stephen's mind as he crosses the Green. Not for him to take any pleasure in the contrast afforded by the eighteenth-century elegance of Clanwilliam House and its pavilion-like grace with the more sober, stately façade of John Whaley's lion-crowned construction and the transition of both by way of Hungerford Pollen's Byzantinish chapel to its pleasant residential neighbour where, in rooms overlooking the Green or with views of the mountains, most of our classes were held. Stephen, 'dim of sight and shy of spirit', did not see the stucco mythologies of No. 85, their garlands and swags upheld by playful *putti,* and the Muses led by Apollo in No. 86, the vine tendrils clustering in the Bursar's office, and the myriad birds circling on the ceilings or clamorously resounding with the fiddles and hunting horns on the walls of the grand staircase. Nothing of this, but only 'above him and beneath him and around him in little dark, dusty rooms .

. . young men were engaged in the pursuit of learning'. Learning's very clothes are seedy: Alfieri is wretched, Machiavelli dingy, Alvarez ragged. And what of these young men of whom I was one and of their 'oppressive life' passed in this 'sombre building'? We were, it would appear, 'a shivering society', 'a company of decrepit youths', a day-school of terrorized boys banded together in a complicity of diffidence, eyes only for their future jobs; to secure these they will write themselves in and out of convictions, toil and labour to insinuate themselves into the good graces of the Jesuits—in common with the other inhabitants of the island entrusting their wills and minds to others that they may ensure for themselves a life of spiritual paralysis. Little wonder if the deadly chill of such an atmosphere should paralyse Stephen's heart.

I find all this insubstantial:

> This bodiless creation ecstasy
> is very cunning . . .

Confronted by this frieze of stooges against which Stephen plays his part as suffering protagonist, I find myself bewildered. I search my memory in vain for these pathetic figures, devoid of intellectual curiosity, not merely docile but servile. An odd chronic medical, a few fanatics, if you like, but not this sad company afflicted with hemiplegia of the will. To my more artless understanding the College presented itself as a single intelligent commonalty split like the atom with a variety of energies, all fascinating. Its virtue, as I have said, lay in its small numbers. Apart from the busy First Medicals there were hardly more than 150 of us in the Arts classes. We passed with healthy appetites from the academic table d'hôte to our own à la carte. Outside class this small company could split up and re-form itself into, someone has reckoned, no fewer than thirty societies. These societies had an active nucleus in students resident in the College. In their working we were all a stage army where the privates in one formation were officers in another. The Literary and Historical was the largest of them and the most vociferously representative; the smaller groupings as accurately and more tranquilly reflected our student interests. They ranged through philosophy, science, languages, music, and athletics. Papers were read and discussed by the specialists but most of us drifted carelessly from one to another, irrespective of our special studies. One, the Library Conference, was like the Literary and Historical another free-for-all, with students from every faculty joining in; the argument might concern itself with the existence of God or Shakespeare or N-rays. The Library Conference was a sort of *viva voce* book-reviewing to which anyone might introduce at his choice any new—or, for that matter, old—publication. My own contribution was Montgomery Carmichael's queer *Life of John William Walsh*. It started me on two diverging lines— Joseph de Maistre and Franciscan literature—pullulating later on my shelves to dozens of volumes. Of one thing about them all I am sure: every man spoke his own mind freely. Indeed, it would be hard to conceive otherwise with men present like Kettle or Skeffington, Felix Hackett or John Marcus O'Sullivan, or others whom I have not mentioned, like John O'Byrne or James Creed Meredith who passed from the Aquinas Society to play a public part in the revolutionary movement. They met again as judges of the Supreme Court and I do not recollect any intervention of theirs in these student debates less pungent or unshackled than their later pronouncements from the Bench.

Joyce took little or no part in such societies although they make the normal life of any university. Apart from his two addresses to the Literary and Historical he spoke but rarely at its meetings. He was present once or twice at the Aquinas or Library Conference but I think these attendances were out of courtesy to a friend. He took no interest whatsoever in the doings of the Choral Union and this was not surprising—its nineteenth-century repertory was not consonant with his idea of music, but he did occasionally make use of its piano for some gentle improvising and like most of the students he entered his name on the sodality roll, but in his first year only.

Aware as I am of this student life from which he abstained, I find it surprising that even in a cancelled work he should see in it stagnation and worse. Even as a *déformation à propos* Stephen's ecstasy in this respect appears to me as something less than cunning and his creation wholly bodiless. He is discussing fustian with his own shadow. Yeats, as I have said, showed more insight and greater detachment in a letter written to the *Daily Chronicle* in January 1899. He wrote: 'The lull in the political life of Ireland has been followed among the few by an intellectual excitement.. . and among the many by that strong sense of something about to happen which has always in all countries given the few their opportunity.' That excitement, let me repeat, ran through every fibre in the College. Such also, I think was John Eglinton's opinion. That devout student of letters, the friend of George Moore, episcopophagous rather than obscurantist, cannot be accused of undue partiality or blind solicitude for any Alma Mater. He was at that time assistant librarian in the National Library and had us daily under shrewd observation. When he came to write of Joyce in his *Irish Literary Portraits,* he introduced him as 'one of a group of lively, eager-minded young men in University College who were interested in everything new in literature and philosophy [and] in this respect far surpassed the students of Trinity College'. This seems no less than the truth.

Still less do I find these young men a servile company contentedly living under an authoritarian regime. One may accept with some reserves the picture of docile youths, mildly bent over their notebooks, patiently recording their professors' definitions. Docile, and why not? Did they not come to be taught? And who more than Joyce used his notebook and his professors' definitions to greater advantage? But, outside class, Stephen's description of a general subservience is grotesquely unreal. I have known no institution of its kind where authority was so lightly exercised. There were, to be sure, examinations to be passed. But for students like Joyce or myself there was obligatory attendance at nothing; no chores; whatever was done was done voluntarily. Professors and students worked on cordial terms and in an unforced relationship. Authority in the College, as I knew it, ran no risk of being corrupted by subservience and I do not think that many students went far out of their way in the interests of their future jobs, as Stephen says, to insinuate themselves into the good graces of the authorities. This cant of Stephen Hero is later and more appropriately placed in *A Portrait of the Artist* in the mouth of Mr. Simon Dedalus, professedly an expert in such things.

On an earlier page I have alluded to University politics as it affected college life. The matter has some relevance here in this point of subservience and I mention two incidents of these years. The first was a demonstration against the University Senate in which the President of the College was an outstanding figure. This 'Organ Row' was a characteristic ebullition of student feeling against the playing of the English anthem at our conferring of degrees. The affair, I may say, ended in the resignation of the Chancellor of the University and in the permanent discredit of the Senate. To avoid further commotion on that afternoon and to dissociate college authority from the action of the students, the President barred the students from the premises and their further demonstration was held about the college steps. It was followed, some nights later, by a students' meeting in an upper room of an old house in Middle Abbey Street over the printing plant of the newly founded Sinn Fein. The place was lit by flaring gas-jets and candles. The room was packed out with students crowded on top of each other, standing on window- ledges, and hanging from window and door cases. Young barristers like Tom Kettle had come down from the Law Library, and with them the brilliant and short-lived John O'Mahony who was to advise us on the legal steps to be taken against the plainly illegal action of the Senate who had, at their formal meeting, gone grievously wrong in a point of fact. For the first time I heard familiar reference to mandamus and quo warranto, this time from the lips of Hugh MacNeill, a professor of Latin at the College, the Professor McHugh of *Ulysses*. The meeting was gusty, deadly serious, tumultuous, and yet orderly. With Carlyle in my mind I saw myself at the Club of the Jacobins with the Mountain in session. I did not imagine myself in a 'shivering society'. Writs, however, did not issue. The threat was sufficient to bring the Senate to its knees. Nor did I observe any notable 'subservience' when a little later I found myself at a function in the Aula Maxima at a period of schism in the Literary and Historical. Many of the students were still cross with their President. They gathered about Cruise O'Brien, protagonist in their quarrel, who had just come in, 'chaired' him with no great difficulty and proceeded in crocodile around the hall and then up the 'staircase, still singing 'God Save Ireland', to deposit him at length at the door of the President's Chamber. Here was no great care on anyone's part for expedient graces. This was, it is true, in 1905—three years after Joyce had left the College. The political atmosphere had sharpened; the university situation had grown more acute; but the temper of the students had not essentially changed. The young cocks were crowing as the old. The tune came from no 'shivering society' but from (I quote the most truthful and outspoken of the Irish Chief Secretaries, Augustine Birrell, who had a close-up experience of the College and saw the students in action) 'a very democratic assembly, by no means very docile and obviously not humble'.[18] I need develop this topic no further. Defence of my fellow-students is superfluous and distasteful, and if I have entered into it at all it is only by way of warning against the blind acceptance of *Stephen Hero* or *Portrait of the Artist* as a transcript of college life, and to set up my own roadblock in the way of the odd mentality to which all Catholic education appears an obscurantist tyranny. Properly regarded, *Stephen Hero* has a high autobiographical as well as a

[18] *Centenary History of the Literary and Historical Society, U.C.D.*, ed. Meenan, p. 317.

literary interest. Not a vain coinage, though the author did his best to obliterate it and withhold it from currency.

It is appropriate to insert here the last of the Cornell letters—a letter written to Joyce in 1917 in acknowledgement of *A Portrait of the Artist*. Since the letter expresses, however summarily, my contemporary opinion, I shall not comment on it save in one respect: I have opened the way to a misconception by reproaching Joyce with unkindness in his references to our Dean of Studies. In using the words 'if harmless and pitiable' I am as certain as the lapse of time permits that I did not use this description as my own. It was never my opinion of the Dean. His idiosyncrasies certainly made him the butt of many stories, and much student mimicry, but we all not merely loved him for his invariable kindness but appreciated and respected his unique quality. It is inconceivable to me that I should ever have used these derogatives, which would explain themselves had I used inverted commas. I think Joyce understood them to be my echo or transcription of something he had himself said or written and that I had clumsily used to shorten argument.

15 Garville Avenue, Rathgar,
Dublin. 26th Febr. 1917.

Dear Joyce,

I am immensely flattered to have from your publisher a copy of your novel and your note. The book is making itself felt and I am only afraid that a *succès de scandale* may obscure its proper virtue. I expect you will have seen by the time this letter reaches you Wells's review of it in the *Nation*. The notice, at the end at least, is amazingly stupid and unctuous but it praises the book highly and will unquestionably sell it. I do a little work at present for the *Nation* and on receiving the novel I wrote to interest Massingham in it and perhaps my letter helped the prompt review. Ezra Pound is doing another article on you for *The Egoist*.

As to my own opinion of it—you have given it an excellent title and the only just criticism must have reference to it and so in regard to the desperate brutalities I am content with your 'this race, this country and this life produced me—I shall express myself as I am'. I admire, too, your courage in scrapping your first draft as I knew it. I think there were passages in that version which might well have been retained but as the chapters were being added to it, it seemed to me that the writer's mood was changing too much from the reminiscent Dichtung of the opening to the literalness and finally to the harshness of the latest chapters I saw.

This version is all of a piece and is much more skilfully and economically worked out. But all the same I regret some episodes in *Stephen Hero*.

On the other hand I think that the student characters are too little individualized within their own group—a good deal of Cranly and Temple not excepted. To us who know them it is easy to distinguish them by personal tricks of speech but they all present too much the same kind of foil to the only character you were really interested in. Secondly I think the pages on aesthetics are too dead, mainly because you talk them at Lynch. I rather think it is a pity that for that side you didn't make Stephen use the old Debating Society. Then I think you are unjust in almost alone mentioning Ghezzi by name and you are unkind to the dean of studies who after all was a kind if harmless and pitiable soul.

But I can't sufficiently praise the fine things. It was a continual pleasure to see so much of the old days in literature—the old songs, 'Turpin Hero', 'Pastime with Good Company'—not so very good perhaps—and the ancient scornfulness. But there were passages of unalloyed joy in the exquisite feeling for words—the girl at the North Bull p. 199 and all that episode; the dance at pp. 257-258, her hand 'a soft merchandise' and the gorgeous thrifty adverb at the top of p. 271. Surely we can still hope for another volume of Chamber Music or rather not Chamber Music but fine poetry none the less when you are still writing these pages or such others as the birds in Kildare St. (Kildare St. by the way reminds me that you have made a mistake in planting the Royal Irish Academy in the passage from 'the duke's lawn' to the National Library. You meant the School of Art.)

I hope to hear from you sometime that you are still writing verse, I have one poem of yours in MS., and to hear of another book. The fact that you have left the whole Abbey Theatre group out in the cold—at which they will scarcely repine—suggests that another volume of unamiable observation is threatening. I cannot help thinking from much of *Portrait* and from *Chamber Music* that when that book is done with you will put that class of work definitely behind you and quarry something less dependent on externals out of your own imagination and deeper experience. I would be glad to hear from you on what you are doing. I have heard vague reports that your eyes have been giving you very serious trouble, and better news to the effect that American publishers are looking for your work. I hope the second is truer than the first.

With best wishes.   Sincerely yours,   C. P. Curran

There has been since a favourable one column review in the *Manchester Guardian* of Friday March 2nd and another in the *Times Literary Supplement* of the same week.

Jimmy Good was on the staff of the *Freeman's Journal* at this date, with John Hooper as the editor. He told (an unconfirmed) story of how John Stanislaus Joyce came to the office one evening with a copy of *Portrait of the Artist* which had just been published, saw the editor, and asked for the favour of an early review of 'his son's first novel'. When John Stanislaus left the editor sent for Jimmy Good who did not happen to be in the office. A subordinate appeared and when the editor was assured that the type had not been 'locked up' he told him to write a review for the next day's issue. The reviewer was going out for his supper. Over sandwiches and beer with his friends he quite forgot the urgency of his commission. Remembering, he rushed back to the office, hurriedly opened the book at the sermon on hell, read, turned over a few more following pages of an edifying character and began his review, 'This is a book which should be in every Catholic home . . .', and so forth. Jimmy Good said that hardened *Freeman's Journal* men blushed to hear the story.

After Joyce and I had taken our Modern Literature degrees in the autumn of 1902, Joyce, as I have mentioned, went to Paris and stayed near the Luxembourg at the Hotel Corneille. It was a modest hotel, celebrated by Thackeray and Du Maurier, but it had earlier and later associations that were purely Irish. Father Prout had lived there, and John Mitchel and John O'Leary and in my own time Synge and Stephen MacKenna; Joyce, no doubt, went to it by reason of its Dublin connections. I stayed there myself later, on the recommendation of some friend of Dr. Sigerson's circle, probably Stephen MacKenna whose way of living there was not less Spartan than Joyce's—he lived, he said, on what he borrowed from Synge, while Synge lived on what he got back from MacKenna, I heard nothing of Joyce from Paris, and, occupied with my own affairs and new studies, saw nothing of him until his mother's death in 1903, and I did not follow all his reviews—some sixteen in number—which were printed in the Dublin *Daily Express* from December 1902 to the following November. Another one—of Ibsen's *Catilina*— was printed in *The Speaker* (London).

These reviews deserve attention. They are composed with uniform care and deliberation. Written at a low ebb in his fortune, they show no trace of haste or half-work. They have complete assurance with due sense of responsibility, occasionally harsh but more usually written with courtesy or a politeness touched with irony. Naturally they reveal the course of his reading and his earlier studies. One of the slighter notices begins with Da Vinci's observation on the tendency of the mind to impose its own likeness upon that which it creates. All show this trait, whether in his indiscriminate eulogy of Bruno, in his unfavourable comparison of Goldsmith's arcadian grace with Crabbe's realism, in his scornful attack on Schiller's pragmatism, or in his sympathy with the wise, passive philosophy of the Burmese and their table of values: happiness founded on peace of mind in all circumstances, the courtesies of life not neglected, all anger and rudeness kept at a distance. And apt epithets are not missing, as when he writes of the agent of the papish plot as 'the monstrous, moon-faced leader—the horrible Oates'.

The articles on Bruno and on Lady Gregory's *Poets and Dreamers* as well as the short, trenchant notice of William Rooney's poems go back to Joyce's Mangan paper, just as the *Catilina* review with its discounting of the Romantic temper and the breaking-up of tradition draws possibly from 'Drama and Life'. All clearly indicate his detachment from national propaganda and our folklore literature. He repudiates both Rooney's patriotic verse and the stories of 'feeble and sleepy' minds brought back by Lady Gregory from her exploration of a 'land almost fabulous in its sorrow and senility'. Yet in this censure of her twilight art he was neither a precursor nor did he stand alone. He was speaking his own convictions confirmed by Ibsen, but he was also repeating what Kettle had said five years earlier when, deriding the literary wardrobe of this art, he found it 'groping in the dust and shrouds of the past not for the lost thread of the labyrinth [of true progress] but for the sorry tinsel of folklore and legend to dress them up for the stranger—a retrospective renaissance with no manly vigour, no spring of action, no fruit but Dead Sea fruit'. The stringency of Joyce's criticism was not lessened by his not being alone in this particular judgement and hardly softened further either by his scorn for Whistler's nocturnes and Mallarmé's verse or, on the other hand, by his studied reservation in favour of Yeats's 'delicate scepticism'. At any rate, this review article (which, unlike the others, was signed or at least initialled) defined clearly enough his relation with our new school of writers and his distance from the majority of his brother bards.

This was also his brief period of dissipation, a dissipation quite foreign to his character. His fortunes were at their lowest ebb. The breakwater of order was less evident than the squalor against which he had sought to build it and to many outsiders it was not plain that there was in fact any citadel to defend. He had published little or nothing: they saw only a 'troop of unmannerly passions'—defiant flags on sand-hills; pretensions and little substance; much cry and no wool. Even the herdsmen of slow, twilight flocks grew impatient and some, angry. Ever since, the amateurs at a distance from the *vie de Bohème* have been fascinated by the violent contrast presented by the heaven-aspiring artist's excursions into taverns and brothels. Their picture of a twentieth-century Dublin Villon or Verlaine is grossly exaggerated. In the first place, the interval of loose living was quite short: it can be reckoned barely in months. It may also be measured quite prosaically in terms of cash and hard work. From the autumn when his home was broken up Joyce was living from hand to mouth, his meals scanty and precarious. A few hours a week of teaching, a handful of reviews, two short stories, three poems, an odd concert engagement, paid or unpaid at Dublin current rates, afforded little margin for excess once landladies' bills were paid. This work of his was punctually discharged and with scrupulous care, while he was still finding time for some musical training. And to this must be added the steadily accumulating mass of the *Stephen Hero* MS. The account does not square with much hectic living, but what there was of it was sufficiently startling, being lived openly and in defiance of convention, and was in plain contradiction with his life before and after the winter and spring of 1903-4. Reckless as he seemed, Joyce never threw down the reins of will. His whole nature was bent excessively in the contrary direction, being perpetually and often preposterously given to method and to elaborate planning, much of it miraculously executed.

It was at this time, in the summer of 1904, that I took the photograph, mentioned above, in the garden of my father's home and in reference to which Edmund Wilson in *Axel's Castle* queried whether without it we should ever have a clear idea of Stephen Dedalus. He also appears in a group of my fellow-students and professors in two other photographs I took in 1902. Both these groups were taken on the same occasion. Having exposed the first plate, I took my position in the second and got the college porter to squeeze the bulb. The photos were taken in the grounds behind the College (Nos. 85 and 86 Stephen's Green) and beside the ball alley mentioned in *A Portrait of the Artist*. The 1904 photograph has a certain humorous bravado in dress and carriage and the same quality, with something more affecting, appears in four notes to me which have survived the vicissitudes of many years. Two I have already quoted in connexion with the *Stephen Hero MS.* The third is a postcard with the postmark of 3 July 1904. It runs:

Je serai à votre bureau demain. Suis dans un trou sanguinaire.

J. A. J.

And the fourth:

60 Shelbourne Road.
30th August 1904.

My dear Curran,

    I am in double trouble, mental and material. Can you meet me tomorrow at half past four at smoke-room Bewley's in Westmoreland Street?

Yours truly,
J.A. Joyce

This letter of 30 August 1904 is the last I had from him before he left Dublin with his future wife for Pola and Trieste. I do not recollect the precise circumstances which provoked it, but I do remember my own bewilderment when Joyce characteristically reminded me thirty years afterwards of what passed between us at that meeting-giving its exact date and place. Nor did I know anything of his fortunate engagement to Nora Barnacle until he came to me one day in October to tell me of their resolution to leave Dublin.

As I have mentioned, I had seen comparatively little of Joyce in 1903 or in the first months of 1904. I had been to Italy for some four or five weeks in February and March and he left Cabra to occupy the Martello Tower at Sandycove with Oliver Gogarty and Chenevix Trench. I did not see him at the Tower nor, indeed until he had moved to Shelbourne Road and was beginning his singing lessons. Nor except for casual meetings, did I really know Trench for another year, though I was to see a good deal of him when with John Marcus O'Sullivan we had entered the Kings' Inns and were attending our first year's law lectures in Trinity College. I can in no way recognize him in the Haines of *Ulysses* and he should not be so identified with him. Trench was an Irishman who had come over from Oxford and grew interested in the Theatre and language movement. He was on the committee of the Theatre of Ireland and as an amateur played the part of O'Hanrahan in Douglas Hyde's *Casadh an t-Súgáin.* As law students at T.C.D., the three of us listened to scholarly lectures on obsolete feudal law from the ageing but hardy pedestrian Vaughan

Hart and with growing indifference we disregarded young Robert Leonard as he sleeked his glossy hair and droned out criminal law. We were more interested in the theatre. We pooled our play-books: John Marcus O'Sullivan fresh from Germany, contributed much Hauptmann, Sudermann, and Ibsen; Trench contributed Shaw and Pinero; and I myself, Maeterlinck and the French dramatists, with more Ibsen. In one term we consumed the European stage, taking a few hours off at the end to run through Stephen's *Digest* before a perfunctory examination. But of the future author of *Ulysses* I heard nothing from Trench.

It was plain enough to me in that autumn that Joyce was at a dead end and that even with the prop of some auxiliary post he could not live in Dublin as the writer he meant to be. In Joyce's family circumstances—with a father who even in middle years had thrown over his responsibility for a numerous family and built all his hopes for himself and them on his eldest son—the situation was quite impossible. Even if the father was not quite the human boa-constrictor of the Mangan paper, even if he was less extraordinary than he was, Joyce was unfitted for that burden. His father has since become something of a legendary character, but the legend hardly outruns the facts. I knew him only in his last days, though like many north-side Dubliners I was familiar with his bristly, stocky figure in the Prince Albert and low topper worn by men of his generation (though in his case the top hat and frock-coat, spruce enough on the first of the month, grew a bit seedy towards its close). He had passed in his time from one employment to another before renouncing all, but his mainstay was a pension of some £250 a year drawn for Government service in the abolished office of the Collector-General of Taxes. Apropos his rate collection, a friend of his told me one story which appears to date from the time the Joyces were living close to Eccles Street at 29 Hardwicke Street. 'Jack', as he was known to his friends, had to get in the Eccles Street rates and he decided he would save himself a lot of trouble by serving court summonses straight away for non-payment of rates, before the regular notices to pay were issued. Court-day came, and Jack attended the Magistrates Court to get his decrees or his money. Then for the first time he discovered, to his horror, that on his list of alleged defaulters was the magistrate himself who, he knew, was in no affluent circumstances. Before the cases were called the magistrate had a hurried word with him, said he noticed his own name on the list, that this was awkward and indecorous, but that he could assure him that his rates in default would be promptly forthcoming. Greatly relieved, Mr. Joyce said: 'Of course, of course, any time at your convenience, etc.' Then the application came on for hearing and one household-er, appearing indignantly, produced his receipt for payment. To the enormous relief of Mr. Joyce the magistrate rapidly intervened, 'We all know that Mr. Joyce is a most capable and conscientious officer. Decree granted.' If his character had been different, John Stanislaus would have been a remarkable social figure in Dublin life. As it was, even during Joyce's school-days his way of living drove him down to always lower levels, commuting fraction after fraction of his pension and insurance policy until little was left to supplement the rent of the house he had once bought in St. Peters Road, Cabra. He passed from lodging to lodging, paying no bills, and dragging after him in his flight his hapless family. This was the position when Joyce was at college. One story I had of a time when they were at Fairview lodging with a Frenchman named Bosinnet. The father and he col-laborated in non-payment of rent but when forced to leave a house after some months Bosinnet, posing as landlord, would recommend Joyce senior as a most desirable, punctually paying tenant and John Stanislaus would enter into possession of the new premises with Bosinnet as his lodger and so on alternately. Another tale told of a night's drinking with friends when he had been living far out beyond Clontarf. Helpless and protesting, he was pushed into the last Dolly-mount tram and put in charge of the conductor. Faithful to his trust and in spite of all protests, the conductor allowed him to alight only when at midnight they had reached Dollymount. His friends met him the next day and made due inquiries as to how he got home. His language was more than usually fearful; unknown to them, a day or two earlier and in customary haste, he had moved camp to Phibsboro, a quite other quarter of the city.

He was a man of unparalleled vituperative power, a virtuoso in speech with unique control of the vernacular, his language often coarse and blasphemous to a degree of which, in the long run, he could hardly himself have been conscious. A notable singer, with a wide knowledge of Italian opera, he would hold the attention of any room all night if there was a piano at which he could sit, play, and sing. He could fascinate indefinitely with stories told with consum-mate art, one neatly fitting into another. And these stories would be of a perfectly drawing-room character till suddenly, as if taken unawares, he would slip into the coarse vein and another side of his nature and vocabulary be revealed.

He was living in this shiftless way long prior to his wife's death in 1903, his family the victim of that tempestuous nature portrayed so admirably by Patrick Tuohy in his portrait of the septuagenarian, where after the lenitive of seventy years the volcano still more than smoulders. He was imposing a quite intolerable strain on those family ties and obligations which in Ireland perhaps more than elsewhere are freely recognized. It was not at all that mutual affection was lacking in the Joyce household or—at least from one side—an exact understanding. At home or on long walks with the two elder boys he had been an inexhaustible reservoir of song and story and racy commentary on life. To his latest days Joyce, like his sisters, spoke of the old man with the same despairing, humorous affection and appreciation, and his more poignant feeling overflows in his 'Ecce Puer' and the closing pages of *Finnegans Wake*. But he could do little to alleviate the misery which followed his mother's death, when his father was a broken man. Deprived of her gentle restraint, demoralization set in and his family, powerless to help, gradually scattered. Presently there was complete collapse, and the old man suffered ignominy before he was at length rescued by friends like Alf Bergan and the Medcalfes, generous, understanding, and forbearing good Samaritans, who took him into their care for his last twelve years or more. All this lay in the future. He was now in the bankrupt stage of his career, accurately enough detailed by Stephen towards the close of *Portrait of the Artist*. For Joyce in 1904 there was no outlet but flight; whatever assistance he might give his family could be rendered from a distance, and it was fortunate for him and for us that it was in the June of this year that he met the woman whose courage and devotion confirmed his resolution to leave Dublin and saw him safely through the difficult years that lay before him. They left Dublin together on 8 October on their way to Pola, where he had been offered a post in a Berlitz school for languages.

It so happened that my friend James Murnaghan and I had already arranged to spend the first fortnight of that month in Paris. Economically we travelled by night and by the Dieppe boat, where there was much talk of Pretty Polly's chances in the *Grand Prix* to be run the next day at Longchamps, and our first conversation at 6 a.m. with the *garçon de chambre* at the Pension Orfilas in the Rue d'Assas was on that momentous topic. Next morning Joyce called to see me as he had promised, but of that meeting I have little other memory than the sudden view of his familiar profile passing the window where we sat after breakfast. We had a later meeting at a cafe and parted in the Rue Monsieur le Prince where he was staying, but I did not then meet Nora and our talk was only of his prospects by the Adriatic.

That was the last I saw of him for five or six years. We kept up a desultory correspondence sometimes upon the appearance of articles of his in the Trieste *Piccolo della Sera*. One of these which he sent me, 'L'Ultimo Feniano', was occasioned by the death in 1907 of John O'Leary. In the same year I had from him *Chamber Music* with the following letter:

Via S. Nicolo. 32. IIIo
Trieste (Austria)

Dear Curran,

I send you by the same post my volume of verses *Chamber Music* which was published in London on Monday last. I trust sincerely that in the future I may be in a position to requite the obligations I am under towards you. I would have sent you also my MS copy but that I feared my doing so would seem to imply a higher conceit of these verses than I now have. However if you wish for it (as I promised it to you) I have it still.

Faithfully Yours

10 May 1907   Jas. A. Joyce

Re-reading this letter, I am desolated not to have promptly seized upon his generous offer of the MS. of these verses. The explanation probably lies in a note to me some weeks later from Stanislaus telling me that his brother had been laid up for more than a month with rheumatic fever and eye trouble. His first brief visit to Ireland in 1909 was in the long vacation when I was not in town, and although he was back again for some months in the following winter as an advance agent to set up the Volta Cinema in Mary Street—the first of a numerous Dublin brood—and I met him not infrequently, my only recollection is of his singing from the score of *Manon Lescaut* and of talk of Massenet and Puccini. His final visit was in 1912, when I was called off the sidelines to take a very casual part in the *Dubliners* imbroglio. Joyce had been to his solicitor about his contract with Maunsel & Co. and George Roberts, and he was of the opinion that the solicitor might be fortified by my opinion of the texts in dispute. Three of the stories had already appeared in the *Irish Homestead* and he now gave me the entire page proofs to read, without comment or any indication as to where the trouble was brewing. During our interview with the solicitor Joyce remained remarkably silent and the solicitor was obviously ill at ease upon unfamiliar ground. We went over the text, the hard-boiled, police-court solicitor showing sensitive reaction to much of its vulgar language. Though I myself was a bit dubious only on the score of 'An Encounter', my view was that no prosecution was anywhere likely and that the public authorities would remain supremely indifferent to its publication. I was surprised and a little amused to find that, amongst all the episodes in question, 'An Encounter' seemed to have aroused the least misgiving. A relic of this interview survives in Joyce's letter to me of August 1912 written immediately before his final departure

19th August 1912   17 Richmond Place N/C/R.
                                                                    Dublin.

Dear Curran

Allow me to thank you before you leave Dublin for your very kind intervention to-day on my behalf and also to wish you a pleasant holiday abroad. Should you be near the 'amaro Adriatico' I hope you will come also to my poor Trieste.

With kind regards and remembrances.

Sincerely yours
James Joyce

3

Joyce Leaves Dublin

JOYCE left Dublin in 1904 not as an Aristides driven out by his fellow-citizens but 'self doomed and unafraid'. He was primarily a victim of economics, his departure the inevitable outcome of his circumstances—in the heel of the reel Shem the Penman out of a job would sit and write. To write he had to escape from the situation created by his father, and to help him do so there came to his side at the critical moment the woman he made his wife. Shem the Penman's problem could only be solved outside Ireland and if he had simply gone to London like many of his contemporaries to pick up work as a journalist and conventional man of letters, his departure would everywhere have been regarded as quite normal. It would have excited no comment, then or later. English critics would have seen it to be in the natural order of things. We should have heard nothing of exile from them, and American expatriates would not have identified it with their own flight from Gopher Prairies. The Greenwich meridian, however, did not run through University College. Italy or France, if not Scandinavia, was Joyce's natural *locus refugii;* the timely offer of a teaching post brought him to Italian-speaking Pola. As always, he went where he could live and write with least disturbance. When he was living in Paris years later, in the full tide of work, he could still write to his friend Frank Budgen, 'Can you tell a poor hard-working man where is the ideal climate inhabited by ideal humans.' He never knew that land, though the go-as-you-please of Paris made it his longest and most congenial abode. I do not pretend that his was not a spiritual as well as an economic exile. He was everywhere an exile of the soul, and an inner detachment made his departure from Dublin all the easier. When I met him in Paris on his way to Pola with Nora, there was certainly no resentful casting of his shoe over Edom. He was as Gabriel in his own story, 'The Dead': 'He felt they had escaped from their lives and duties, escaped from home and friends and run away together with wild and radiant hearts to a new adventure.' Like Falk in Ibsen's play: 'Out into God's world he carried within his breast a two-stringed lute. The upper string vibrated to the joy of life, the lower had its own secret notes quivering long and deep.'[19]

I do not ignore the parting shafts of his 'Holy Office' let loose against some of his acquaintance. My note to him in August 1904 (quoted on pp. 46-47) gives ample reason to think the lines were written independently of his departure. At any rate they were earlier in their sharpening and unlike the 'Millennial Ode' which Ibsen wrote in flight. The squib which had been offered me for *St. Stephen's* is no more than a tart *jeu d'esprit*. It is obviously of a quite different origin from the 'Gas from a Burner', written twelve years later, which singed Maunsel and Falconer with a more scorching flame. That burner was first lit by an English publisher and English printers. His misadventures with them inflamed his later trouble at home with Maunsel and his printer, and this quarrel in the long run became for him a symbol, magnifying the trolls which always beleaguered his imagination. The trolls he divined in Dublin he was to find ubiquitous. As he presented them—and as they were more and more inflated by some contemporaries—Ireland appears as their unique habitat and their victim an Ishmael driven into exile.

Much of the writing of these commentators is negligible, arising from ignorance or preconceptions. What Stanislaus Joyce has written comes, however, with a different authority—by reason of his early intimacy and his own literary capacity. His critical discernment however, and the admiration in which he held his brother's early work do not exclude a great deal of prejudice, some bitterness, and much misconception of the Ireland to which from 1905 until his death he was an utter stranger. His elder brother watched Irish affairs from abroad with interest. He maintained many contacts with his homeland; Stanislaus had none outside his family, and in his later years he had comparatively little communication with his elder brother. At all times he gave heated expression to his opinions on Irish contemporaries and these *boutades,* whether his own or shared between them, I take with some reserve. They were the habitual rhetorical exercises in the vernacular 'contraps', in Joyce's phrase, 'of

[19] *Love's Comedy, Act III, trans. C.H. Hereford.*

fermented words'. In part I see them as an inheritance with which, on the shores of the *amaro Adriatico,* they comforted themselves in the racy accents of their father.

In his *Recollections*[20] Stanislaus Joyce describes the relations he supposes to have existed in 1904 between his brother and those whom he calls 'the other writers of what later became the Celtic revival'. His statements are definite and categorical. He finds amongst Joyce's fellow writers a latent hostility arising first because he separated himself from any purely national movement and later from their consciousness of his superiority to them in culture, talent, and moral courage; and again he writes: 'At a time when he had all the little literary world of Dublin against him, when his every activity was balked and everything that came from his pen was censored. . . .'

In these years from 1902 I was familiar with the figure of Stanislaus Joyce, long-coated, buttoned up, and with collar upturned, accompanying his brother on evening perambulations through the city. He had not been a student at college. He seemed to me a silent, devoted companion, imitating his brother's manner but standing apart when Joyce met an acquaintance. I never saw him except when alone or with his brother. On the few occasions I had speech with him, it was as his brother's emissary and, so far as my observation went, he had no acquaintance with Joyce's literary friends. His judgement of them, I must think, was formed at a distance out of youthful loyalty and later coloured not only by his own strong prejudices, but, more reasonably, by Oliver Gogarty's writings after Joyce's death. I do not know how far Gogarty's hostility was latent before the emergence of Buck Mulligan in *Ulysses*—I do not think there was any. But, with that single reservation, I find no truth at all in Stanislaus's sweeping charges and I speak from personal acquaintance with, I believe, every one of the writers concerned. If, furthermore, I were to seek out Gogarty's opinion of Joyce at this date, I would resurrect one of the many limericks in which he poked fun at his friends. It was written about 1903:

> There is a weird spectre called Joyce
> Re-arisen from Monasterboice
> His whole occupation
>
> A walking negation
> Of all his acquaintance's choice.

[20] Most of what I have written in this chapter was written before the appearance of Stanislaus Joyce's *My Brother's Keeper.* I have the less hesitation in disputing his statements since some of them were the subject of friendly interchange between us in his last years.

Not a very hostile manifestation one would say; in no way different from limericks he wrote at the same time on his other friends, e.g. Tom Kettle and A.E.,[21] or from Shem the Penman's description of himself as one of those who 'sleep at our vigil and fast for our feast' (*Finnegans Wake,* p. 189) or from the confession with which Stanislaus concludes his own paper: 'I admit without hesitation that Joyce was a very difficult person.'

I take a more explicit illustration to show the light in which his own generation saw Joyce at this period. It is from the review of Joyce's *Chamber Music* in the *Freeman's Journal* written on Saturday 1 June 1907 by Tom Kettle, the clearest voice in our college group and representative of his literary generation:

Those who remember University College life of five years back will have many memories of Mr. Joyce. Wilful, fastidious, a lover of elfish paradoxes he was to the men of his time the very voice and embodiment of the literary spirit. His work, never very voluminous had from the first a rare and exquisite accent. One still goes back to the files of *St. Stephen's,* the *Saturday Review,* the *[Irish] Homestead* and to various occasional magazines to find those lyrics and stories which, though at first reading, so slight and frail still held one by their integrity of form. *Chamber Music* is a collection of the best of these delicate verses which have, each of them, the bright beauty of a crystal. The title of the book evokes the atmosphere of remoteness, restraint, accomplished execution characteristic of the whole contents. There is but one theme behind the music, a love gracious and in its way strangely intense but fashioned by temperamental and literary moulds too strict to permit it to pass ever into the great tumult of passion. The inspiration of the book is almost entirely literate. There is no trace of the folklore, the folk-dialect or even the national feeling that have coloured the work of practically every writer in contemporary Ireland. Neither is there any sense of that modern point of view which consumes all life in the language of 'problems'. It is clear, delicate, distinguished playing of the same kindred with wood birds and with Paul Verlaine. But the only possible criticism of poetry is quotation.

Briefly reviewing Irish literature for 1907, the Sinn Fein *Irish Year Book* mentions *Chamber Music* as proof of Joyce's 'very delightful and delicate lyric talent'. I ingeminate that here again there is no evidence of hostility, latent or overt, in my parish or of ostracism, any more than in the matter of 'The Day of the Rabblement' and

[21] On Tom Kettle: On A.E.:
A holy Hegelian Kettle
Has faith which we cannot unsettle
If no one abused it
He might have reduced it
But now he is quite on his mettle.

There is a weird poet called Russell
Who wouldn't eat even a mussel
When chased by an oyster
He ran to a cloister
Away from the beef and the bustle.

The cloister he called the 'Hermetic'
I found it a fine diuretic
A most energetic
And mental emetic
Heretic, prophetic, ascetic.

its *amende honorable* in the publication of 'Mangan', with which I have dealt earlier. If this was the attitude of Joyce's immediate contemporaries between 1901 and 1907, how did his seniors react to the publication in 1901 of this first raking attack on their literary programme? How far did they attempt to balk his activity? Having no evidence, I pass over the mention in *Stephen Hero* of an offer by the University College authorities of some tutorial work about 1902. I never heard of it, but Mr. Mason apparently refers to it as a Jesuit lure.[22] Quite as jesuitically, and at the same date, Yeats introduced Joyce to Arthur Symons and used all his good offices to open for him the doors of London editors. George Moore's dramatic work was the target of Joyce's sharper criticism, but neither then nor at any later time did Moore show any resentment. Quite the contrary, and when it fell to him to express a literary judgement there was no trace of hostility. He came to his support later in the matter of a Civil List pension when Joyce's fortunes were at a very low ebb. Writing with some reserve on his other stories, he said that 'The Dead' seemed to him perfection when he read it and regretted he was not its author. Joyce in his turn, suffering no wrong, but inheriting, rather, Moore's 'mimetic ability', harboured no ill feeling. He did not, in fact, meet Moore until a few years before his elder's death. Writing on that occasion, he expressed the hope that he paid him 'the respect due to his age, personality and achievement'. To Yeats, as is well-known, he showed on all occasions a special courtesy and regard. He never failed to acknowledge the debt he was under to him.

A.E. has received unmannerly and undeserved treatment at Stanislaus Joyce's hands on the same score. But, in this critical year (1904) of his departure from Dublin, A.E. printed three stories by Joyce in the *Irish Homestead* which later appeared in *Dubliners* and subsequently one of his poems. The *Daily Express* had been printing his reviews for twelve months before and *Dana,* edited by John Eglinton and Fred Ryan, had published one of his poems. It is true that *Dana* declined the offer in 1904 of some draft or introductory chapter of *Stephen Hero*. John Eglinton has left his account, which I have given above in Chapter 2, of the proffer of this bulky MS. In declining it he did not overstep an ordinary editorial function nor did it appear so to Joyce then or later, when his comment to Miss Harriet Weaver on *Stephen Hero* was succinct but humorously unjust to himself: 'What rubbish it is.'

What becomes, then, of his brother's wild statement that every-

[22] Stanislaus Joyce and Ellsworth Mason, *The Early Joyce: Book Reviews* 1902–3 (Colorado Springs, 1955), p. 30.

thing that came from Joyce's pen at this date—about 1904—was censored and that he had all the little literary world of Dublin against him?

His other charges of concerted Catholic or nationalist intolerance are more profuse, equally unfounded, contradictory, and wholly ill- defined. A.E. was a nationalist and a theosophist. T. P. Gill was a nationalist and a Catholic and though he had just relinquished his editorship of the *Daily Express* it was he who had made it one of the champions of the new theatre movement and had settled its literary attitude. John Eglinton and Fred Ryan, in their conduct of *Dana,* were declared anti-clericals, but John Eglinton was an imperialist and Fred Ryan a socialist and nationalist of the same temper as Frank Skeffington and in his outlook not very far removed from Joyce himself. In this variety of opinion, where is the evidence or likelihood, amongst either Joyce's seniors or his equals, of a banded hostility?

Stanislaus Joyce's charge reaches egregious expression when, after the long-drawn-out discussion and ultimate breakdown of the contract with Grant Richards, *Dubliners* was offered to the Irish firm of Maunsel. Into the ensuing Maunsel-Falconer tangle he introduces an imaginary 'vigilance committee . . . presided over by the Viceroy's wife, but the Jesuits were widely represented on it, both directly and indirectly',[23] at whose behest the edition was destroyed.[24] I can only stare and gasp at this nonsense. This indeed is 'bodiless ecstasy' *à la* Eugene Sue or such as possessed the begetter of the rule in *Mac-Naghten's Case* wherein an Ulsterman, conceiving himself the victim of a conspiracy between Peel, the Pope, and the Jesuits, assassinated Peel's secretary in mistake for the Prime Minister.

I have nothing to say in defence of the ambiguous transactions which culminated in the precipitate destruction by the printer of the sheets of *Dubliners*. It was a harsh experience for Joyce in the house of his friends and left its permanent mark. However rough the deal, there is no reason to import into it any political or sectarian bias. The directors of the publishing firm and their printer were, as it happened, of three or four different religions and of equally varied brands of politics and their behaviour did not differ materially from Grant Richards's hesitations, prolonged over nine years from 1905, and the recalcitrance of the English printers. There is nothing in the history of publishing that makes the Maunsel story exceptional. Watchdog biting dog, Thackeray closed down Ruskin in the *Cornhill* and Froude stopped him in *Frasers*. Leslie Stephen censored Hardy in the *Cornhill*, Mudie banned Meredith, and Dreiser

[23] *Recollections*, p. 9.
[24] *The Listener*, 25 March 1954.

was withdrawn after publication. Max Beerbohm did not escape scratching and the B.B.C. and the Home Office were later to make difficulties for Joyce. Those things being so, I see no reason why my parish should be the peculiar butt of obloquy or why Stanislaus Joyce should reiterate direful assertions of hidden forces and hands raised in darkness against his brother. The simple explanation of caution on the part of printer and publisher, dubious of their legal position, was not, at any rate, accepted by him.

Joyce's own resentment helped to colour his record of earlier happenings when, in the company of Stanislaus, he was reducing the MS. of *Stephen Hero* into *A Portrait of the Artist as a Young Man*. Both of them saw all Irish affairs in the light of an inherited family trait which cannot fairly be ignored. A corrosive, sceptical suspicion was a characteristic of the father. It appears in Joyce's delineation of him. Stanislaus, recognizing it in himself, wrote, 'My character is permeated with suspicion.'[25] This element of suspicion cropped up in Joyce's own talk with disconcerting frequency though usually with a comic twist. Joyce recognized it in himself in *Stephen Hero* as 'the divining of intrigue' and as part of the 'ineradicable egoism' that conceived all the thoughts and deeds of his microcosm as converging on himself. The sensitive victim beheld 'the pack of enmities come tumbling and sniffing . . . after their game', and as Shem the Penman the tragic jester mocked in himself the dislocated reasoner, the seeker of the nest of evil in a good word, the blind porer over suspicion and auguries (*Finnegans Wake*, p. 189). This faculty of divination lay dangerously close to persecution mania. I say this with difficulty, conscious as I am of the genuine obstacle against which he resolutely struggled and of his own share in creating them. It had early, preposterous expression in his appeal to Lady Gregory in 1902.[26] The same charge of 'a deliberate conspiracy of certain forces in Ireland to silence me' is repeated to the London publisher, Elkin Mathews, in 1913[27] but it gains no greater force by his complaint in 1921 that he has then 'been a year in Paris and in that time not a word about me has appeared in any French periodical'.[28] It was a trait which was only gradually coming to my notice and was in later years to make me often stare at him in bewilderment. Living abroad, it was fed by ill-formed, perhaps obsequious, gossip. Paradoxically, the sceptic was too often credulous. Joyce in Paris was like Ibsen in Dresden, of whom it is written that 'he missed not one item of anything written or said or whispered about him in Norway or elsewhere even though

[25] Stanislaus Joyce, *Dublin Diary* (London, 1962), ed. Healy, p. 38.
[26] Stuart Gilbert (ed.), *Letters of James Joyce* (London, 1957), p. 53.
[27] ibid., p. 73.
[28] ibid., p. 166.

it were spoken in Chocktaw at some Burmese altar'.[29] He attached importance to scribblers and their wildest inventions made a permanent lodgement. He had little sense of proportion either in what concerned his own work or in his activities on behalf of his friends. When his interest in the theatre brought him into relation with the English Players in Zurich and into a complicated row with a British Consul, he sent to me, as to others in 1919, a long dossier on the affair for urgent publication. At that time I was Irish Correspondent for the *Nation* and I mentioned the matter to its editor, H. W. Massingham, as well as to Jimmy Good, the Irish Correspondent of the *New Statesman*, and to the *Freeman's Journal*. Nothing, so far as I recollect, followed at either end. Joyce took this silence as deliberate indifference. He made small account of the absorption of Ireland in its own acute revolutionary business and could still think it possible his little rumpus in a Zurich office had an interest for a Dublin editor who was about to see his printing-press smashed up by the Black and Tans. When his wife and family were travelling in a Galway train carrying soldiers during our subsequent civil commotions, this train was fired on and his family flung themselves on the floor of their compartment. Joyce persuaded himself that the attack had an ulterior motive and, incredible as it sounds, that he was being aimed at through his family. I do not yet know whether I succeeded in disabusing his mind. Equally, he is reported as believing some silly, quite groundless, story that his books were burned at some date or another on the steps of the National University, by which I suppose was meant University College, Dublin. One could multiply such instances of credulity. Some were entertained in pure ignorance; some were wrong deductions from a grain of fact; many were mere dialectical perversions thrown at one's head by way of humorous retort. But, whether well- or ill-founded, they did live in corners of his mind as symbols of forces gathered in the shadows against him, and, if it were not for his own stronger will and his antiseptic humour and for his wife's gay and unfailing common- sense, they might have taken a more tragic turn.

I recall Rousseau in Byron's words of *Childe Harold*:

> His life was one long war with self-sought foes,
> Or friends by him self-banish'd; for his mind
> Had grown Suspicion's sanctuary, and chose,
> For its own cruel sacrifice, the kind,

[29] Edmund Gosse, *Life of Ibsen* (London, 1908).

'Gainst whom he raged with fury strange and blind.
But he was phrensied,—wherefore, who may know?
Since cause might be which skill could never find;
But he was phrensied by disease or woe,
To that worst pitch of all, which wears a reasoning show.[30]

Such misconceptions give rise to others, as the Surinam toad sprouts as it goes. It is regrettable, however, that they still find credit in the minds of competent critics. Writing to me in 1940 on the publication of *Finnegans Wake,* Joyce found its most curious notice to come from a Finn in Helsinki and the best from Professor Levin of Harvard. Professor Levin's later book confirms Joyce's tribute and I read, therefore, with all the more astonishment its statement that 'Joyce's books could not and cannot be published or sold in his native country'.[31] I have dealt with his early pamphlet 'The Day of Rabblement', published in Dublin in 1901. As to all his other writing, it is incorrect to say that any book that Joyce ever issued could not at any time or cannot be bought and sold in market overt in the Republic of Ireland. For a few months, but a few months only, *Stephen Hero* was on the index of books prohibited by the Censorship Board. No other book of Joyce's was ever banned by the Board, though it is true that the customs authorities—acting under a British Parliament Act of 1878 stopped *Ulysses* at the port of entry on several occasions.

During Joyce's two visits to Dublin after 1904 I saw no trace of any resentment towards his old associates apart from the quarrel with Maunsel & Co. Absent from Dublin in the long vacation of 1909, as I have mentioned, I saw comparatively little of him at that time. The Volta Cinema project was then occupying his main attention and his friends were naturally intrigued at his sudden appearance in this new role as a man of business, which he took very seriously. Whenever we met, there seemed little in him of the dedicated man of letters, and the evenings went in music and talk of opera. In 1912 he was still the man of business concentrated exclusively on discussion of the Maunsel affair. His resentment, however, went no further than the four corners of his contract. I heard nothing of the language of the embittered exile but very much indeed of the iniquities of publishers. The change from his student years was apparent. The reserve which was second nature to him had become more marked. His self-possession had grown even greater, but there was nothing at all of the artificial aloofness of the early D'Annunzian

30 *Childe Harold,* III, 80.
31 Harry Levin, *James Joyce* (London, 1944), p. 13.

sovrouomo. In company there was little talk of literature and, though his talk ran willingly enough on continental music, in fact he took no initiative. On the other hand, he spread no embarrassed pools of silence about him and seemed a tranquil part of a friendly atmosphere. This perhaps reflected, from widening experience, what he had earlier, though in a special context, already written to his brother from Trieste in 1906:

Sometimes thinking of Ireland it seems to me I have been unnecessarily harsh. I have reproduced (in *Dubliners* at least) none of the attraction of the city, for I have never felt at my ease in any city since I left it, except Paris. I have not reproduced its ingenuous insularity and its hospitality; the latter virtue, so far as I can see, does not exist elsewhere in Europe.[32]

Ibsen had the same second thoughts: 'The man who has made his home abroad in many foreign countries feels himself never at home in the depths of his soul. Perhaps not even in his own fatherland.'

Dublin was more to Joyce than Norway to Ibsen even though, as Yeats said, 'when driven into exile by, as he thought, his fellow- countrymen Ibsen never forgot the little seaboard towns of Norway'.[33] Joyce wrote in 1902 that the epic poet must keep at a distance from his work. He was following this instinct when he kept Europe between him and his subject. Only from a distance could he modulate the rumour of its streets, set the dream-stage for the dance of its images, and subject its form and history to his kaleidoscopic recreation.

[32] Herbert Gorman, *James Joyce* (New York, 1939), p. 170.
[33] W. B. Yeats, *Explorations* (London, 1962), p. 161.

4

Joyce in Paris

WARS at home and abroad intervening, I saw nothing of Joyce from 1909 until 1921. He had come to Paris from Zurich in 1920 and, I being in France in the autumn of 1921, we arranged a meeting. Our rendezvous was on the Pont des Arts under the shadow of the Institut and I went there with a picture forming in my mind of a meeting years before on the Blacquiere Canal Bridge in Dublin and of the changes the troubled years must have wrought in his appearance. Knowing enough of the hard struggle he had had in Trieste and Italy and of the glaucoma with which he was afflicted, I expected a ravaged apparition. I was therefore gladly surprised at the elegant figure which alighted from a taxi. A slight moustache and beard accentuating the lines of his face were new to me; his eyes were shaded with powerful lenses; but his carriage was brisk and his debonair carrying of a cane diverted one's attention from his defective sight. Of that afternoon as of all our later meetings I have the friendliest recollections but, from the point of view of literature, recollections of little worth, for Joyce preferred to gossip about Dublin than talk literature. We went to lunch, at my suggestion, to a restaurant near the Luxembourg—*not* Foyot's. I was only gradually to level up my awareness of Joyce's choice in the matter of food. Never gourmand, considerations of health made him here as selective as in all things. But, anyway, we ate oysters and I answered all his questions about Dublin and his Dublin acquaintances and realized how he loved to reconstruct its streets in the precise succession of shops, houses, and their occupants. The only flaw I could find in his rebuilding was his omission of the recent asphalting of the streets and the increasing smell of petrol. There was no trace left in his speech of his former abrupt silences, no needless reticence, but a quiet gravity and some courteous reserve. He told me, however, of Miss Weaver's princely generosity and his freedom from financial worry. He liked Paris as a place to work in, a place where you could be and let be; Nora and his family liked it better than his own possible preference for some place nearer the Mediterranean. On a later occasion he was more explicit and emphasized the debt he was under to the generous recognition extended to him by French writers in Paris. This I was to see for myself.

Joyce had been sending me copies of the *Little Review* and the *Egoist* in which episodes from *Ulysses* had been appearing since 1918. After lunch we crossed over to the Café d'Harcourt and talked of the completed work which was to be published in the following spring.

I made it evident that, however much I appreciated the sections I had read, I had formed no idea of the Homeric framework and had only a rough notion of many of the secondary associations. Such lapses of intelligence happen when a strange planet swims into the literary firmament. Nor did I carry every detail of the *Odyssey* in my head. No Grecian, I had read, like Joyce, Lamb's *Adventures of Ulysses* at school and in later years, with less attention, I had read Butcher and Lang's at one time esteemed translation. Joyce was at pains to take me step by step through all the wanderings of Bloom and Dedalus, plotting out the Homeric parallels, courteously but quite erroneously assuming that I knew every splinter from the *Wandering Rocks* and that I had not failed to observe and remember the meshing of every cog in his mechanism of time and space. This patient courtesy was characteristic of him but it was also deliberate. I was presently to see in print the evidence of similar conversations and like instruction. Joyce was a serious artist. When writing, he thought of his work only. He made no concessions in the interests of easy and immediate communication. But, when his work was finished, he treated it objectively and did not underestimate the necessity of smoothing its path to ultimate intelligibility. When I had heard him out, I said tritely that this Homeric scaffolding was no doubt helpful to him in composition but mattered little when the building was up. He seemed to agree, but I felt his assent was no more than a politeness. I began to think as I think now that these and similar parallels and correspondences had begun to be of great importance to him. They lay at the foundation of Joyce's experimental and characteristic work where time is expanded or folded up like a concertina with the same overlapping of planes and with metamorphoses or liquefaction of objects. In his own art Braque was making not dissimilar experiments in space control in the series of *Ateliers* on which he was working off and on from 1939 to 1954.[34]

I recall only one other instance of any sustained conversation on the work he was engaged on. It was five years later in his apartment, and we were discussing a section of *Work in Progress* which had appeared in the *Criterion*. Again I could not conceal my far greater bafflement at a form as strange as that by which old Jacopone da Todi *nova mundum arte delusit*. Like everyone else I wanted to know why he was doing it. His reply was succinct: it was a night-piece and the language of night is not the language of day. Had Paul Valéry written a letter which in fact he did not write until a year later, Joyce might at this point have invoked it as an authority for Ear- wicker's prolonged dream and indeed for Molly Bloom's monologue:

Figurez-vous que l'on s'éveille au milieu de la nuit, et que toute la vie se revive et se parle à soi-même. . . . Sensualité, souvenirs, émotions, sentiment de son corps, profondeur de la mémoire et lumières ou cieux antérieurs révus etc. Cette trame qui n'a ni commencement ni fin, mais des nœuds, —j'en ai fait un monologue auquel j'avais imposé, avant de l'entreprendre, des conditions de forme aussi sévères que je laissais au fond *de liberté.*[35]

Settling down to closer discussion, he tried to make clear to me its polymorphism—the transmogrifications by which his figures, animate or inanimate, obscure or famous, *urbi et orbi,* were liable to sudden change, dissolving and re-forming themselves in Earwicker's dream at any point of time.

He set out for me H. C. Earwicker's omnipresent role, but he did not tell me of something I dropped on much later in a collection of sketches by the Victorian caricaturist, Harry Furniss.[36] These caricatures from Mr. Gladstone's days include one of H. C. E. Childers (p. 44). It has the caption 'H. C. E. Childers' with the sub-title 'H(ere) C(omes) E(verybody)CH-LD-RS'. The sketch is of a smallish, stout figure, strutting forward importantly—as well he might if he knew himself the eponymous ancestor of the Finnegans.

But Joyce did on that earlier occasion introduce me to the *Scienza Nuova* and Vico's theory of history, pointing out its relation with his own *Work in Progress*. Before I left he took down and lent me Michelet's translation of the *Scienza Nuova*, directing my attention to the passage in the introduction which begins:

[34] Braque's *Ateliers;* and John Richardson on Braque in the *Burlington Magazine*, June 1955. I find the analogies irresistible.

[35] Quoted in G. Brereton, *Introduction to the French Poets* (London, 1956), p. 263.

[36] *M.P.s in Session 1882-1890, Five hundred sketches of eminent members of the House of Commons 1882—1890* (London, n.d.).

Le malheur c'est qu' arrivé là, il se trouvait seul: personne ne pouvait plus comprendre. L'originalité des idées, l'étrangeté de langage l'isolait également. Généralisant ses généralités formulant, concentrant ses formules il employait les dernières comme locutions connues. Il lui était arrivé le contraire des Sept Dormants. Il avait oublié la langue du passé et ne savait plus parler que celle de l'avenir. Mais si c'était alors trop tôt aujourd'hui peut-être c'est déjà bien tard. Pour ce grand et malheureux génie le temps n'est jamais venu. . . . Malgré l'obscurité qui en résulte, malgré l'emploi continuel d'une terminologie bizarre que l'auteur néglige souvent d'expliquer, il y a dans l'ensemble du système présenté de cette manière, une grandeur imposante et une sombre poésie qui fait penser à celle de Dante.

La science nouvelle puise à deux sources: la philosophie, la philologie. La philosophie contemple le vrai par la raison; la philologie observe le réel, c'est la science des faits et des langues.

The passage continues after the enumeration of those fundamental principles which Tacitus calls *foedera generis humani* to Vico's classification of the three ages of human society which Joyce adopts, the divine or theocratic, the heroic, the human or civilized. These pages from Michelet's introduction to his translation of the *Scienza Nuova* bear closely on the plan, structure, and language of *Finnegans Wake*.

I had hardly got back to our hotel when a packet arrived from Joyce, and I turned from Michelet to my first reading of *Anna Livia Plurabelle* in the October 1925 issue of *Le Navire d'Argent*. For its better understanding I found myself reading it aloud to my wife. Turning over a page I dropped on this note written on thin paper which he had enclosed: 'You may wish to have A. (Anna) before the corrected version appears in the October *transition*. The piece should be read half aloud, without a break and rather rapidly. J.J.', and with these two keys I had to unlock its secrets before rejoining the Joyces for dinner at Les Deux Trianons. The time and place, however, and the necessity to introduce my daughter, not yet in her teens, to a dish of frogs, excluded further exegesis. Many years before, Dr. Sigerson had introduced me to these delicate morsels at the Cafe Vefour. Such traditions had to be maintained and passed on while Anna Livia flows. But before the evening was out Joyce did tell me—as no doubt he told others—that when he had finished the Anna Livia episode his heart was filled with misgivings. He went down that evening to the Seine and listened near one of its bridges to its waters:

... sans cesse vagabonde
Caquetant pur ton gravois
D'une floflottante voix.

He came back, he said, content.

Joyce was not a table-talker. With me, as I have said, his talk was
of Dublin all the time, Dublin, old and new, with every possible pic-
turesque revival of its familiar figures of the eighties and nineties out
of our own and our fathers' time. In such exhumations he could be
extraordinarily entertaining. At other times, with strangers present,
you became one of a secret society. A party to his grotesque invention, these intricate leg-pulls which he would conduct with enormous
gravity now seem a farcical shadow-play anticipating *Finnegans
Wake*. His talk never ran on books and, as much from disinclination
as from his failing sight, he seemed to read little of his contemporaries. He listened more than he spoke. He was insatiable for fresh local
and personal details, question following question, the answers being
turned over and collated carefully and critically in his mind and filed
as it were for future reference, before giving place to further queries.
As if still 'divining intrigue', there was the usual slight but noticeable
interval between what you said and his next question. There was
no scrap of malicious talk—ever since I knew him he scorned such
gossip—but he took a real and undisguised interest in people's attitude and behaviour and in the fortunes of his acquaintances. There
was nothing intrusive in his inquisition. It ran along with caustic
appreciation and much spirited burlesque and came, plainly, from
his determination to keep the picture of his town clear and firmly
established in his mind. He loved best to talk of singing and the
theatre but did not disdain discussion of food and drink in different
countries and liked to classify his friends' tastes in such minutiae. In
all his conversation he was simple and unaffected, obtruding none
of his preferences intolerantly, but while speaking clearly on many
matters that touched himself personally he would not go beyond an
obviously predetermined point in regard to the progress or process of
his own creative work. He never entered with me on his profounder
beliefs, but showed an equally studied consideration for those of his
friends. Throughout all this later period I found no embarrassment
but only great and watchful courtesy; even when at a distance and
at his blackest hours some twist of wry humour would appear, making the strain tolerable. In company his high spirits abounded, but

neither then nor at any time in my recollection was there any bawdy in his talk—Sancho Panza and Don Quixote in plenty but Panurge never and Pantagruel only on the satiric side. When we met in Paris on later occasions he was increasingly preoccupied with his daughter's illness and his mind was never free from the dread of war and further dislocation. He shrank from all violence and with a sort of stoic passivity watched the terrors gathering in the dark. Yet, in front of this fatalism, his interest in life was so vivid and the pleasure he took in his friends and family circle, and most of all in his wife's challenging and gay intelligence, so engrossing that my Paris memories of him are most exhilarating. They are associated with afternoons in apartments which were never the same—the Joyces seemed perpetually to be changing or about to change their flat—and with evenings at the Deux Trianons, the Taverne de l'Alsace, Chez Francis, and Fouquet's. But there was nothing memorable in such meetings other than the evidence of friendship.

One supper party at Fouquet's remains in my mind because we had Marlene Dietrich as our nearest neighbour. Fouquet's was a then fashionable resort of theatrical and cinema stars. Going there one evening from his flat, whether of malice aforethought or not, Joyce conveniently forgot a book he wished to give me and so—sending our wives ahead—Joyce with Eugène Jolas and myself went back to fetch it and, ignoring warnings given us, we interposed an interval *en route* for pernods. Warned I suppose by the earlier arrival of our wives, there was a great to-do when we made our appearance. Piccolo and commissionaire were strung out on the pavement. Piccolo signalled commissionaire, commissionaire passed the signal to the *maître d'hôtel* advancing from the doorstep. I almost saw a red carpet. Commissionaire took and handed Joyce back his cane, piccolo took and passed on hats and coats, and the *maître d'hôtel*, preceded by the piccolo carrying my two-volume Lasteyrie, which I did not choose to lose sight of, led us in procession to what I suppose was Joyce's accustomed place. I found Nora pointing out the celebrities to my wife as they arrived, both forgetful of reproaches in their anxiety not to miss Marlene's usual moment of arrival. But the manner of our entry was a challenge—hers was no more distinguished—and when she did arrive I kept my attention fixed on Joyce and our conversation and for the rest of the evening did not remove my eyes from his. I imagine that Nora did not fail to appreciate my sense of values. At any rate the pernods were forgiven.

I remember only the gaiety of those evenings and recollection of them is now mingled with my daughter's account of similar later meetings when she was working in Jeanne Bucher's gallery in Montparnasse and seeing the Joyces each week. Joyce loved the theatre, whether it was opera or Jules Verne at the Châtelet to which he took my wife, or the Odéon to which he took my daughter to see *L'Abbé Constantin* in honour of her father's name. I missed all such occasions but more greatly regret absence from his birthday celebrations, honoured each year in set form, Joyce wearing an ancestral waistcoat in brocade and at a given moment executing his ritual dance, a special slip-jig. In one of these, however, which was attended by my daughter I took part from a distance. It was in 1938 and was notable for us inasmuch as Radio Eireann signalized it with a Joyce programme in which I took part. Joyce, as I have already said, attached high importance to any family occasion and this time there was more than usual fuss. Preparatory letters and telegrams were vigorously interchanged between us, and exact synchronization of time established with New York and Mitteleuropa, wherever a Joyce might be at the moment. The evening when it came was divided into two parts: one at the Joyce flat to hear the broadcast, and the second for dinner at the Jolas's, but perhaps I had better with some discretion quote from a letter written to me by my daughter at four o'clock in the morning on her return from the dinner:

We heard the broadcast at the flat with Sam Beckett and an Italo-Swiss music and art critic from Zurich. Joyce fussed around there for some time inspecting the presents and wires and finally proceeded after violent argument over the lost record of Yvonne Printemps to the Jolas's in a taxi full of bottles of wine and cheese, crackers and records and us, of course, singing. At the party were the Gormans, John—greatest-singer-in-the-world— Sullivan, pompous but amusing, the Pelorsons, Paul Léon and Peggy Guggenheim. . . . Dinner was aided and abetted by a fascinating Russian waiter called Conrad. There was a big cake in the middle in green and white with THE BOOK and the Liffey *et tous* raised on it and 56 candles, We ate that with champagne after dinner and lots and lots of Alsatian wine. I remember .. . Claire Gorman shrieking about Beethoven and .. . Léon yelling at me trying to persuade me that Whistler was a Russian . . . and guessing games about the title of W.I.P. only known to Mrs. Joyce—a secret which she has kept sixteen years and did not propose to keep a minute longer; but she was silenced and we took to pulling crackers and then we all with hats on went inside to the salon. First there was Giorgio (who was then in New York) singing on the gramophone and then the piano got going and whiskey and brandy flowed and Philippe Soupault came in and Joyce sang from *Ulysses* and come-all-ye's and *Siubhail a rúin* and then Mrs. Jolas and Sullivan together—he should not be let do it within a radius of 50 yards—and then Joyce sang *Phil the Fluther* and danced and pretty well went on dancing until after three. I talked to everybody far too much, and had a grand time. . . . Mrs. Joyce is thrilled that the broadcast happened in Dublin. Everybody loves Daddy's little moustache and reckons Joyce will be put on the map in Ireland. Finally we got away out on to the rue Borghese, Joyce capering along on Léon's arm still with a yellow hat on while Conrad went chasing ahead for a taxi. Seven of us got in and we saw the last of the *Geburtstagskind* singing on his own doorstep. After that Beckett and the rest of us went and had fruit drinks to sleep on. We were all pretty jaded . . . but the plum pudding came just at the right moment. ... It is nice to hear of people quietly planting sub-hirtilla but of course Europe is one thing, Ireland another. Now I'm going to bed for a change.

Joyce was ever at pains to study his friends' tastes and to serve them. His anxiety to give them pleasure and his sense of hospitality were so embarrassing to me that at times I had to keep him in the dark as to my own holiday movements so as not to disarrange unduly his own plans and mine. When we did meet there was no gainsaying him. You were body and soul at his disposal. He had a planning mind and your days were blue-printed for you. At home in Dublin I was amused to find this servitude in a more distinguished instance than my own. On a May afternoon in 1937 at the Courts I had a telephone message from my wife to say that a French academician, whose name was unfamiliar to her, was calling that evening to our house and that I should be prepared to meet him. It appeared that Louis Gillet, editor of the *Revue des deux mondes,* member and perpetual secretary of the French Academy, son-in-law of René Dominic, brother-in- law of Henri de Régnier, nephew of the late (the more than late, Joyce said) José-María de Hérédia, had somewhat unexpectedly arrived that morning and was met by his hosts of the French Legation and by Professor Roger Chauviré. Chauviré had just rung up my wife to tell her that Gillet's first inquiry at Dun Laoghaire pier was as to my whereabouts. He wished to meet me. That could easily be arranged, Chauviré said, as the day was Wednesday, when we kept open house for our friends. When he arrived, Gillet told me he was a friend of Joyce who wished him to call on us. Before we separated that evening, I tried to arrange for some excursions with him during his stay. He knew Dublin from at least one previous visit. Should we not therefore drive through the mountains and see Glendalough? Chauviré supported me, but Gillet in his slow, deep voice murmured something about rhododendrons in Howth. Were they not now in bloom? We said they were but Glendalough was a famous site and more worth seeing. Gillet said he understood that the rhododendrons in Howth made a very pretty sight. We said they certainly did but that Glendalough had a spectacular situation in the mountains, a sanctuary with historical and architectural associations going back from the thirteenth to the sixth century. Gillet said he would like to see the rhododendrons. We left it at that for the moment. Armed with maps, we met for lunch next afternoon at Jammets and renewed our proposals but, finding him still obdurate, to Howth we went. We were sitting at the foot of the rhododendron cliffs admiring their blaze of colour when I suddenly remembered that on leaving my house that morning I had got a letter from Joyce which I had put, unread, in my pocket, his handwriting requiring some quiet attention. I took it out now to read it and found that it was to announce Gillet's visit; it made also a quite casual allusion to the rhododendrons which should be blooming in Howth. So Gillet's obstinacy was explained. Joyce had blue-printed his programme. Gillet had obviously received his instructions that he was to report on the rhododendrons and he had to obey.

Louis Gillet, whose facial appearance was not unlike that of the sculptured Christ on the Romanesque tympanum at Moissac, had a wide and deep knowledge of European art and literature. The generosity of his intellect had brought him close to Joyce in an intimacy which was none the less valued because he possessed a fine bass voice and had at one time trained for a musical career. He has left his own memorial of friendship in his *Stèle pour James Joyce* (Marseilles, 1941) and in the introduction he wrote for the edition of *Chaucer's A.B.C.* which was decorated by Lucia Joyce. That edition was indeed made at his prompting. The poem had its origin in an address to the Blessed Virgin written by the Prior of the Cistercian Abbey of Chalis, and what still stands of that thirteenth-century foundation had become Gillet's home, more loved than his apartment in the Rue Bonaparte. Lying in the midst of the forests of the Île de France, amid ponds that drank the moonlight—his own description— my wife, daughter, and I were his guests there and learned to appreciate his generous culture and his friendship for the Irish writer whose work he vindicated against the open hostility and more shabby intrigues of Sir Edmund Gosse. In my copy of Lucia Joyce's work I am proud to have my own name linked with his in his inscription of it: *Tibi Constantino Jacobi amico ego Jacobi amicus Louis Gillet.*

Bereft of medical attention, Gillet died in hardship in 1943 in unoccupied France, a victim of the Nazis. In that, he was only a little less unfortunate than Paul Léon who was last seen half-carried by his companions in misery in a wretched procession to a concentration camp. Léon, with whom I had much correspondence, was a lawyer and sociologist interested in international jurisprudence and most unselfishly devoted to Joyce, transacting for him all his business. My last days with Joyce and Nora were spent part in his company at Fontainebleau, driving in the forest, eating *sucre d'orge des réligieuses* at Moret, loafing happily in the sun in quiet ripples of chaff and reminiscence.

In between these rare meetings, from the time Joyce left Dublin, we had maintained a dropping correspondence. Quick interchanges alternated with long silences, but contact was never broken. Not many letters passed between us when he lived at Trieste but he sent me an article or two from those he wrote for the *Piccolo della Sera* such as 'L'Ultimo Feniano', written in 1907 on the death of John O'Leary. I seem to remember one such article—or was it only a conversation—that described an entertaining encounter which Joyce had when he took a *carrozza* outside Milan, at Gorgonzola, with the intention of driving in it to Venice. The horse was recalcitrant, it shied at all uniforms, including, most inconveniently, all policemen. Joyce gradually learned its history. It began its adult career as a Dublin tram horse; was sent out with the Dublin Fusiliers to the Boer War; miraculously escaped the attention of De Wet, and now was ending its days in Lombardy. And its name, believe it or not, was Dublino. But perhaps this story only existed in a conversation !

His books came to me with brief notes as they appeared. But the surviving letters are few. I find I have no more than thirty, a slender garner for a series that began in 1904 and ended in 1940 when growing blindness forced him to supplement our correspondence with messages from Paul Léon. Those that remain are therefore discontinuous. Furthermore, though they are never without a vivid mordant phrase, and their own unmistakable character, few bear directly enough on his work to make them part of literary history. There is no abstract discussion of literary criticism and there are no passages of set description. They are direct and practical, humorous, scathing, or preoccupied with some anxiety. Joyce was no more a letter-writer than a table-talker, and these letters were certainly not written with any idea of ultimate publication. They turned, for the most part, on his family affairs or on some immediate business with such exchanges and inquiries as pass between friends at a distance. Of those I have, a sad number were written in distress of mind during crises of illness in his family and are poignant memorials of his affection for his father and children. In spite of any early repudiation of 'castellar rights' he remained closely knit in spirit with his father. His family, however scattered, was an ever-present concern with him; himself thoroughly domesticated, he kept his correspondent in touch with his family affairs and, just as he welcomed every recognition of a domestic occasion, he was also punctilious and mindful with regard to his friends' domesticities.

In a letter of 1937 he recalls that at Clongowes Father Conmee used to say that his letters home were like grocers' lists and confesses *sono sempre quello*. He was right except that now his demands were prepaid—Joyce was very scrupulous in transactions involving money. But his requirements were numerous and *recherché* and not the easier to meet when the neat handwriting of his early days became more difficult to decipher. I sent him once a long list of theatrical engagements from a file of Dublin eighteenth-century newspapers only to find that what was requested was, more reasonably, from the nineteenth century. On another occasion I was almost misled into a rendezvous with him at Parame instead of Paname.[37] The requests were diverse. One was for Irish poplin of a certain colour to make book-markers or to decorate a book for Nora. Others, and they were plentiful, were for pantomime librettos, music-hall songs, etc., and their yield is submerged in *Finnegans Wake*. From many he wanted the music more than the words, for his own singing and as a keepsake for his son Giorgio. These sent me ransacking music shops in Capel Street and along the quays for the songs of Ashcroft, Wheatley, Val Vousden the elder, and Percy French.

Alone amongst these, Percy French's songs are still on the air. His name alone is written in the stone and water of a public memorial. The others are recorded in a more obscure and more lasting monument. The moralizing type of Val Vousden's entertainments is now long out of date, entertainments in which songs such as 'Let Each

Man Learn to Know Himself' were interspersed with dancing in a variety of character-sketches ingeniously linked to make one-man shows— *The Unity of Nations* and *The Rosicrucians*. In these productions in the Antient Concert Rooms, words, music, dialogue, and dancing were all his own work and—unless for reasons well-known to his audience and not unexpected—his performance was exemplary in its smooth elegance. He lived to a fine age. Joyce knew Vousden and his songs and it is regrettable that the last he saw of him was, he wrote, when he was making a patriarchal entry into the Black Maria outside Store Street police station. He had a long white beard, typifying, he said, the wisdom of the morning after. In earlier years, in his morning glory, by an advertisement in the next day's papers the entertainer would excuse his failure to appear on the stage, pleading an accident to his ankle.

Horace Wheatley was a nearer contemporary of ours and was to be seen at the Gaiety and Queen's Theatre pantomimes throughout the nineties. The indispensable Widow Twankey and watchful mother of all our Christmas heroines, his gags and songs like 'Morgan the Hatter' were clearly localized and informative. Ashcroft, The Solid Man, reigned a little earlier in our music-halls. He had graduated at the Grafton Theatre of Varieties in South Anne Street. His reputation was established in the eighties; his songs, however, were sung in our period. One of Joyce's particular requests to me was for his famous 'A Quarter to Two' and I can now guess the reason, since the victim of the inaccurate timekeeper in that song was of the same avocation as the eponymous hero of *Finnegans Wake*.

> She wakes me up in the morning,
> Calling the hour of six,
> I'd the deuce of a race,
> To get to the place
> For work of carrying bricks.

The family 'flitting' is still remembered:

> McGovern carried the crockery ware,
> The cradle was handed to me,
> Murphy sat on the top of the cart,
> Houldin' the clock on his knee.
> The horse set off at a funeral trot, etc.

Another letter mentions James Gunn of the Gaiety, a good friend of Joyce's father's, and another friend, R. J. Thornton, told him of Guiglini who sang with Tictjens here in 1857 and flew his big kite on Sandymount strand when he was a boy. Dubliners, he said, ranked Guiglini, as a tenor, above Mario. Joyce, however, did not mention that, favourite though Guiglini was with Dubliners, he suffered once at their hands. Piccolomini had made his farewell appearance with the company in 1858 and was escorted in a torchlight procession from the Gaiety to the Gresham. Guiglini was with him and had to address the demonstrators at Nelson Pillar. 'I thank and love you' was all he could say in English. His love was diminished when he discovered his watch had been lifted in the crowd.

His father's friendship with the Gunns continued in the second generation. Michael Gunn's son, Selskar, used to go to the opera with the Joyces, and his sister Haidée told him of the many allusions to her father and mother she had seen in *Work in Progress.* As for myself, I saw Haidée Gunn with Viola Tree make her debut in the Gaiety as a very tall, very charming Juliet. She also appeared in a scene from *The School for Scandal* playing Lady Teazle, one of her mother's notable parts. In *Finnegans Wake* the allusions to Haidée's mother are to her appearances when she was still Bessie Sudlow, captivating Dublin by her beauty and charm in pantomime. She excelled also in light Shakespearian parts like Ariel, but it was in pantomime—as the hero in Edwin Hamilton's *The Yellow Dwarf* and in *The Babes in the Wood,* but most particularly in *Cinderella,* that she had Dublin at her feet. She made her last appearance in that role in 1877, directly after her marriage to Michael Gunn, and her glorious apparition in ballroom splendour remained long in the memory of our parents. The afore-said Edwin Hamilton was unique in winning the Vice-Chancellor's medal for English verse in Trinity College by his comic rhymes. He became an assiduous pantomime librettist and I was enlisted in Joyce's quest for the texts of these ancient masterpieces—*Turko the Terrible, The Yellow Dwarf, The Babes in the Wood,* and *Rhampsonitus.* To uncover their rhythms in *Finnegans Wake* is the task of thesis hounds. For Joyce they were a part of his father's estate—voices from a Dublin that was slipping away and which he would blend with the waters of Anna Livia. Not easily fobbed off from the completion of his collection, he noted the absence of Val Vousden's 'Let It Pass' and Percy French's 'Andy McElroe' from one of my consignments. Paul Léon sent me other reminders; on one I note an endorsement:

97

Percy French's 'Mulligan Masquerade', Ashcroft's 'Quarter to Two', already mentioned, 'McGinty the Swell of the Sea', 'Mind You That Now', and Vousden's 'Time and Tide'. Paul Léon's letter goes on, 'I have just received from Mr. Joyce a letter and a card where he adds to the list a song the name of which I cannot decipher. I think it is "The Soldier's Song". In case it is unobtainable he would like it to be copied.' Paul Léon, of course, was unaware that the song had become our national anthem. So Joyce spun his web.

At Christmas 1933 I had a letter from him telling me he had asked his friend Antoine Establet who owned a vineyard at Avignon to send me a case of Clos S. Patrice, 1920, *rouge*. It was like him to remember our different taste in the matter of wine and my preference for red burgundy.

I never drink it myself [he wrote] as I dislike red wine but it is really wine from the royal pope. The vineyard is at Château-neuf du Pape, the oldest in that part of France and Establet who inherited it says that before the sojourn of the Popes at Avignon the wine of the country was known as *Vin de S. Patrice*. I never met a fellow-islander who had heard of it but I mentioned it to Count O'Kelly, the Irish Free State envoy here and to Dulanty in London and they said they would get it for dinner, etc. There is another S. Patrice below Tours but it is only a *Vin de pichet*.

It was equally like him that having learned the history of this *cru* which had hitherto not been particularized other than as Châteauneuf, he should have set himself to revive its original name and to get Establet to issue his product with the old title on specially designed labels indicating its Irish connexion and to secure its appearance on the tables of our legations abroad. At first its issue in the special form was deliberately limited, but the wine is now on general sale under its original name.

A gift of this sort had to be treated with respect and accordingly I produced it only on St. Patrick's Day under *geasa* that my guests should be men of letters worthy of it. My first party included Stephen Gwynn, my elder in vintage lore, and to him it was a novelty. Then, in soaking off and sending him the wine label, I anticipated a request from him. To my surprise, a year or two later, I saw in Charles Berry's book—I speak of the well-known expert of St. James's Street—a quotation from a letter of mine to Gwynn with reference to another French-Irish vineyard:

I think you and I will agree that this [S. Patrice] vintage should be our national drink at this season and should be admitted to this country free of all duty except that of drinking it. When this objective has been reached it will be our next business to have restored to the Dublin diocese that portion of *Hibernia irredenta* which includes the Archbishop of Dublin's vineyard at Beaune.[38]

Mr. Berry also noted that in 1822 the topographer Jullien mentions the same *cru*, S. Patrice, as 'worthy of being considered of the highest class'.

Next Saint Patrick's Day the poet-philologist Osborn Bergin, most learned of my friends, and the poet-historian Edmund Curtis sat in to our table.[39] The ritual toasts to Saint Patrick and James Joyce having been drunk, our talk turned to folk-songs. Singing by way of illustration kept pace with our meal. A day or two later I met Bergin on the Rathmines bus and he silently fished some Latin verses out of his pocket. They were commemorative of our dinner. I praised them and said they had everybody in them except Petrarch and Vaucluse. As silently he put them back into his pocket, but next evening, stimulated by a hexametrical postcard, I had from him a full version. The lines are a more than sufficient excuse for my long story. Here they are:

De Vino Patriciano
Artificum nutrix multorum et blanda noverca,
qui procul a patria continuere gradum,
Gallia purpureis hoc Narbonensis in uvis
laetificum vinunt coxit amoena tuis.
Saepe duo calices juvenem fecere disertum,
et tribus exhaustis concinuere senes
Ipsum hoc Petrarcam redimitum tempora lauro
fontibus arcebat, Sorgia dare, tuis.
Talia Magnorum lenibant pocula curas
Pontificum, stabat dum furor Urbis atrox.
Dolia deinde pio mercator nomine signat,
Pontificisque nova captat ab arce notam.
Quamvis dulce tamen maturat Avenio vinum,
dulcior a titulo fit meliore sapor.
Felix qui repetens volventibus impiger amis,
restituit priscam, nobilis ille, notam;
Qui tardos gressus cognovit Ulixis Ierni
(quid latet in tumido, Daedale, corde tuo?)
Qui, quo splendidior reddatur debita vino

---

[38] c. f. *Crede Mihi*, No. LXV, for the purchase of this vineyard by Henri de Loundres, Archbishop of Dublin.

[39] Curtis had already been celebrated by Bergin in Gaelic verse commemorating their visit by boat to Clonmacnois with Seán Fraser. That was in 1910, *'agus Éamonn geal dár stiúradh'*.

gloria, 'Patricius tale bibebat' ait.
Advena Patricius colies (quis nescit?) amavit,
qua Rhodanus ridens sole calente ruit.
Tune feres umbram veteris, Provincia, laudis,
immemor et tanti semper amantis eris?
Nunc saltern cyathus venerabile nomen habebit:
Patricianus erit. Prosit, amice, bibe!
Constantinus adest, ruris, laris, urbias amator,
Musarum cultor, dives amicitiis.[40]

There are other allusions in the letters which I should gloss. In September 1929 Joyce refers to a proposed reproduction on the cover of an instalment of *Work in Progress*', there is a reference, I think, to an *objet trouvé* I sent him about this time. On my way to the Courts I had seen on the quays a wood-carving of the arms of the City of Dublin, painted in gesso. It might have come from the old Tholsel or city council or some guild-hall. Believing it would amuse him, I had it packed and dispatched. Later I saw it in Joyce's rooms together with Jack Yeats's pictures of the Liffey. However, the reproduction might have been from a finely engraved early nineteenth- century map I sent him—the course of the Liffey from its source above Lough Bray. Plentiful of place names, it was bound to be received with favour.

In September 1935 Joyce mentioned in a letter his sittings to Seán O'Sullivan, R.H.A., for a drawing. The painter had mentioned he was going to Paris and I arranged with Joyce for a drawing. Seán returned with three from which I made my choice; one of the others is now happily in our National Gallery.[41] Joyce said he had found my friend, as I expected, *très sympathique*, but actually the sitting came at an unfortunate moment. He was suffering badly, as his letter suggests, from a deep-seated malady. The drawings betray evidence of this and show him under a strain.

Finally I would refer to certain passages in the correspondence which run counter to the notion that Joyce had a settled determination never to return to Ireland. In March 1920, writing to Frank Budgen from Trieste, he was speculating on the chances of meeting him in England in the summer, 'Perhaps I too might go to Cornwall and then to Ireland.' It was an ill-judged moment for a visit. Dublin lay under curfew. The armed resistance to England was general, and Lloyd George's Black and Tan terror at its height. It was to this situation that Joyce referred in writing to his aunt in Dublin in 1921: 'If the country had not been turned into a slaughterhouse of course I should have

[40] Or, as translated by my friend, Mr. Niall Montgomery: Fair France—enchanting foster-mother, nurse of many artists whose footsteps mingled, far from their native lands, west of the Alps—out of your purple grapes, you made this gladsome wine. Two glasses oft have loosed a young man's tongue—three drained, and old men join in song. Clear-flowing Sorgues, this wine kept from your springs Petrarch himself, his temples bound with laurels. Draughts of it lightened the great pontiffs' cares, as, outside, the city's dreadful frenzy raged. Thenceforth the shipper marks his flagons with the honoured name and pirates a trade-mark from the Pope's new castle. (However sweetly Avignon matures the wine, that nobler style makes it taste sweeter still!) Blest he who active in the rush of years remembered and nobly restored the ancient name, he who knew of the late wanderings of the Irish Ulysses · (Say, Daedalus, what lies hidden in your swelling heart?), that the debt to the wine be repaid in greater glory, cries: Of such a vintage Patrick drank! Patrick, in exile, may well have loved those hills, where warmed by the sunlight rolls the smiling Rhone. Can you, then, bear the memory of that ancient praise, Provence, unmindful yet, for ever, of so great a lover? Now at least the wine which bore a revered name in future will be called Patrician. Good luck, my friend; drink up! Here with us is Constantine, lover of heath, hearth, and market-place, learned in the arts and with a wealth of friends.

[41] A portrait of James Joyce by Seán O'Sullivan dated 1935 is held in the National Gallery of Ireland. Red chalk and charcoal with white highlights on blue paper.

Joyce, Paul Léon, and the author outside the Hotel Savoie, Fontainebleau.

Joyce in 1937, drawn by Seán O'Sullivan, R.H.A.

gone there and got what I wanted.' To any question of mine on the topic his reply was the evasive: 'Have I ever left it?' In August 1937 he had been writing to me about a proposed visit of his wife to Galway on family affairs. Nora Joyce had an invincible dislike of sea-travel. 'She has never been able', he said, 'to cross water and she will not even trust herself into one of the *bateaux mouches*. It is a frightful job when we get to the channel on rare occasions.' This time Joyce had some idea of accompanying her at least as far as Holyhead, but 'I am trying to finish my W.I.P. (I work about 16 hours a day it seems to me) and I am not taking any chances with my fellow-countrymen if I can help it until that is done, at least. And on the map of their island there is marked very legibly for the moment *Hic sunt Lennones*[42] But, every day, in every way, I am walking along the streets of Dublin and along the strand. And "hearing voices". *Non dico giammai ma non ancora.*

Letters from my daughter to me in 1938 from Paris show that his friends did not believe that he held to any idea of permanent exile. In the February of that year she gathered from Mrs. Joyce and the Jolas's that a combined trip over was in question, 'But I cannot quite fathom how much is in such talk. At least Mrs. Joyce and Jolas are keen but *Work in Progress* must be finished first.' In June of that same year she wrote me:

Went to the Odeon with Joyce on Thursday—*L'Abbé Constantin* in memory of you. Romantic comedy but he mostly laughed at my stories about Newmarket-on-Fergus.[43] Apparently he has been keeping Mrs. Joyce awake at night ever since laughing. He has started speaking at last about finishing his book which I think is really true this time. Then they are coming to Ireland, but of course will have to be kept up to it. I am given a long list of questions to be worked out in Dublin before he can finish it all the same. More work for the stooges.

I do not think that Dublin for permanent residence would, at any time, have suited Joyce's way of working or way of living. Had he lived, he might have come back for some stay, short or long. But I also believe that, although he was arriving at a juster estimate of the appreciation in which his work was held at home, he felt his pride involved. I see him postponing any return until some public recognition of the position he had won after much hardship was offered. Ibsen may still have been in his mind. Anyway, time passed and the opportunity never came. This 'high, unconsortable one' rests with his life's companion in a grave in Zurich.

[42] The allusion is to an ill-conditioned article in an old number of the *Catholic World* (Canada).

[43] The stories, I understand, related to her experiences when assisting in an archaeological 'dig' in Co. Clare.

Part Two

5

Joyce's D'Annunzian Mask[44]

REVIEWING the student years we passed together and figuring out to myself the new moulds in which Joyce's ideas and conduct were then forming, I have been for many years convinced that D'Annunzio was one of the mould-makers. Ibsen, like Yeats, was another and his influence has escaped the attention of none who has written on Joyce. But the 'radiant simultaneity' with Ibsen which Joyce so gladly recognized in 1901 extended even before that date to his Italian contemporary and Joyce for some years lay fully in his orbit. None, save his brother, has pointed in this direction and these brief references of Stanislaus Joyce in his *Letteratura* article, significant as they are, travel even further than they may appear to at first sight. D'Annunzio's influence was as early and almost as strong as Ibsen's. Its evidence lay indeed on the surface, plain to anyone with the clue, and while it lasted it was consonant with Ibsen's and was stylistically more apparent. In Joyce's student years when *fin de siècle* masks were still the fashion it was strong enough to lead to deliberate identification and self-dramatization on his part and to affect his personal behaviour as well as his credo and style.

D'Annunzio, whatever his limitation, takes a place in the train of the great nineteenth-century egotists—Byron, Hugo, Wagner. Like Joyce he did, as Arthur Symons suggests, help to shift interest from the 'exterior' novel to the hidden, inner self which 'sits silent through all our conversation'. In 1901 Joyce found him the culmination of the tide that rose with Flaubert and certainly with him a new style was born, a theatrical pastiche and a manner which deeply affected a whole section of Italian society.[45] He saw himself as a 'redemptive' writer like Ibsen. With superb mastery of language and magnetic eloquence, however overwrought and feverish, he built up

[44] With grateful acknowledgement to the editor of *Studies*, in which part of this chapter first appeared in Summer 1962.

[45] See Luigi Barzini's article in *Encounter*, January 1956.

a fictitious stage for the Italian superman's choreographic existence.

Abroad, thanks to Eleonora Duse, D'Annunzio was then perhaps more generally known as a dramatist than as a novelist. Led by his own early interest in the theatre, Joyce's attention was drawn to him in 1899 but he knew him in both fields—as did Symons who found place for D'Annunzio's one symbolical novel, *Le Vergini delle Rocce,* in his collection of literary essays. In May 1900, after the publication of his Ibsen article in the *Fortnightly Review,* Joyce, as we know, crossed to London to see Duse's performance in *La Gioconda* at the Lyceum. I have in my collection of books once owned by Joyce, three by D'Annunzio.

D'Annunzio was little read in the Dublin of those years. His plays and poetry, to say nothing of his novels, came slowly to the shelves of the National Library, though Huneker, in 1890, was writing of him as one who with Ibsen and Hauptmann personified the thoughts of the new generation with its contempt for 'the conventional lies of our civilization'. But not later than 1900 Joyce was defending a novel —plainly by D'Annunzio—in Ghezzi's Italian class in University College (*Stephen Hero,* p. 170). It is evident from this, and from his interest in *La Gioconda,* from his reference to *Il Fuoco* in 'The Day of the Rabblement', from the Leonardo-D'Annunzian epigraph with which it opens, and from what I believe to be D'Annunzian echoes in his paper on James Clarence Mangan in February 1902 that Joyce was following all he could of D'Annunzio's work with special attention. Alone in Dublin, I imagine, he had this admiration. One will, I suspect, search in vain for D'Annunzio's name in *Beltaine* or *Samhain* amongst the Ibsens, Björnsons, Hauptmanns, Sudermanns, Tolstois, Maeterlincks, and Echegarays freely mentioned in these organs of the promoters of the Irish Theatre movement. And this is not surprising, for in spite of Yeats's interest in Arthur Symons's explorations there was as much in D'Annunzio at that stage to repel as to attract our Irish poet. The Yeats of 1900 was occupied with folk-lore and magic and with dreams of a theatre whose personae could step clear of any more tangible nets. He lent an ear to Raftery, the Irish folk poet, rather than to the Italian Renaissance. He had not yet made the journey to Urbino and Byzantium.

The traces of D'Annunzio may, I believe, be discerned in many aspects of the youthful Joyce: in his early artificial attitude and bearing towards his fellows; in the methods of his self-discipline as an apprentice-writer; in his Messianic outlook and in his aesthetic gospel. Let us consider these from old recollection and in the light of *Le Vergini delle Rocce* and *Il Fuoco*.

First as to his personal bearing. Joyce left Belvedere for University College in the autumn of 1898. He was then no more than sixteen years old, exceptionally gifted but in no other way singular. None of his Belvedere school-friends describes any undue, habitual aloofness in him at this time or any detachment from school routine. We have authentic recollections from two of his school fellows. William Fallon told me that as a small boy Joyce made a notable Red Indian in spite of his frail physique. He was by all accounts cool and imperturbable, though he took no part in regular school games. Judge Sheehy has written of his useful initiative in school plays and of his talent for satirical improvisation. On the other hand, as I have mentioned earlier, from 1899 none of his University College friends failed to note aloofness and detachment as a special characteristic. It is true that this reserve appeared in different measure. It affected only in a slight degree his old schoolmates and the one or two acquaintances whom he was making his partial confidants. But reserve there was, although open at times to irruptions of sudden merriment. His detachment took more often the form of studied politeness but it fell little short of arrogance in the eyes of many of his fellow-students and it was not less known as such to the group of writers outside the College—generically known as 'the bards'—whose acquaintance he was making and who were later to be the unflattered recipients of his 'Holy Office'.

This change over from normal companionship to an increasingly defiant, arrogant isolation lasted some four or five years and it began quite suddenly—within the space of a twelve-month. It was, of course, part of that 'enigma of a manner' which Stephen describes himself as constructing in his first year at College (*Stephen Hero,* p. 27). Becoming evident in 1899, it is not unreasonable to look for the origin of this change in his reading in that year. Its progression is the subject matter of the *Portrait of the Artist,* but its form and definition are so curiously forecast in D'Annunzio's *Le Vergini delle Rocce* and the parallels so exactly drawn that, when every allowance is made for experiences common to adolescent genius, one cannot escape finding in this novel a direct influence. Long persuaded of its bearing on Joyce's early writing and opinions, I am confirmed in this by Stanislaus Joyce's categorical references to its effect on his personal behaviour, building up no less than a life in advance. *Le Vergini delle*

Rocce certainly helps to explain the mask he wore in his early years. Joyce at seventeen deliberately modelled himself on D'Annunzio and Ibsen. However incongruous his two exemplars were, they had just enough in common for Joyce to build up out of them or their pages a new personality for himself, unconsortable and scornful of public opinion, and with a settled programme and plan of conduct. Ibsen's moral fibre fixed his intransigence but D'Annunzio's heroes left no less unmistakable traces on his public behaviour.

We turn to *Le Vergini delle Rocce* and to supporting passages from *Il Fuoco,* examining their pages not in full detail—for that in view of D'Annunzio's prodigality of lavish language would require too copious transcription—but summarily and with sufficient particularity.[46]

Le Vergini delle Rocce is a novel indeterminately symbolist and allegorical—calculated therefore to attract Joyce as did Yeats's *Tables of the Law.* It begins, as Symons says, with a discourse and ends as a poem—a description which might, indeed, cover Joyce's whole achievement from his essay on Mangan to *Finnegans Wake.* The discourse occupies the first section. Its race-conscious hero, Claudio, seeks to recreate in himself the mannered and masterful personality of an admired Renaissance ancestor and in a degenerate age he faces the self-imposed task of reanimating the exhausted race of his fellow countrymen with his antique spirit. Under the tutelage of a Socratic demon and of da Vinci he conducts a self-examination which establishes the framework within which he will fulfil his destiny. His faith is in himself and in aesthetics. He believes in the grand manner, defined by Henry James in this immediate D'Annunzian context as 'the sense of the supremacy of beauty, the supremacy of style and, last not least, of the personal will, manifested for the most part as a cold insolence of attitude'.[47]

This virtuoso has learned from Leonardo *se tu sarai solo, tu sarai tutto tuo* and that there can be no greater mastery than of oneself. In 'The Day of the Rabblement' Joyce is equally urgent that the artist should isolate himself; he formulates this as a radical principle of artistic economy and as Stephen Dedalus in *Stephen Hero* he repeats it as a first principle (p. 33). Claudio seeks in silence to lift his life above its circumstances and by his will, by selection and exclusion, to prepare himself for his creative work *(The Virgins of the Rocks,* p. 14). So Stephen 'built a house of silence for himself' (*S.H.,* p. 30). He erects his 'breakwater of order', just as Claudio 'after the inev-

[46] I use Agatha Hughes's translation of *Le Vergini delle Rocce: The Virgins of the Rocks* (London, 1899).

[47] Henry James, *Notes on Novelists* (London, 1914), p. 221. In his essay 'Poetry and Tradition', W. B. Yeats wrote, as Mr. Niall Montgomery reminds me: 'In life, courtesy and self-possession, and in the arts style, are the sensible impressions of the free mind, for both arise out of the deliberate shaping of all things, and from never being swept away, whatever the emotion, into confusion and dullness.' This comes closer than cold insolence to Joyce's later attitude.

itable tumult of early youth' raised a barrier 'against the confused and multifold overflow of sensations' (*V.R.,* p. 14). The analogies with Stephen grow as we proceed to passages inculcating 'methods to conduct thy being to attain perfect integrity ... to concentrate the purest essence of thy spirit, and to reproduce in . . . art the deepest vision of thy universe . . .' (*V.R.,* p. 52). Stephen also 'strove to pierce to the significant heart of everything. He doubled backwards into the past of humanity. . . . He seemed almost to hear the simple cries of fear and joy and wonder which are antecedent to all song. . . . And over all this chaos of history and legend ... he strove to draw out a line of order, to reduce the abysses of the past to order by a diagram' (*S.H.,* p. 33).

But Claudio also has realized his necessity. He also has learned the benefits of order and the ruled design: 'Day after day I felt my whole nature grow, under the rigorous discipline of meditation, selection, and exclusion ...' [Its marvellous virtue was], 'that although it drove me to order my inner life with the exactness of a ruled design, it did not dry up the spontaneous springs of emotion and imagination . . .' *(V.R.,* p.28). This passage in which the verbal resemblance with the text of *Stephen Hero* is so close is immediately followed by sentences which recall the flowing forth over Stephen's brain of the verses in *A Portrait of the Artist.* Of a sudden a 'jet of poetry would burst from my inner being, filling my whole soul with music and ineffable freshness, and causing desires and hopes to burn higher in a happy flame' (*V.R.,* p. 28). A further passage seems to me again to reflect the young college student's ambitions in point of discipline and design. It is when Claudio learns 'to seek and discover in my own nature genuine virtues and genuine defects, that I might arrange both in accordance with a premeditated design, striving with patient care to give a seemly appearance to the latter, and to raise the former upwards towards the supreme perfection', excluding 'everything which was discordant with my ruling idea . . ., which could slacken or interrupt the rhythmical development of my thought' (*V.R.,* p. 22).

Such passages from *Le Vergini delle Rocce* appear so similar in language and ordonnance to others in *Stephen Hero* and *Portrait of the Artist* that I hardly know from which text I transcribe. It is true, of course, that they also depict the experience of many another young poet but the analogies grow close in other particulars. Claudio's Socratic demon counselled him 'to compose and cultivate music'. In our college days, if we were alone together and a piano at hand, Joyce would inevitably drift to the keyboard and into snatches of song and recitative. It was then I heard him first sing to his own music certain lyrics by Yeats. As well as being a 'cultivator of music' Claudio is a poet and a master of style. His demon assures him: 'Thou dost possess the gift of poetry and must study to acquire the science of words.' As an avowed student of Leonardo da Vinci he notes down his 'terse, proud sayings' and is drawn by 'the pithy significance of an incisive axiom'. Are we not here alongside Stephen the word-catcher, the lexical student—in the workshop of young Dedalus, fabricating those definitions and terse, proud sayings which he or his creator will throw down at any interlocutor? D'Annunzio endows Stelio, the hero of *Il Fuoco,* with his own exultant mastery of language. Consciously he tries out his mental agility and the facility of his speech. Like Claudio he is prodigal of quotations drawn from carefully recondite sources and spreads embroidered cloths of didacticism before his audience. He cultivates language at two extremes: one, the concise 'da Vincian epigraph'; the other, evocative of dream, unfolding itself in purest verbal music. These are again conspicuous traits marking Stephen Dedalus. Other passages or sentences in *Il Fuoco* carry to me fainter overtones of Joyce's youth. I do not refer so much to the title 'Epiphany of Fire' borne by Part I of the novel, though his appearance of a favoured word may well have now first caught Joyce's attention. I allude rather to other touches descriptive of Stelio which recall Joyce: his liking, for example, for ceremonial (p. 10 [48]), his passion for opera, and more particularly the description of Stelio's voice and Stelio's own account of his public speaking. 'I can speak only', he says, 'about myself. Obliged to speak to my audience only of my dear soul I must speak under the veil of seductive allegory and with the magic of gracious cadences'; and he speaks with 'a clear penetrating voice, icy at the start'. Was this passage present to Joyce's mind when he was preparing his paper on Mangan? I conceive no more concise description of this piece of veiled allegory and semi-autobiography and of Joyce's manner in its delivery.

These stylistic and personal details have drawn me away from Joyce's assumption of that 'cold insolence of attitude', which Henry James finds in D'Annunzio's heroes stemming from their sense of the supremacy of beauty and of the personal will. Claudio, meditating on the counsel of Socrates's demon, learns that the real duty of a man of worth is to discover in the course of his existence a series of harmo-

[48] *Il Fuoco* (London, 1899). English trans.

nies, varied indeed, but controlled by one dominant motive, and bearing the impress of one style. *... In his supreme wisdom the ancient sage made his Ideal* 'the living centre of his being and deduced his own laws from it. . . exercising with calm pride such rights as they permitted him, and separating—he, a citizen of Athens under the tyranny of the Thirty, and under the tyranny of the plebeians— deliberately separating his moral existence from that of the city. (*V.R.*, pp. 15, 16.)

And accordingly Claudio, like Stephen, breaks with God and the State. *Non serviam,* says Stephen; and Claudio says that 'I will be obedient to God only' means 'I will be obedient only to the laws of that genius to which, in order to fulfil my conception of order and beauty, I have subjected my free nature' *(V.R,* p. 16).

Claudio, poet and man of action, conceives himself 'destined to engrave on new tables of stone new laws for the religious guidance of the people' *(V.R.,* p. 29) and, as Stephen would forge in the smithy of his soul the uncreated conscience of his race, so Claudio dreams of 'the iron for the plough which shall furrow afresh an exhausted land' *(V.R.,* p. 25). Meanwhile he is harrowed by the ignominy which surrounds him:

the arrogance of the populace was not so great as the cowardice of those who tolerated and supported it. Living in Rome, as I did, I was witness of the most ignominious breaches of faith . . . which ever dishonoured a sacred spot.... Like the overflow of sewers, the flood of base desires was invading the market place and the cross-roads. . . . (*V.R.*, p. 24.)

The 'turbid seething of servile passions' surrounded Rome 'like a river of Tartarus'. The sacred city is populated by a miserable race stricken with leprosy re-iterating their dreary complaint. The ancient Persians, as the ever-fresh Herodotus relates, used to attribute this foul infirmity to offences committed *against the Sun.* And these slavish people had indeed offended against the Sun. A certain number of them, hoping to be cleansed, had bathed in great fonts of piety. . . . But the sight of these was quite as repugnant. *(V.R;* p. 35.)

He envied the young Garibaldian soldier who had 'ceased to form part of a compact and unanimous band, and assumed an individuality of his own, a singularly warlike aspect, consecrated to a new onward movement' *(V.R.,* p. 26).

The poets, meanwhile, 'have exhausted their store of rhymes in evoking images of other days, in weeping over their own dead illusions .... Only some magnificent power armed with ideas more brilliant than past memories could be able to raise its head above the monstrous phantoms. . . .' Again, is it Claudio who speaks—or Joyce in his criticism of Mangan?

Claudio's integrity must at all costs be preserved in this 'Day of the Rabblement' and of *La Bestia Trionfante:*

The gaze of the crowd is worse than a splash of mud, the breath of it is poisonous. Go far off while the sewer discharges itself. . . let not thyself be contaminated by the crowd. Thy hour will come *(V.R.,* p. 53.) [And his demon declares:] Everything that is born and exists around thee is born and exists by reason of the breath of thy will and thy poetry *(V.R.,* p. r50). Defend Beauty! [cries Claudio to the poets] Defend the vision that is within you . . . defend yourselves with all your weapons, even with jests, if such are of more use than invectives. Be careful to sharpen the point of your scorn with the bitterest poison. Let your sarcasm have corrosive strength. . . . Let your frenzied laughter rise to the very heaven when you hear the stablemen of the Great Beast vociferating in the Assembly. . . . Defend the Thought which they threaten, the Beauty which they outrage! A day will come when they will attempt to burn the books, shatter the statues, rip up the canvases. *(V.R.,* pp. 36-37)

These are some draughts of the heady wine Joyce was drinking in 1900 and such passages—denunciatory or hortatory—from *Le Vergini delle Rocce* can be multiplied. They confirm at every point the attitude Joyce was assuming; the deliberateness of his plan and purpose, his reserve, his aloofness from his fellows and scorn of the rabblement, his faith in an autonomous art controlled only by the laws of his own genius. True that, however defiantly borne, these are the not uncommon insignia of many young artists, but they seem peculiarly to bear upon Joyce's attitude in the years following 1900 and they are accompanied by enough echoes in Joyce's first writings and in *Portrait of the Artist,* to make it difficult or impossible to exclude an immediate influence. Claudio's *cave, adsum* and his *sub se omnia* are heard in 'The Day of the Rabblement' and in his paper on Mangan; and the assurance of Claudio's demon that his 'hour will come' was hardly absent from Joyce's ear when he prefigures himself as the minister who 'will not be wanting when his hour comes. Even now that hour may be standing by the door'. The parallel already mentioned between the forge in Stephen's smithy and Claudio's ploughshare is accompanied by another passage in *Il Fuoco* where the protagonist finds in 'the beating of his own heart. . . the repercussion of the hammer on the hard anvil where human destiny is forged'. The Herodotean offenders against the sun are glanced at in the Mangan paper. In *Ulysses* (Paris, 1922, p. 34) Mr. Deasy reproaches these sinners against the light with darkness in their eyes; they reappear in the Oxen of the Sun episode and indeed are implicit everywhere in Joyce. The cunning Ulysses (*V.R.*, p. 40) is not absent, nor the birds of Daedalus whose screams and wingings fill the souls of Claudio (*V.R.*, p. 102) and of Stephen (*Portrait of the Artist*, p. 263[49]) with ancestral terrors and exultation; their hawk-cries are finally heard as night falls over *Anna Livia Plurabelle*. Very assuredly, also, Joyce fulfilled in due time Claudio's divination of 'the power which the genius of place can exercise over the responsive soul'.

These promptings find other support in the general character of D'Annunzio's novels. Meditations taking their departure from some casual sight or phrase stick in my memory as characteristic of the *Stephen Hero* MS., which I was reading in 1903-4, but the resemblance between Joyce's first published work and D'Annunzio can be more clearly indicated. Arthur Symons finds in D'Annunzio's novels not so much a plot as the progression of states of mind. The interest lies in the hidden, inner self which sits silent through all conversation. He finds D'Annunzio the attentive and wholly unreticent recorder of the primary sensations of pain and pleasure. Beginning with intent waiting upon sensation, he expands his creature of acute sensibility into a kind of amoral Renaissance personality.[50] Add D'Annunzio's ever-present vein of lyricism to this exacerbated sensibility and to the minute inquisitorial distinctions he observes in the world of the senses, and we seem to be very close to the youthful Joyce and can understand the attraction D'Annunzio had for him.

I do not wish to stretch these analogies too far or to ignore other literary influences which ran parallel with that of D'Annunzio. Blake, for example, was ever on the lips of Yeats and A.E. in those days, and was also a favourite of Joyce. The inquisitorial distinctions just mentioned may have had equal encouragement from Blake, who founded all sublimity on 'minute discrimination' and held that 'to Particularize is the Alone Distinction of Merit'. It matters little or nothing whether it was from D'Annunzio or Yeats or even Huys-

[49] London, 1916.
[50] A. Symons, Introduction to *The Child of Pleasure* (Boston, 1898).

mans (whom Joyce disparaged) or some other that he borrowed the trick of esoteric discourse, whether he got his word-catching from Ben Jonson or, spurning the rabblement, joined the sleeve of communication with D'Annunzio, Bruno, or Leonardo, or with old Seneca who said: 'Flee the crowd, flee from a small group, shun even a single companion.' It is enough to say that like sought out like; that D'Annunzio had Joyce's attention when he was writing on Mangan and *Stephen Hero,* and that in those years he wore a D'Annunzian mask. I do not say that reserve was not as innate in him as a wild humour. But enigmatic detachment was more publicly paraded in his college years; the breakwater was breached only in private fun. D'Annunzio remained all his life inhumanly humourless. Joyce's developed work is notably different in this respect from his early writings. Picasso says it takes a long time to grow young. The young artist treads delicately in the sanctuary and only in his maturity is at ease in Sion. So it was with Joyce, who in his first years drew very strict lines in his aesthetics—stricter and more finely drawn than D'Annunzio's—before giving full play later to his natural humour. There was a second difference in their aestheticism. Both were race conscious. D'Annunzio's passionate *italianità* clad him with a Messianic mission to transform his fellow-countrymen into 'an ideally potent and perfect race'. Preaching first the efficacy of aesthetics, he turned later to air-bombing. Joyce found the writing of books more life-enriching. When all were thinking of national resurgence, he abstained from any political manifestations. Then and always. But those are gravely mistaken who think him un-Irish or anti-Irish because he quarrelled with one or other expression of a general feeling. He was primarily European but his Irish attitude is significantly enough expressed in a letter written about 1906: 'If the Irish programme did not insist on the Irish language I suppose I could call myself a nationalist.' He placed a faith greater than D'Annunzio's in aesthetics and grounded thereon his prophecy for the future of his race. To the end he was content to observe Leonardo's epigraph cited in *Le Vergini delle Rocce:* '*Io farò una finzione che significherà cose grandi.*'

6

Ibsen and Others

ITALY is not more different from Norway than D'Annunzio from Ibsen. It approaches a paradox, therefore, to say that Joyce modelled his behaviour on both writers. It is more correct to find the root of Joyce's intransigence in Ibsen's moral fibre and to find his D'Annunzian affinities associated only with certain early attitudes and literary echoes. Ibsen was the earlier and more enduring model and we do not need Joyce's own confession of 'radiant simultaneity' to be persuaded of a more than merely literary influence. This is so plainly understood that I shall refer here only to a detail or two which might have struck Joyce with some special sharpness in the course of his reading of the Scandinavians in 1899 and the years immediately after.

This reading pivoted, no doubt, on the dominant figure of Ibsen but was not confined to him. It covered Brandes extensively; Björnson, who also was to his hand in translations, entered into it; also Jacobsen, whom he introduced in 1901 into 'The Day of the Rabblement'. That reference, it is true, was no more than might have been derived from an encyclopedia article, but Joyce's Danish was something more than rudimentary and the particular contribution which Jacobsen made to Danish literature was such as to arouse his special interest. Joyce, at any rate, was fully conversant with the Danish literary movement from the 1880s. By and large, it was a breakaway from conservatism and an inbred self-sufficiency into the fuller currents of European experience and experiment. With Brandes in its critical vanguard, it was a compound of naturalism, symbolism, and satire, and its expression was as much through the novel as the drama. Jacobsen looks askance upon Brandes's programme 'which would make literature a floor for socio-political debate', but 'fulfilled his demands for a psychological novel'.[51]

[51] P. M. Mitchell, *A History of Danish Literature* (Copenhagen, 1957).

It is to this fulfilment that Joyce alludes in 'The Day of the Rab-blement' when he places Jacobsen between Flaubert and D'Annun-zio in the development of the psychological novel, which goes along with his abstention from political and social problems as matter not befitting the artist. Jacobsen was, furthermore, 'a stylist, a word ma-gician . . . and achieved unusual effects by his handling of paragraph and sentence structure. Long descriptive sentences are broken off by curt momentous remarks'.[52] Such abrupt transitions from reverie and a subjective intricacy to external reality are, as I have said ear-lier, perhaps my clearest recollection of my reading of the MS. of *Stephen Hero*.[53]

To revert now to Ibsen, Georg Brandes had published his *Ibsen and Björnson* in 1899. Joyce would certainly have read the copy in the National Library when he was preparing his paper 'Drama and Life'. He would have found in its pages the story of a young writer living with a bankrupt father in a home which was beginning to have no great attraction for him. Stephen Dedalus also found it in him to refer to the unpleasant character of his home. Ibsen was enter-ing a literary arena which had many resemblances with the Dublin scene. He was sharing in the activity of the Norwegian theatre—a part, like the Irish Theatre movement, of a general, national resur-gence. He found himself fighting on two fronts. The Norwegian stage was beginning to supplant the ascendancy of Denmark and its conservatism. Its writers were pledged to two loyalties: the cult of Norse sagas, and the cult of the Norse peasant. Ibsen's allegiance was given to neither. He used, to be sure, saga material but his mod-ern treatment of these consecrated national themes was only less shocking to the public than his disrespect for the peasant ideal. The public thought him envenomed and he found himself, as Brandes says, continually at war with his countrymen. His first lyrical mood passed over into satire and critical detachment. 'I had not', he him-self wrote later, 'the gifts that go to make a good citizen nor yet the gift of orthodoxy and what I possess no gift for, I keep out of.' For this isolation Ibsen makes Dr. Stockman, enemy of the people, his mouthpiece who declares the strongest man to be he who stands alone. The real enemies were 'surrender to the trolls and the spirit of compromise'—the spirit which reappears in *Peer Gynt* in the form of the *Boyg*, 'embodiment of all that is cowardly and yielding in man'.[54] Even in the desert he would still preach and not abandon his ambi-tion 'to awaken his people and teach it to think big', but, reduced

52 ibid.
53 I am not competent to say whether or not Jacobsen's *Maria Grubbe* left any traces on Joyce's *Dubliners*. Its sub-title, *Interiors*, and still-life detail as described by Mr. Mitchell may have been in his mind when he turned to the short story but such resemblances, if they exist, had become common property. Flaubert and George Moore were exemplars closer to hand.
54 *Ibsen and Björnson.*

by poverty and unimpressed by or unwilling to meet the demands of his elders for support (I still quote Brandes), this 'full- blooded ego-tist' retired abroad to fulfil his mission from a distance. From abroad he retorted fiercely to the critics of his *League of Youth* that 'he had studied the ways and manners of their pernicious and lie-steeped cliques'. As Falk in *Love's Comedy*, or as he shows himself in the bitter lines of his 'Millennial Ode', he took up the staff and weeds of the exile:

> My people gave me the exile's staff,
> The badge of care, the wanderer's shoe of pain,
> The pilgrim's shirt with hardship over-wrought. . .

and remained in self-exile for twenty-seven years.

Joyce was certainly in Ibsen's forge when he was writing 'Drama and Life' in 1899 and watching the development of the Irish Literary Theatre. I do not find it accidental that Ibsen's lines 'To the Poet, H. O. Blom', from which a quotation is made in that paper, echo clearly in Joyce's paper on Mangan as well as in some of his later writing. This poetical epistle to a poet whose name rings another bell is a racy and vigorous repudiation of Blom's lament that with the retirement of a certain conservative Danish actor the end of a Danish tradition meant the ruin of the Norwegian stage. C. H. Herford's adaptation in *Beltaine* runs: 'Never fear, the twilight of the gods will come to an end, a new day is dawning behind yonder hill; and you shall yet see that the daylight can burn the rotten lumber of the past; you shall yet see that beyond the ruined Valhalla rises the new Heaven.'

Herford's quotation is from the last stanza of Ibsen's poem— not, as he says, from the first. To judge its purpose, one should consider the parable in the poem's sixth stanza. The poet sees an embalmed corpse emerging from the shades of the pyramids. Pride is on its strong face and a disdainful smile; long unconscious of the sun's majesty, knowing nothing of life's intoxication, it still worships age- old, bankrupt powers; the mummy-mouth smiles scornfully because time will not stand still.

I believe Joyce had this vision before him when he finds Mangan —however admirable a poet, and matchless at times—ultimately the type of his race enclosed so straitly in history that even his fiery moments do not set him free from it. The fair flowers in the queen's garden have become the husks of history and food for boars. A more eager spirit would cast down with violence the high traditions of his race which Mangan has too passively accepted. The vision was still before his eyes when, reviewing Lady Gregory's *Poets and Dreamers* in 1903, Joyce renewed his assault, quite in the Ibsen vein, on the effete traditions of 'feeble and sleepy' minds. The same vision from Ibsen's last stanza holds its place in the closing paragraphs of the Mangan paper. 'Dusk veils the train of the gods' and he who listens may hear their footsteps leaving the world but, though there is dusk about their feet and darkness in their indifferent eyes, the miracle of light is renewed eternally. A new, serene spirit, entering cities and the hearts of men, will sing the glad, underlying life of the earth.'

> As you shall yet see, highest of all the heavens
> Is not Valhalla—it is the dawning Gimli

Passing from the assault on tradition, Georg Brandes tempts me to mention one other dominant theme common to Ibsen and Joyce. Brandes emphasizes Ibsen's early preoccupation with the relation of father and son. It appears notably in *John Gabriel Borkman* where the pleasure-loving young Erhard will be neither a redeeming genius nor a family wage-earner. Repudiating all 'castellar' claims, he will go out into the wide world with the partner of his choice.

Stressing such points is superfluous; it is more trivial still to pick out other personal details from Ibsen's biography. Yet, aware of Joyce's curious interest in correspondences between himself and his friends, I confess myself struck by the parallels between Ibsen's early ambition to be a painter and Joyce's to be a singer; by their reaction from a short-lived bohemianism in dress to their natural, almost ex- aggerated, neatness; and by their appeals, when in an emergency, in the one case to the Swedish and in the other to the British crown. To escape such further entanglements I revert to Joyce's Italian reading at college when he was first translating his life into literature.

What really mattered was that he continued at college the Italian he had begun at Belvedere. He grew to love that language and liter- ature so that when, later, he resolved to leave Dublin, it was choice more than chance that led him to Italy rather than to Scandinavia or France. Italian had become, in effect, his second language. He liked speaking it, he loved the sonority of its vocables and the grace and precision of its classics. His Italian class in college was, indeed, the only one he followed with any pretence at assiduity and the texts with which he grew acquainted there from 1899 to 1902 included Tasso, Machiavelli, Maffei, Monti, Manzoni, Petrarch, Castiglione, Dante, and Leopardi. He encountered them more or less in that order. From one or two of them I pick up some threads which seem to tie up, however tenuously, with his early experience.

Leopardi, for example, was included in his 1901 course. This was the year before his Mangan paper and Leopardi is introduced into that discourse by way of contrast with the Irish poet and as a spirit stronger than his—a heroic pessimist with the patience and courage of his own despair. Joyce presented Mangan in his home as a sensitive boy living amid much coarseness and misery. Would Joyce at the same time have remembered that Leopardi also was the victim of a family despot and lived under the sway of what Stephen Dedalus was to call 'castellar rights'? And would he have found in the poet's father, as I like to think, another and more sympathetic trait? Joyce used to say that he would sooner be Lord Mayor of his city than head of the State. Count Monaldo Leopardi reckoned a man's pride should not extend beyond his town. 'One's patriotism', he wrote, 'is not due to the whole nation, not even to the state; one's true country is only that morsel of the earth in which one is born and spends one's life. That alone should awaken any interest in its citizens.[55] In spite of his D'Annunzian ambition to forge a new conscience for his race, could not Joyce, here, have found something to confirm his dedication to his native city, as indeed also in a text of Edmund Burke which he was reading in the same year wherein Burke's wider comprehension could still find a place for 'attachment to the sub-division, the love of the little platoon we belong to'?

In his reading of the history of Italian literature he would, of course, have met the names of Giordano Bruno and Vico; but, though his feelers may have been stretching out in their direction, I see small evidence in those years of any real familiarity' with their work. I refer later to a sonnet attributed to the former, but with that possible exception I do not think he was reading consecutively, or, indeed, at all, in any of the characteristic texts of these very divergent philosophers. Such deliberately casual allusions as he made to Bruno he could have gathered in plenty, and he was plainly held and horrified, as by every instance of barbarism, by the Nolan's tragic destiny. But, notwithstanding the genuine feeling, eloquence, and youthful parade exhibited in the article he devoted to Bruno in

[55] Iris Origo, *Leopardi* (London, 1935), p. 2.

1903, I see no proof of any wide, textual acquaintance. On the other hand, in 1901 he was reading Fornaciari's *Disegno Storico della Letteratura Italiana* as part of his college course and even in that slender outline—apart from other sources—the references to Bruno and to Vico, to the intuitional and pantheistic mode of Bruno's thinking, to the indeterminate, encyclopedic sweep of mind which makes Vico, as Fornaciari says, an inexhaustible mine for future quarrying are sufficient to set an intelligence less alert than Joyce's upon inquiry. At any rate, Joyce alludes twice to Bruno in 1901 in 'The Day of the Rabblement' and again, more obscurely, in his Mangan paper of 1902, as well as (yet more doubtfully) to Vico. Passages in that paper treat as one the poetic and the philosophic vision and Joyce defends, as against the historian, poetry's intuitional approach to reality. In its closing sentences, where he invokes the vast courses which enfold us and a memory greater and more generous than our memory, one may feel a current deriving as much from Vico's cyclic view of history and from his *sapienza volgare* as from the theosophic airs which, in those days, were blowing about A.E. and Yeats. If this is so, the circle from 'Mangan' to *Finnegans Wake* over which Vico presides, already begins to be drawn.

This paper on Mangan is the most noteworthy memorial we have from Joyce's college years. It is a significant reminder of his struggling idealism, reflecting through the images it calls up the writer's attempt to arm himself with patient fortitude against difficult days crowding upon him. Other comfort and promptings he might have won from Machiavelli. There was more to this unlikely name than 'the dull, wooden words' of his 'dingy chronicle' falling piecemeal from Stephen's lips. There was in Machiavelli the irony which De Sanctis called his real muse and to this Joyce would willingly bend an attentive ear. And he had also perhaps for Joyce, at this moment, if not for Stephen Dedalus, something more than irony. To externalize the crudities of life, to set them down in all their harshness, is one way by which the writer vindicates the supremacy of the spirit. And so Joyce who, as I have said in an earlier chapter, had seen Baudelaire's swan lifting its plumage from the soiling mud of the city, might in his grievous hours have recalled words from the Florentine's selfstory: 'And wrapped in that baseness I take my brain out of the mud and let the malignity of this fate of mine burst out of me, being glad that it should trample on me like this, just to see if it can be ashamed of itself.'[56]

[56] De Sanctis, *History of Italian Literature* trans. Joan Redfern, (London, 1932), vol. 2, p. 571. May we regard this as a whisper

These are speculations and we end them again with Bruno whom he had invoked in 1901 as one who would have the lover of the good and the true abhor the multitude and again in 1903 as one who had cast away tradition. When Joyce came to write *Portrait of the Artist* he could have found in him, as I imagine, promptings, images, or allegories as urgent. In the sonnet attributed to Bruno, 'Poi che spiegate', he could have met Ovid's man and the son of Daedalus.

Bruno's name appears in the pages which end *Portrait of the Artist*. In its last sentences Stephen Dedalus feels the air thick with the company of his kinsmen and their voices calling to him, making ready for flight, shaking the wings of their exultant and terrible youth. Is it not possible after this juxtaposition of Bruno's name to overhear in these closing sentences the words of Bruno's sonnet as it proceeds:

Out on the air I hear the voice of my heart saying, 'Whither dost thou carry me, thou fearless one': And the answer, 'Fear not, though utter ruin should come to thee. Hold to the clouds and if thou die, be happy that Heaven has destined thee to so glorious a death.'

LIST OF FIGURES

[ALL IN CURRAN-LAIRD COLLECTION, UCD, UNLESS NOTED OTHERWISE]

Part Three

Town and Generation:
The Currans and the Colums

Margaret Kelleher

'I write in vindication of my town and generation and out of "the attachment", which Edmund Burke approved, "to the subdivision, the love of the little platoon we belong to".' So writes Constantine Curran in his preface to *James Joyce Remembered (JJR)*.[1] That little platoon, whose friendships were forged in Dublin town in the first decade of the twentieth century, would prove to be a major force in Ireland's cultural and political future. As Padraic Colum, himself a core member of Curran's 'subdivision', concludes in his foreword to *JJR*, 'Several were to leave a mark on the formation of a new state, some on the history of their country.'[2]

One of the striking features of Curran's book of 'memories'[3] – underlined by the inclusion of Colum's voice in the foreword – is that a volume titled for one famous man should also provide such a vivid portrait of a generation. As such, it anticipates a key recent turn in Irish historiography towards the prosopographical – collective biography rather than single biography – most fully realised in Roy Foster's 2014 work *Vivid Faces: The Revolutionary Generation in Ireland 1890–1923*. In his 'group portrait', or 'group biography', Foster explores the 'unexpected lives of that extraordinary generation', redirecting historical attention to the ways 'a revolutionary generation comes to be made, rather than born'.[4] And as Curran recognises, the group portrait, with what Foster calls its 'networks of interests and preoccupations'[5] is inextricably bound with the biography of the city. Here also from Foster: 'The more one reads the accounts, letters, diaries and reflections of this generation, the more one

[1] Constantine Curran, *James Joyce Remembered* (hereafter '*JJR*') (Oxford, 1968; Dublin, 2022), preface, vi
[2] Curran, *JJR*, foreword by Padraic Colum, viii
[3] Curran, *JJR*, preface by Curran, vi
[4] R. F. Foster, *Vivid Faces: The Revolutionary Generation in Ireland 1890–1923* (London, 2014), xxii–iii
[5] Ibid., xxi

gets the sense of an intimate but complex city, with certain areas defined by political subcultures'[6] – the town, generation and its subdivisions.

In her memoir *Life and the Dream*, Mary Maguire (later Colum) – another member of the platoon, and near contemporary of Constantine Curran and James Joyce at University College – recaptures the fervor and excitement of living in an intimate, complex city during the Revival years:

> Dublin was a small city, the suburbs stretched out to a distance, but the centre, the old part of the city, was circumscribed and bristled with movements of various kinds – dramatic, artistic, educational; there were movements for the restoration of the Irish language, for reviving native arts and crafts; for preserving ancient ruins, for resurrecting native costume, an array of political movements; here, too, were the theatres and the tearooms and pubs which corresponded to the café life of the Continental city. In the centre, too, were the headquarters of the clubs and societies, some at war with each other, but all exciting and, somehow, focused towards one end – a renaissance. Between Abbey Street and College Green, a five minutes' walk, one could meet every person of importance in the life of the city at a certain time in the afternoon.[7]

Similarly, Curran remembers the 1903–04 period as one in which 'all sorts of converging lines were carrying from disparate, newly tapped sources unsuspected energies which in that very decade founded a new school in literature and in the next established a new State'.[8] Both Maguire and Curran's descriptions differ sharply, and deliberately, from Joyce's portrait of a centre of paralysis: notably, the characterisation of a 'shivering society', as termed in *Stephen Hero*, is explicitly rebuffed by Curran in *JJR* who aligns himself, more than once, with Yeats's 1899 prophecy of 'intellectual excitement' and 'that strong sense of something about to happen'.[9]

Within such a circumscribed city centre, the hospitality offered not only by people (Æ, Augusta Gregory, the Sheehy family) but also by places was vital. Colum rightly pinpoints this distinctive trait of Curran's

6 Ibid., xxii
7 Mary Colum, *Life and the Dream* (London, 1947), pp 94–5
8 Curran, *JJR*, p. 55
9 Yeats, *Daily Chronicle*, January 1899, quoted in Curran, *JJR*, p. 60

observations: 'He meets Joyce on his own social and intellectual level: the houses, the teachers, the books that formed one student are part of the other student's daily life.'[10] And in diplomatic terms, he welcomes Curran's rebuttal of 'some mis-statements that are in the Joyce texts', one of which concerned 'the appearance of the College he attended: the houses were dignified, and one had style; the classrooms were from a great house.'[11] Recollecting Joyce's reading of his Mangan paper to the Literary and Historical society on 1 February 1902, the eve of his birthday, Curran reanimates the old Physics Theatre with student life (those familiar with the room, and especially those of us who are ourselves teachers, will note a layout designed perhaps to turn the student gaze indoors):

> The meeting was held as usual in the old Physics Theatre, a large, octagonal room lit from its end bay by tall, ogival windows against which the benches rose as in an amphitheatre, crowded in the day-time with joint classes of medical and arts students, and filled on Saturday evenings by the members of the Literary and Historical and its camp-followers. On such occasions, the guest chairman, auditor, and officers of the Society had their places at the long demonstration table facing the rising tiers and the reader of the paper stood to its left.[12]

For Colum – whose family's financial circumstances did not allow him to attend university – the National Library (and what Curran calls its 'free pastures'[13]) was the educational centre. Writing in *Our Friend James Joyce* (1958), he recalled the significance of an institution then only 'in existence a generation':

> Young people have no aptitude for evaluating what is theirs by inheritance; they step into it – that is all they know about it. So it was with the students and the casual intellectuals among the youth of Dublin. In the reading room of the National Library they had a handsome place in which to read, to view each other, to converse in the portico below, to make the encounters that permitted couples to

[10] *JJR*, foreword by Padraic Colum, viii
[11] Ibid
[12] Curran, *JJR*, pp 12–3
[13] Curran, *JJR*, p. 28

walk together to their quarters. The library thus provided something of a social life as well as an intellectual life. It was hospitable.[14]

The friendships between Constantine Curran, Helen Laird (later Curran), Padraic Colum and Mary Maguire (later Colum) were forged in 'the theatres and the tearooms and pubs' of early twentieth-century Dublin and most especially in its theatres. On 3 April 1902 Padraic Colum wrote to Helen Laird from his digs in Longwood Avenue (and using the stationery of his employer the Irish Railway Clearing House). Helen was then in her family home in Rathbane Cottage Limerick and Colum's reason for writing was to keep her appraised of events in the Dublin theatre, specifically the Fays' successful production of Æ's *Deirdre* and Yeats' *Cathleen ni Houlihan* in St Teresa's Hall on Clarendon Street. Addressing Helen as 'a chara dhil' (your dear friend), and signing himself as 'do cara go buan' (your eternal friend), he reported of the performances: 'They were indeed successful. People were walking on each other ten minutes after the door was opened. So successful were the costumes that they worried George Moore, he came up to tell us they had not found favour in his sight.' The confidences shared by a younger generation, unbeknownst to their elders, continue in Colum's account of his plans for that evening: 'I am going round to Miss Gonne's to-night to inflict the "Kingdom of the Young" on Yeates (sic). Wish hard that it may impress him.'[15]

Subsequently, and using her stage name 'Honor Lavelle', Helen Laird played the role of Anne Kilbride in Colum's play *The Broken Soil*, first produced by the Irish National Theatre Society at the Molesworth Hall in Dublin on 3 December 1903. Weeks later, on 25 January 1904, Lavelle played Maurya in the first production of Synge's *Riders to the Sea* also for the I.N.T.S at Molesworth Hall. That early solidarity and friendship with Colum may also have motivated Laird's decision (to the surprise of Gregory and Synge) to join him, Máire Nic Shiubhlaigh, Thomas MacDonagh, Edward Martyn and others in the breakaway group Theatre of Ireland (1906–12). For Colum, what was at stake in this conflict was his

14 Mary and Padraic Colum, *Our Friend James Joyce* (1958; Mass., 1968), p. 21

15 Letter from Padraic Colum to Helen Laird, 3 April 1902, University College Dublin Special Collections Library (hereafter 'UCDSC'), CUR L10/a

view of the Abbey as 'national drama' versus that as 'personal adventure' (the view he ascribed to Gregory and Yeats), and his departure would impact seriously on his future career prospects as dramatist.[16]

Meantime, the young college student Mary Maguire established a theatre club, the Twilight Literary Society, for her fellow 'literary enthusiasts', who attended not just one performance of each Abbey play but 'every performance until we almost knew the plays by heart'.[17] In her memoir she also recounts being deputed as President to seek a discount from the Abbey box office, the cheapest ticket then being a shilling; Yeats, emerging from rehearsal, and to quote his delighted observer, 'exhausted and remote from the world, his lips still murmuring lines', readily agreed to an eight-pence ticket for the club's twelve young members.[18]

Mary Maguire and Padraic Colum married in 1912, Helen and Constantine Curran in 1913. The lives and careers of the two couples took very different forms following the departure of the Colums to America in 1914. Yet their correspondence shows a continuing closeness and network of personal and professional connections: on a visit to Paris in November 1922, Padraic fondly remembered his and Mary's recent visit to Garville Avenue, the Currans' home, writing 'Don't let Elizabeth forget us, and tell her she'll have to keep some of her stories "about the neighbours" for us. We were immensely flattered by her passionate outburst at parting with us.'[19] Eight years later, in 1930, and writing again from Paris, where the Colums' longer stay was enabled by Mary's winning of a Guggenheim fellowship, Mary ('Mollie') sought help from 'my dear Con' in introducing French Catholic philosopher Jacques Maritain to Dublin circles, including permission to give 'the usual letter to you'.[20]

Helen Laird died on 5 October 1957; Mary Colum on 22 October 1957. The Dublin hospitality provided by his friend Conn would prove especially valuable to Padraic in the years following Mary's death, and the friendship between the two aging and widowed men deepened over these years. Correspondence between Colum and Curran from the 1960s captures Colum's financial worries and publishing concerns, but also his delight at the

[16] See letter from Padraic Colum to W. B. Yeats, 18 February 1906, Berg Collection, NYPL; quoted in Richard J. Finneran, George Mills Harper and William M. Murphy (eds), *Letters to W. B. Yeats* 2 vols (London, 1977), vol. 1, p. 160

[17] Colum, *Life and the Dream*, p. 100

[18] Ibid., pp 133–4

[19] Letter from Padraic Colum to Constantine Curran, Paris, 4 November 1922, UCDSC, CUR L 200/b

[20] Letter from Mary ('Mollie') Colum to Constantine Curran, Paris, 1930, UCDSC, CUR L 11/a

Padraic Colum and Constantine Curran
UCD Special Collections

imminent publication of Curran's Joyce volume. Writing from New York at Halloween 1965, Padraic remarked: 'I love being in at the finish, and it will be a great joy to know that your good account of our times will be ready to go to a public that has had so little chance to know about a glorious period that we were fortunate enough to live through – you, especially, dear old friend.'[21]

The Colum and Curran biographies of Joyce – *Our Friend James Joyce*, co-authored by Padraic and Mary and published in New York 1958 soon after Mary's death, and *James Joyce Remembered* published in 1968 – contain few explicit cross-references. Padraic drew from Curran's recollections of his student days explicitly on one occasion, for his discussion of Joyce's Mangan address, which he too recognised as a notable 'event in the literary history of his time'.[22] Curran cites Colum directly in one instance, with reference to Padraic's recovery and publication of Joyce's early verse in *Our Friend James Joyce*.[23] More significant resemblances are implicit: their early recognition of Joyce's distinctive intellectual ability, their sympathetic but unshrinking commentaries on his personal complexity, and the determination of both to tell the history of their times as more than the life of one, albeit acclaimed, individual.

Colum's recollection of his first conversation with Joyce is vivid and engaging, but also revealing as to the very different choices then being made by these two young men within this intimate but complex city life. Knowing Joyce by 'recognizing distance', Colum encountered him leaving the National Library one evening and engaged him in conversation; in the course of their 'promenade' along Kildare Street and onto O'Connell Street, the youthful Joyce declared: 'I distrust all enthusiasms.'[24] Published over five decades later, Colum's account has the benefit of historical hindsight but retains a powerful immediacy:

> It was natural to think, and I suppose I thought it, that a young man who distrusted all enthusiasms was a singular character. And for Joyce to say this in the Dublin of the day was to set himself up as

[21] Letter from Padraic Colum to Constantine Curran, New York, 1965, in personal ownership of Helen Solterer
[22] Colums, *Our Friend James Joyce*, p. 20
[23] Curran, *JJR*, p. 5
[24] Colums, *Our Friend James Joyce*, p. 16

a heretic or a schismatic, one who rifles the deposit of the faith…
To us at that time, belonging to 'a movement' meant fellowship,
exhilaration. It meant moving away from the despondency of the
generation before and toward a new national glory. Who would not
be in such a movement? And it was animated by enthusiasm.

I am trying to find a word for the way that young man standing
on that street corner said, 'I distrust all enthusiasms.' It was not with
any youthful bravado. It was rather like one giving a single veto after
a tiring argument.[25]

Curran's portrait is less hesitant and offers pragmatic insights into how
Joyce was best 'met' or handled, in company:

Joyce was not naturally a good 'mixer', but he was not anti-social.
He was difficult but not uncompanionable. At no time, then or in
later years, do I remember him in company taking part in any general
discussion. For anything approaching serious talk he preferred the
company of one to many, and even then you had to meet him on his
own ground… He was ready enough to enter into explanation of his
attitude towards many things, but irony, wry humour, grotesquerie,
courteous evasion, or silence – each in turn was enlisted to build up
an impregnable defence against intrusion on the inner sanctuary.[26]

How then to reconcile a commitment to write in vindication of a
generation, with public interest in the life of its most famous member?
This was a challenge encountered earlier by Colum with respect to how
the history of Irish theatre would be written. Almost 20 years prior to
the publication of *JJR*, his impassioned essay on the 'Early Days of the
Irish Theatre', was published in the *Dublin Magazine* 1949–1950.[27] Here
the target of his ire was a growing trend among critics and memoirists
to write the history of Irish theatre as the story of one great man, Yeats.
Colum's spirited defence of the value to the national movement of what
he termed 'the fermenting minds' is worth reproducing at some length:

[25] Ibid. For a valuable overview of Colum's life-long engagement with Joyce's work, see John McCourt, '"Patrick What-Do-You-Colm": Reading Joyce with Padraic Colum', in Emma-Louise Silva, Sam Slote and Dirk van Hulle (eds), *James Joyce and the Arts*, European Joyce Studies vol. 29 (Brill, 2020), pp 199–219
[26] Curran, *JJR*, p. 36
[27] Padraic Colum, 'Early Days of the Abbey Theatre', *Dublin Magazine* 24 (October 1949), 11–17, 25 (January 1950), pp 18–25

My conclusion will be a comment... Plutarch lied: the great thing cannot be altogether the creation of the one great man... When Willie Fay wrote about the foundation of the theatre, when Lady Gregory wrote about it, they were on the side of Plutarch, the side of the historian who is there to tell us that the great man, the hero, does everything. There are certain imponderables working through minor men and women that instigate great men to give form and scope to what the others are reaching towards. ...Without these imponderables, without the fermenting but unkeyed-up minds surrounding the great man, no dominating work is ever achieved. The fermenting minds, the man who can give them focus, were present in the moment that created a national theatre for Ireland. My recollection assures me that behind the writers and players was a national feeling that manifested itself through the young men and women belonging to the politico-cultural clubs in the Dublin of the time; it was they who gave the project spirit and the breath of life.[28]

For Curran, writing a decade later, the burgeoning international Joyce industry posed a new historiographical foe, but his targets also included some of Joyce's own writings, and specifically *Stephen Hero* and *A Portrait of the Artist as a Young Man*. What is at stake, and to be opposed, is most clearly stated in the lines which end page 20 in the 1968 text: 'These texts have made everyone familiar with the picture of the artist-student absorbed in the aesthetics of literature, jealous of his independence, scornful of his fellows, standing on his defence, arrogantly aloof. He moves with an occasional companion against a frieze of figures.'[29] In a happy coincidence – or clever visual design – Curran's publication counters these lines not with other words but with the facing image and the group biography that it tells. This is of course the well-known graduation photo entitled 'The B.A. degree class of 1902 with its professors'.[30] An alternative caption might be the line quoted approvingly by Curran some pages later, from Æ's comment to Yeats following his first meeting with Joyce: 'the new generation was knocking at the door.'[31]

[28] Ibid.
[29] Curran, *JJR*, p. 20 of 1968 edition, p.19 of this edition
[30] Ibid, facing illustration
[31] Ibid., p. 34

C. P. Curran's photographs of Joyce and Dublin

'An untrustworthy composite doubly and trebly overlaid'

Hugh Campbell

'Cityful passing away, other cityful coming, passing away too: other coming on, passing on.'[1] Thus muses Leopold Bloom on the transience of cities in the *Lestrygonians* episode of *Ulysses*. What that novel copiously demonstrates is that no version of the city ever really disappears, that every city contains within itself all its past iterations. Thus, Dublin as it was in the summer of 1904 is still available to us, both directly through the streets and spaces and buildings that survive from that time, and indirectly, through memories, through written and visual records.

Among such records are a number of the better-known photographs from the Constantine Curran and Helen Laird Collection held at UCD Library. A set of images of Eccles Street and its environs show the 1904 address of Leopold Bloom, while, in a photograph made in 1904 at Curran's home, James Joyce stands hands in pockets, head tilted, staring into the lens.[2] In the nature of photographs, each – the Eccles Street set and the Joyce portrait – is bound to the facts of its making and the view it records, but, like the city itself, each also has more complex spatial and temporal dimensions. In these photographs it is always Dublin in the summer of 1904, but it is always other times and other places as well.

In this same spirit, recalling some 40 years later his reading of the manuscript of *Stephen Hero*, Curran notes, 'I believe I read all the text written before he left Dublin in 1904, but my recollection of it is insecure. It is an untrustworthy composite doubly and trebly overlaid with my

[1] James Joyce, *Ulysses* (the 1922 text) (Oxford: Oxford University Press, 1993), p. 156
[2] Curran–Laird Collection, Special Collections, The James Joyce Library, University College, Dublin, CUR P1 and CUR P15 a–e

acquaintance with familiar places and people and later talk about them, with my knowledge of happenings as they actually occurred, and with the recurrence of episodes in the Portrait of the Artist, where they are more abruptly and sharply delineated.'[3]

Such uncertainties notwithstanding, a composite of evidence of different kinds allows us to be reasonably precise about when and where the 1904 photograph of Joyce was taken. Of course, the photograph is reproduced in duotone on the cover of Curran's James Joyce Remembered and although even in this book it is sometimes credited as 1902, Curran confirms in the text that 'It was at this time, in the summer of 1904, that I took the photograph… in the garden of my father's home.'[4]

The Curran home was at 6 Cumberland Place on the North Circular Road. This was the easternmost of a terrace of six houses completed in 1851.[5] The terrace was among the earliest to be completed along what was still a relatively undeveloped stretch of the road, which, together with its counterpart, the South Circular Road, was often taken to demarcate the city perimeter.[6] The individual plots of the terrace were quite narrow (24 ft/8 m) but deep, with a 60 ft/20 m garden to the front and another 100 ft/35 m garden to the rear.

When, during 1902 and 1903, Joyce lived with his family at 7 St Peter's Terrace – another set of six houses, of more modest scale and more recently built – it would have taken less than 10 minutes to walk to Curran's house. But following the death of his mother and his sojourn in Paris the previous year, Joyce had become more peripatetic. Since late March 1904 he had been living in 'a very large room which spanned the first floor of a house' at 60 Shelbourne Road on the other side of the city.[7] From there, the journey to Cumberland Place would have taken over an hour on foot. This was therefore more likely a pre-arranged visit than a casual call on a neighbour.

Curran and Joyce did meet relatively frequently during this period, with Curran engaged in reading the Stephen Hero manuscript from early June. 'Most often,' Curran writes, 'we met in some café, Bewley's in

[3] C. P. Curran, *James Joyce Remembered* (hereafter *JJR*) (London: Oxford University Press, 1968), p. 50
[4] Curran, *JJR*, p. 66; The 1902 date is given in, for instance, David Pierce, *James Joyce's Ireland*, (New Haven: Yale University Press, 1992) p. 154 and the Beinecke Library; Yale also gives this date for its copy of the photograph.
[5] www.buildingsofireland.ie/ buildings-search/building/50070029/ cumberland-place-north-201- 211-north-circular-road-annamoe- parade-dublin-7-dublin Accessed 12 July 2021
[6] The 1847 Ordnance Survey Map shows almost no development between the junction with Cabra Road at Phibsborough and the Phoenix Park. By the time of the 1907–09 OS Map, this stretch was more or less completely developed. See https://geohive.maps.arcgis. com/apps/webappviewer/index.
[7] Richard Ellmann, *James Joyce* (London: Oxford University Press, 1959, 1982) p. 151; also Vivien Igoe, *James Joyce's Dublin Houses and Nora Barnacle's Galway* (Dublin, 1990)

Westmoreland Street was our favourite, but I recall no higher "altitude" than Blaquiere Bridge over the Royal Canal at Phibsboro' where once I found him waiting, stretched along the parapet in the pose of the Elgin Marbles Theseus with no other resemblance to the Greek than appears in the photograph I took of him at that time in the garden of our house.' As if prompted by the memory, Curran then asserts: 'This photograph may well have been taken that particular day.'[8]

Meeting at the bridge – which spanned a part of the canal subsequently filled in during the 1930s to create the Blessington Basin Park – would make sense if Joyce were coming on foot from Shelbourne Road. His most likely route would bring him over Butt Bridge, up Gardiner Street and Eccles Street.[9] If he were on the tram, it could have come from Sackville Street and dropped him at the bridge, although the tramline did also run along the North Circular Road past Curran's house.

Despite the tramline, this area would still have felt somewhat undeveloped, even rural. A trainline brought cattle into the large market that lay across the road, just beyond the boundary wall of the Grangegorman grounds. And directly behind the lane at the back of Curran's house, fields extended north and west. However close to the centre, this was still the city's frontier. How freshly odd this liminal condition must have felt to Joyce, recently returned from metropolitan Paris.

So when, in the summer of 1904, was the photograph taken? A closer look at the site yields more clues. From the 1909 Ordnance Survey 6" map, it is evident that the glasshouse in front of which Joyce stands was built against a north-facing wall in front of a storage shed that spanned the width of the rear of the site and was accessed from the lane as well as from the garden. A sun-path analysis of the shadows cast by the joists of the glasshouse confirms that the photograph must have been taken on a mid-afternoon between late April and late May.[10] Given Curran's own reference to the photograph being taken in summer, it seems reasonable to assume the later end of this date range. The level of growth of the foliage in the garden accords with this early summer timing.

8 Curran, *JJR*, p. 49
9 Appropriately for this meeting place, there is now a café called *Two Boys Brew* next to the bridge
10 I am grateful to my colleague Dr Paul Kenny for this analysis made in April 2021

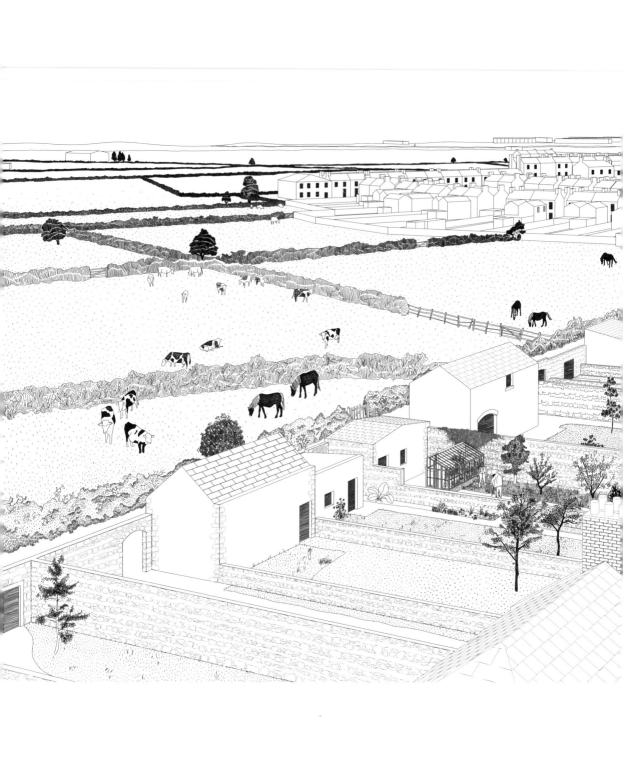

Curran had been away in Italy in March and notes that he didn't see Joyce 'until he had moved to Shelbourne Road and was beginning his singing lessons'. In fact it was a loan from Curran that allowed Joyce to move a small grand piano into his new lodgings.[11] This was a period during which Joyce was regularly seeking loans, so his often-cited response to the question about what he was thinking about when Curran took the photograph – 'I was wondering if he would lend me a few shillings' – may have been more factual than humorous.[12]

In one of the few detailed discussions of Curran's photograph, Eloise Knowlton compares it to a formal graduation portrait of Joyce from 1902 (Curran also made two well-known group photographs on the occasion, including himself in one). She opposes the staged realism of that photograph to the more informal aesthetic of Curran's: 'The 1904 snapshot of a lounging, full-face, hands-in-pockets Joyce partakes of the camera's ability, newly wielded by ordinary people, to re-present, rather than represent an arbitrary, fleeting, casual instant in time.'[13] She goes on to assert that: 'While the graduation portrait presents us with a controlled, determinate, and clearly intended signification, the Curran photo participates in a different notion of image, one understood as casual, accidental, arbitrary, mechanical, objective, contingent, efficient, and historically embedded.'[14] The point is somewhat undermined by the fact that the photograph is not the product of one of the new portable Brownie cameras that had just come on the market, but was instead taken with a more old-fashioned view camera. To take a photograph such as this requires time and deliberation, and the willing participation of the subject. Curran would have had to set up the camera on its tripod, adjust the lens and bellows, duck beneath the black cloth to study the composition, reversed and inverted, on the gridded viewfinder, before opening the shutter and fixing the image on the 6 ½" x 4 ¾", half-plate glass negative.

This is by no means a 'snapshot'. It is more posed and deliberate than that. Accordingly, Joyce has time to strike and hold a pose for the camera: Curran refers to him showing 'a certain humorous

[11] Ellmann, *James Joyce*, p. 151
[12] The line seems to appear for the first time in the caption to the cropped version of the photograph which appears, courtesy of Curran, in Ellmann, *James Joyce*, Plate VIII. Ellmann does record that Curran 'made him several small loans with uncomplaining generosity' in early July 1904, Ellmann, *James Joyce*, p. 162
[13] Eloise Knowlton, 'Showings Forth: *Dubliners*, Photography and the Rejection of Realism', in *Mosaic: An Interdisciplinary Critical Journal* 38:1 (March 2005), pp 133–50; Later, Knowlton elaborates the point: 'In contrast, the Curran snapshot, caught incidentally in a spare moment, seems to lack this kind of heavily intentional discursive meaning. In fact, Joyce was asked to supply one, as if to his friends' and family's eyes the picture suffered from a lack that must be filled. Asked what he was thinking when the shutter snapped, Joyce said, "I was wondering would he [Curran] lend me five shillings". Full-length and full-faced, Joyce is posed in the straightforward documentary attitude peculiar to the photograph. Curran's picture does pose Joyce – this is not a candid photograph – but its candor is far greater than that of the graduation portrait. This is the everyday Joyce; incidentally caught in an incidental moment, he is not quite entirely in the frame of the picture: Curran has stepped on his toes. It is taken against the backdrop of a dilapidated greenhouse, with a wall behind, a specific context, a particular moment. Anyone who knows about Joyce will have no difficulty generating meanings for this photograph.'
[14] Knowlton, 'Showings Forth', 2005, p. 148

bravado in dress and carriage'.[15] This was a period when Joyce was occasionally performing concerts and practicing hard for the Feis Ceoil (a competition in which he would eventually place third, having refused to sing the sight-reading composition). It may be serendipitous that the *Irish Times'* notice on 17 May of Joyce's third-place commendation is placed beside a cropped version of the 1904 photograph in Ellmann's biography. Might the photograph have been taken to mark the achievement? Or perhaps it was on this visit that Joyce asked Curran to read and comment on the manuscript of *Stephen Hero*, which he would deliver to him in early June. Certainly, it is made with a degree of deliberate intention.

While the photograph lacks, in Knowlston's terms, the 'kind of heavily intentional discursive meaning' found in his graduation picture, it nevertheless seems, if only in retrospect, to occur at a pivotal moment. Here is Joyce, returned from a first foray to the continent, having just completed his first manuscript, about to meet the love of his life, months from leaving Ireland for good, impecunious but emboldened, looking to the future. Bound to the specific circumstances of its making, the photograph almost immediately resonates beyond them.

In his essay on 'Appearances' in *Understanding a Photograph*, John Berger discusses the photograph's capacity for what he calls 'revelation' in terms that seem related to Joyce's understanding of epiphany.[16] For Berger, the photograph's capacity for revelation is in direct proportion to the extent of significant information it can incorporate within the instant of its taking. Thus a resonant photograph extends the event of its making beyond itself, acquiring larger significance: 'The photograph which achieves expressiveness [...] works dialectically... it preserves the particularity of the event recorded and it chooses an instant when the correspondences of those particular appearances articulate a general idea.'[17] While Berger is considering the validity of photography as an art-form, his notion of the event of the photograph's making being able to extend in space and time can also be applied to the Curran photograph.

[15] Curran. *JJR*, p. 67

[16] 'The epiphany was the sudden "revelation of the whatness of a thing", the moment in which "the soul of the commonest object ...seems to us radiant"'. Ellmann, *James Joyce*, p. 83. The quotes are given without citation. Later Ellmann explains how the epiphany 'seeks a presentation so sharp that comment by the author would be an interference... The artist abandons himself and his reader to the material.' Ibid., p. 84

[17] Berger John, Appearances in *Understanding a Photograph* (London: Penguin, 2015), pp 119–121

In very straightforward terms, considerable time seems to have elapsed between the instant captured on the plate and the subsequent printing of the photograph. While it would be usual for the plate itself to be developed at home – presumably in a makeshift darkroom in Curran's home, maybe even in the shed behind Joyce in the photograph – making prints from the glass negative would usually be done professionally. In the UCD collection, the envelope containing this and the two 1902 graduation pictures comes from Ashmore's International Pharmacy in Dawson Street, which was not established until April 1909. So these three plates were presumably sent to have prints made, but not till at least five years after the latest of them was taken. In fact, Curran's note on the envelope gives the dates of the pictures as 1902, 1902 and c.1904 [emphasis added]. He would of course recall 1902 as his graduation year, but seems to be sufficiently distant from the taking of the later picture to have to estimate the year. This suggests a date for the printing considerably later than 1909.

It is beyond the scope of this paper to trace the first appearance of these photographs in circulation or in print, but given that Ashmore's pharmacy has disappeared by 1930, the print must have been made before then, and we know that James Joyce signed a copy of it in 1924 (now in the University of Buffalo's Joyce collection).[18] Suffice to say that as it appeared and began to circulate, it was already referring back to a period in the past, a period that was critical to Joyce's development as an artist and that also provided the temporal setting of all his oeuvre. In other words, the photograph's facts had begun to merge with Joyce's subsequent fictions. Curran himself asserts that 'Edmund Wilson in *Axel's Castle* queried whether, without it, we should ever have a clear idea of Stephen Dedalus.'[19] In fact Wilson, writing in 1931, posits a more general question: 'should we have a clear idea of Stephen if we had never seen photographs of Joyce?' He makes the distinction between how little is known of the character's physical appearance and the way 'their eternally soliloquizing voices become our intimate companions and haunt us long afterwards.'[20]

[18] https://digital.lib.buffalo.edu/items/show/9195. Accessed 12 July 2021. The description notes 'Signed by JJ "James Joyce | Paris | 30 · x · 1924."' Thanks to Eugene Roche for this reference
[19] Curran, *JJR*, p. 66
[20] Edmund Wilson, *Axel's Castle*, (London: Harper Collins, 1985), p. 199. The full passage is as follows: 'And in "Ulysses" we hear the characters far more plainly than we see them: Joyce supplies us with descriptions of them in sparse, scrupulous phrases, one trait here, another there. But the Dublin of "Ulysses" is a city of voices. Who has a clear idea of how Bloom or Molly Bloom looks? and should we have a clear idea of Stephen if we had never seen photographs of Joyce? But their eternally soliloquizing voices become our intimate companions and haunt us long afterwards.'

Joyce's emphasis on the interior lives of his characters meant that, in all his writing, their physical environment mostly stayed in the background.[21] Were there to be a Joycean rendering of the Curran photograph, we might well know exactly what Joyce was thinking, but very little of the physical setting. '[I]t is [….] singular', noted Curran, 'that, in one who so assiduously paced the stones of Dublin, so little of its most characteristic aspect enters into his writing. Its life was an unfailing stimulus, its skies and the furniture of its streets reflected his mood but the graceful untenanted shell gave him no special pleasure.'[22]

By the time Curran began assembling the 'memories' gathered in *James Joyce Remembered* at the end of the 1930s, Dublin's 'graceful untenanted shell' had become his own main subject. His 1940 article on Dublin's plasterwork was the first in a series that culminated in the 1967 book *Dublin Decorative Plasterwork*.[23] He also produced knowledgeable and astute publications on The Rotunda Hospital (1945), the Bank of Ireland (1949) and, returning to the site of his education, Newman House and University Church (1953). His attentiveness to the built environment is evident too in some of the later photographs included in the UCD Special Collection – specifically the set of five taken of Eccles Street and its environs.

While it has sometimes been thought that these pictures were taken by Curran at Joyce's behest as part of his research for *Ulysses* (in the same vein as his requests to friends to consult street directories and newspapers for details), it is clear that they actually date from considerably later. The type of film used attests to this, and, as with the 1904 photograph, the envelope containing the developed contact prints offers further clues. The chemist Joseph Smith, on Terenure Road East in Rathgar, only became active in the 1930s. The five-digit phone number suggests a date between 1930, when the five-digit system became uniform, and the late 1940s, when six-digit numbers begin to appear.[24]

There are clues too in the pictures themselves. The dress of the children, particularly the girl in the photograph of The Dorno shop – which was located at the corner of Dorset Street and Dominic Street

---

[21] As Frank Budgen noted, 'the city was as native to them as water to a fish' and hence in need of no conscious attention. Frank Budgen, *James Joyce and the Making of Ulysses*, (Oxford: Oxford University Press, 1936), p. 70

[22] Curran, *JJR*, p. 40

[23] Constantine P. Curran, *Dublin Plaster Work*. Extracted article from *The Journal of The Royal Society of Antiquaries of Ireland*, vol. LXX, Part I (vol. X Seventh Series), 1940

[24] The Growth and Development of the Irish Telephone System*, A. J. Litton, B. E , BSc, M.I.E.E. (Read before the Society on 15 December 1961), www.tara.tcd.ie/bitstream/handle/2262/4617/jssisiVolXXPart5_79115.pdf?sequence=1&isAllowed=y. Accessed 12 July 2021

←― The Dorno, shop on corner of Dominic
Street and Dorset Street, early 1940s,
photographer Constantine P. Curran
UCD Special Collections, CUR P 15a

―→ Houses on Eccles Street early 1940s,
photographer Constantine P. Curran
UCD Special Collections CUR P 15c

[25] Thanks to the eagle-eyed Joe
Brady for discovering these clues

[26] C. P. Curran, 'When James Joyce
Lived in Dublin', *Vogue*, 1947,
pp 144–9, 197–9, 202; The Lee
Miller photographs were exhibited
at the James Joyce Centre, Dublin
in 2014 https://jamesjoyce.ie/lee-
miller-exhibition/. Accessed
13 July 2021

[27] In the UCD Collection there is
also a 1947 letter from J. F. Byrne,
author of the 1953 *Silent Years:
Memoirs of Our Ireland and James
Joyce*, seeking his memories of
Joyce and '*any snapshots he may
have of Eccles Street*' [emphasis
added]. Curran–Laird Collection,
Special Collections, The James
Joyce Library, University College,
Dublin, CUR L 147

rather than on Eccles Street as the catalogue suggests – hint at a date in the 1940s. A reflection of a telephone box in the window of the shop confirms that it is one of a type with *Telefón* written across the top, which only appeared after 1932.[25] A long view of the Eccles Street terrace containing No. 7 (of those visible, it is the second house from the left) shows a billboard on the gable to Dorset Street advertising Battersby's Auctioneers and Estate Agents. This same billboard appears on a shot of Eccles Street from Hardwicke Place taken by the American photographer Lee Miller as one of a portfolio of shots of 'Joyce's Dublin' which were published in Vogue in 1947.[26]

Taken together, this evidence suggests the pictures were taken around the same time as Miller's, perhaps somewhat earlier. Curran actually provided the brief text for the Vogue piece – it was his earliest published reminiscence of Joyce.[27] Might he have been prompted by the commission to revisit and photograph a part of the city he had long since left? In photographing Eccles Street, he would be looking back to his own walks with Joyce through that part of the city at the turn of the century, while also, of course, acknowledging the street as the fictional address of Bloom. In some senses, these are just as much photographs of Dublin 1904 as the photograph of Joyce that Curran took that year. This ambiguous status of the street – as a physical location, a site of memory and a fictional setting – is accentuated by two of the prints being accidental double exposures, such that the streetscape seems to shift and dissolve. 'Double exposure – Eccles St is not being taken down' a handwritten note on the back of one print reassures us. It is not in Curran's hand, but must have been written before the threat of this part of Eccles Street being taken down became real and before its eventual demolition in 1967.[28] Curran's photographs now number among relatively few records of Bloom's residence.[29]

Photographing this part of the city would also transport Curran further back to his own childhood, largely spent in the environs of the O'Connell School he attended. The children included in each image (the same group recur) directly evoke memories of the kind he would later describe in his memoir *Under the Receding Wave*:

> Then my vision explodes into a whole city quarter, a pattern of rectangular streets on the north side of Dublin, slipping down from Mountjoy Square to wide traverses at the foot of the North Circular Road. [that undeveloped stretch where he and Joyce would later live.] Here the small boy with his companions had the franchise of quiet streets and with the extraordinary faculty and facility of children perceived and entered into the life of inanimate things. Every street had its own personality, every hall-door and window its own physiognomy, every lamp-post its known number and its allotted role in our existence.'[30]

In his earlier short memoir essay 'The Side Walks [sic] of Dublin', Curran describes himself at the outset as a 'witness to the charming variety of Dublin, my native city and as the friend of many masters of their crafts

[28] The slow deterioration of Eccles Street from the 1930s onwards is detailed by Ian Gunn in his article *The Demise of Ithaca*, James Joyce Online Notes, www.jjon.org/joyce-s-environs/no-7-eccles-street. Accessed 12 July 2021

[29] Among the best-known of these is the frontispiece to J. F. Byrne, *Silent Years: Memoirs of Our Ireland and James Joyce* (New York, 1953). There is also a 1950 photograph by Harvard professor Philip Philips included in the Rosenbach Collection in Philadelphia, https://rosenbach.org/collection-highlight/photograph-of-7-eccles-street/ Accessed 12 July 2021

[30] C. P. Curran, *Under the Receding Wave* (Dublin: Gill & McMillan, 1970), p. 10

who practiced there'.[31] In both memoirs, it is in his accounts of childhood that the fabric of the city looms largest. The urban environment, in all its detailed specificity, is vividly recalled, its fundamental role in the shaping of identity acknowledged. And even when the city later fades into the background as Curran's attention shifts to the dramatis personae who inhabit it, its presence continues to be felt.

As has already been noted, Joyce exhibited little interest in the architecture of the city, and yet, as Curran described, '[h]e knew the streets of Dublin by heart and his memory was a map of the town. But his interest in its buildings… was for their associations.'[32] What Joyce understood was that this dense web of associations, of past and present connections, was bound up with, and could not be separated from, the buildings themselves. The fabric of the city was abstract as much as physical, a rich weave in which the past and the present as well as aspects of the future (Joyce was always describing it retrospectively) were simultaneously available.

Curran's photographs capture something of this simultaneity, operating in, and giving access to, multiple temporal and spatial registers. Relatively unremarkable in their own right, they acquire this resonance by virtue both of the circumstances of their making and of the subjects and settings they record. Like Curran's recollected city, they might be considered as 'untrustworthy composite[s] doubly and trebly overlaid'. Certainly they evade complete explication: they can never be completely knowable. Nevertheless, the facts recorded do make possible the kind of retrospective re-enactment attempted here. So it is that today one can still stand in the garden of what is now 211 North Circular Road. The greenhouse is gone, the boundary wall is lowered, and beyond it the city has expanded and changed enormously. But the essential lineaments of the scene, the location within the garden and the way the sun strikes it, remain. Here, in front of Curran's camera, on the cusp of the encounter and the exodus that would shape everything he subsequently achieved, Joyce stood and posed for his portrait.

[31] C. P. Curran, 'The Side Walks of Dublin: Self-Portrait', *Studies: An Irish Quarterly Review* 51:201 (Spring 1962), pp 108–116, www.jstor.org/stable/30084123. Accessed 28 June 2021

[32] Ibid., *JJR*, p. 39

IN A NUT SHELL

For **THIRTY THREE YEARS** Parliament have been considered **Bills.**

The English Parliament, though time an Irish Party demanding Rule, **never gave us**

But **IN THREE WEEKS** passed a Conscription same Irish P

'the right to speak on behalf of Ireland'
Conn Curran and the Nation, 1917–22

Diarmaid Ferriter

During the Irish War of Independence from 1919–21 the absence of poet W.B. Yeats from Ireland caused tension between him and his close confidante, playwright Lady Augusta Gregory. Living in Coole, County Galway, Gregory was irritated when Yeats complained from Oxford that 'the constant bad news from Ireland kills my power of poetical work.' She recorded privately: 'Yeats only knows by hearsay while our troubles go on.'[1] Gregory's own allegiances had shifted, from unionism in the 1890s, to support for home rule, to considerable sympathy for republicans after 1916. Both Yeats and Gregory had strong contacts in London but, unlike Yeats, Gregory was able to write about what was happening in Ireland as a close observer.

In April 1920, at the suggestion of playwright George Bernard Shaw, Gregory was asked by the radical journalist and editor H. W. Massingham to write about the escalating conflict for the weekly journal the *Nation*. During his time editing the *Star* and *Daily Chronicle* in the 1890s Massingham had been committed to Irish home rule and after the first world war as editor of the *Nation* (which he edited from 1907–23) he was 'equally devoted to the cause of Irish independence'. Massingham made the most of his acquaintance with prominent Irish figures, and Gregory's anonymous articles appeared in five issues of the *Nation* as the 'diary of an Irish writer and landlord'.[2] She referred to 'atrocities' and 'outrages' directed against the Irish, viewing the activities of the forces that had been sent to Ireland to bolster the Royal Irish Constabulary

[1] Colm Tóibín, *Lady Gregory's Toothbrush* (Dublin, 2002), p. 101
[2] Alfred F. Havighurst, *Radical Journalist: H. W. Massingham (1860–1924)* (Cambridge, 1974), pp 283–4

(RIC, policing Ireland since 1836) with horror, as indiscipline, brutality and reprisals increased.

While the *Nation's* circulation was limited, it was often remarked that 'it reached a highly select reading public.'[3] Its coverage of Ireland has been neglected; more attention instead has been devoted to British newspaper editors such as C. P. Scott of the *Manchester Guardian* and Henry Wickham Stead of *The Times*, who 'played a part in keeping the focus on Ireland by publicising the ongoing strategy of reprisals carried out by Crown forces'.[4]

Massingham's interest in Ireland was deep and enduring, despite the multitude of national and international journalistic challenges and preoccupations during the first world war. The British government's policy after the Easter Rising in 1916 'brought from him expressions of dismay, anger and lack of confidence in the Coalition'. He had an intense dislike of David Lloyd George, appointed prime minister in December 1916, and the *Nation's* attacks on him 'rose to a new crescendo' in late 1917; Lloyd George, in turn, depicted Massingham as 'just like a shrieking shrew'.[5] Massingham had travelled to Dublin the month after the Rising and in the *Nation* advocated for home rule immediately and a promise of complete independence in the future. He also returned to Ireland in June 1916 to attend a convention of nationalists in Belfast and that summer urged the reprieve of decorated diplomat turned republican rebel Roger Casement from his death sentence while considering him legally guilty of treason. Massingham's desire was that Ireland and England 'would be equals in the new Imperial Federation'.[6] The distinguished war correspondent H. W. Nevinson (who was also in Dublin after the Rising and regarded as 'another friend of Ireland') described Massingham as 'the greatest editor I have known' and Massingham was also lauded as 'a great humanitarian', a reminder that he did not think about the Irish question in abstract terms.[7]

Like Massingham, Lady Gregory was conscious of the need for a British audience to know what was being done in their name in Ireland

3 Ibid., p. 227
4 Oliver O'Hanlon, 'Press Coverage from Abroad', in John Crowley, Donal Ó Drisceoil and Mike Murphy (eds), *Atlas of the Irish Revolution* (Cork, 2017), pp 479–82
5 Havighusrt, *Radical Journalist*, p. 259
6 Ibid., pp 245–6
7 Harold Herd, *The March of Journalism: The Story of the British Press from 1622 to the Present Day* (London, 1952) p. 296

and partly wrote her articles for the *Nation* to encourage others to do the same: she records entertaining a *Daily Herald* journalist at her homestead in Coole: 'It is a great relief to my mind that these horrors are being made known by so competent a writer.'[8] Gregory felt some resentment that her contributions to highlighting the Irish crisis were not being adequately recognised, lamenting that 'my *Nation* articles, not being signed, don't count.'[9]

But there was another observer based in Ireland who was also writing for the *Nation* and who did sign his articles, albeit using a pen name: Constantine (Conn) Curran, the UCD graduate, writer and lawyer who, during the war of independence, was appointed registrar of the High Court and was married to the Irish actress and suffragist Helen Laird. Curran used the penname Michael Gahan as the *Nation's* Irish correspondent – McGahan was his mother's maiden name and Michael a Curran name – and Massingham's biographer, Alfred Havighurst, has noted that in Curran 'the *Nation* had a remarkable correspondent in Dublin.'[10]

Curran later wrote glowingly of Massingham as one who gave 'the most unselfish undeviating and influential support to the Sinn Féin movement of any foreign publicist. This is his first title to Irish respect.'[11] Massingham's trip to Dublin in May 1916 had proved to be an important turning point for Conn Curran. In a self-portrait written in 1962 he referred to his working life as mostly spent in the Four Courts and that 'his free hours were passed on the fringes of the arts in the company of… poets, painters, musicians, theatre men and a few scholars.'[12] But there was another significant string to his bow as when Massingham was in Dublin, Curran took him around the city and 'the result was that, for the next six years, until the paper was sold over his head, I was its Irish correspondent, dealing with books and politics.'[13]

Curran's casual reference to 'dealing with books and politics' for the *Nation* was typically understated. During his time with the *Nation*, the Anglo-Irish political stakes were very high, and the resultant emotions, divisions and settlements had profound and lasting consequences. The war of independence generated 'an extraordinary amount of attention

8 Lennox Robinson (ed.), *Lady Gregory's Journals: 1916–1930* (Dublin, 1946), p. 139, entry for 20 November 1920
9 Ibid., p. 161, entry for 18 October 1921
10 Havighurst, *Radical Journalist*, p. 283
11 Anthony F. Tighe, 'The Constantine Curran Letter Collection: A Catalogue, Analysis and Critical Interpretation' (University College Dublin PhD, 1997), p. 91
12 Constantine P. Curran, 'The Side Walks of Dublin: Self Portrait', *Studies: An Irish Quarterly Review* 51:201 (Spring 1962), pp 108–16
13 Ibid.

from the world's press', attracting correspondents 'convinced that universal principles were at stake'.[14] The activities of the Black and Tans and Auxiliaries, ex-soldiers and demobilised officers of the British army sent to Ireland in 1920 to augment the RIC, garnered much coverage in the *Manchester Guardian* and journalists altered perceptions, connected Ireland to the world and did much, if not more, for the rebels than their own political efforts.[15] In tandem, British based republican activists did their utmost to highlight the Irish crisis; the IRA in parts of Britain was even more active than in some parts of Ireland and the Irish Self-Determination League of Great Britain was inaugurated in 1919 in Manchester. In February 1920 'an overflowing attendance of over 10,000 people attended a rally in the Albert Hall, London' to hear speeches from Conn Curran's friends Eoin Mac Neill and Arthur Griffith.[16]

Irish republican propaganda efforts were, by their nature, selective and elided ugly domestic realities but also successfully communicated the idea of 'the underdog confronting and sometimes besting the big wig, the brass hat and the bully.'[17] Sinn Féin's newspaper *The Irish Bulletin* ran from November 1919 to December 1921 and was edited by, at various stages, Desmond FitzGerald, Erskine Childers, Frank Gallagher and Robert Brennan while Kathleen MacKenna was chiefly responsible for its production and printing and later accompanied the Irish delegation to the Treaty negotiations.[18] By May 1921, 650 copies of the *Irish Bulletin* were being produced and sent to newspapers and politicians around the world: 'The *Bulletin* was quoted in many English papers and its reports were cited by members of parliament critical of Irish government policy in Ireland, a fact which caused the Chief Secretary of Ireland, Hamar Greenwood, to denounce the paper in the House of Commons.'[19]

Separately, Childers also wrote articles for British newspapers, and their impact was 'more successful even than the *Bulletin*'; one series in particular, 'Military Rule in Ireland' became a sensation in 1920 and was also widely circulated as a pamphlet. Childers was also helped by journalists Hugh Martin of the *Daily News*, H. W. Nevinson and

[14] Maurice Walsh, *The News from Ireland: Foreign Correspondents and the Irish Revolution* (London, 2008), p. 3
[15] Ibid., p. 5
[16] Gerard Noonan, *The IRA in Britain 1919–23: 'in the heart of enemy lines'* (Liverpool, 2014), pp 4; 54–5; David M. Leeson, *The Black and Tans: British Police and Auxiliaries in the Irish War of Independence, 1920–21* (Oxford, 2011), pp 172–4
[17] Arthur Mitchell, *Revolutionary Government in Ireland: Dáil Éireann, 1919–21* (Dublin, 1994), pp 101–2
[18] Ian Kenneally, 'The *Irish Bulletin*', in Crowley et al. (eds) *Atlas of the Irish Revolution*, pp 483–6
[19] Ibid.

Massingham. Childers's voice was compelling as he cut to the marrow of the issue in a way that chimed with how Massingham, Curran and others were thinking: 'The army takes over civil functions, supresses every meeting, gathering… makes raids at all hours of day and night… This Irish war, small as it may appear, will, if it is persisted in, corrupt and eventually ruin not only your army but your nation and your empire itself… what right has England to torment and dominate Ireland? It is shameful.'[20]

That was the wider context for Curran's writings in the *Nation* and he was therefore part of a very broad effort. His contributions also invite a reconsideration of the assertions that he was extremely reticent (nicknamed 'cautious Con') and 'never drawn into politics'.[21] Through his personal life and wider contacts, he was surrounded by politics. His wife Helen was a political radical and his brother, Monsignor Michael Curran, who was secretary to the Catholic Archbishop of Dublin during the Easter Rising and beginnings of the war of independence and then, in 1920, appointed rector of the Irish College in Rome, was in full sympathy with the republicans, mediated between Sinn Féin and the Catholic Church and helped to author a claim to Irish independence presented at the post-war Paris Peace Conference.[22]

Conn Curran's family ties and range of friendships, many dating from his time as a schoolboy with the Christian Brothers in Dublin and his subsequent years as a UCD student, underlined the complex, layered allegiances and ideologies in the Irish melting pot during the first world war. He believed his close friend Tom Kettle, the politician and writer, to be 'the most brilliant of my generation'. Kettle died while serving in the British army and regarded the cause of European civilisation as greater than that of Ireland. Curran also lauded the integrity of Eoin Mac Neill who as chief of staff of the Irish Volunteers had sought to prevent the 1916 Rising: Curran described him as having 'returned the inverted cone of Ireland to its true base… MacNeill's study was not a cell, but the sally-fort from which our state was established. He was the most dangerous of all revolutionaries, the student revolutionary.'[23] Curran had also served with Patrick Pearse on the committee of the Catholic Graduates

[20] Michael McInerney, 'From Union to Republic', *Irish Times*, 25 June 1970; article commemorating the 100th anniversary of the birth of Erskine Childers.

[21] Pauric J. Dempdey and Bridget Hourican, 'Curran, Constantine Peter ('Con'), 1883–1972' in James McGuire and James Quinn (eds), *A Dictionary of Irish Biography: From the Earliest Times to the Year 2009* (Cambridge, 2009), vol. 2, pp 1102–3

[22] Irish Military Archives, Dublin, Bureau of Military History, Witness Statement 687, Michael Curran

[23] Michael Tierney, *Eoin Mac Neill: Scholar and Man of Action, 1867–1945* (Dublin, 1980), p. 369

Association and was close to Arthur Griffith, the founder of Sinn Féin, enjoying long walks with him in Wicklow.[24]

It is true that as a UCD student Curran was more likely to speak on cultural than overtly political matters but he did not engage in much public speaking at all; as his contemporary James Meenan was to record about debates at UCD, 'I have never been able to understand why so gifted and versatile a man was not more often propelled to his feet in the physics study.'[25] Perhaps it was because he knew he was more effective with his 'nimble pen'.[26] Curran was from a home rule background but like so many others, was caught up in the intense political awakening after the 1916 Rising as Sinn Féin became 'the fad or the craze of 1917'.[27] His mission at the *Nation* consisted of five main strands: to encourage the British government to offer Ireland dominion status within the commonwealth; in the absence of that, to defend the legitimacy of Sinn Féin and its quest for Irish independence, to denounce the Irish Parliamentary Party (IPP), to expose the excesses of Crown forces in Ireland and, subsequently, to defend the Anglo-Irish Treaty of December 1921 that created the Irish Free State.

There was nothing understated about Curran's commentary for the *Nation* on both the rise and righteousness of the Sinn Féin movement, but he did acknowledge in February 1917 that 'its methods and ultimate aims are still obscure' and that it housed both 'moderate and extreme'.[28] Curran was somewhat cautious that year; wary of the 'extremists' and keen to stress that Arthur Griffith's 'conception of Sinn Féin was in essence constitutional'.[29] He reported on the Sinn Féin National Convention in October 1917, attended by 1700 delegates, when Éamon de Valera, who had been spared execution after the Rising and was now its sole surviving commandant, was elected president, replacing Arthur Griffith who became vice president. They pledged Sinn Féin to achieving a republic with a promise that a referendum on the precise form of government would follow, a pragmatic, temporary burying of the differences within the movement. Curran declared Sinn Féin 'the dominant factor in Irish politics… it must be regarded as essentially a

[24] Curran, 'The Side Walks of Dublin'
[25] James Meenan (ed.), *Centenary History of the Literary and Historical Society of University College Dublin* (Dublin, 2005; originally published Kerry, 1955) p. 71
[26] Ibid.
[27] Michael Laffan, *The Resurrection of Ireland: The Sinn Féin Party 1916–1923* (Cambridge, 1999), p. 94
[28] Michael Gahan, 'Sinn Féin and North Roscommon', *Nation*, 17 February 1917
[29] Ibid.

stable and enduring force.'[30] But the disparate views within the Sinn Féin movement were notable; Eoin Mac Neill, for example, was elected to the Executive of the party, alongside those of a more radical, separatist hue.

The party's winning of 73 seats in the general election of December 1918 (unionists won 26 seats) was not just a resounding and defiant victory – its manifesto had promised it would abstain from the Westminster parliament, convene a parliament in Dublin and use 'any and every means available to render impotent the power of England to hold Ireland in subjection by military force or otherwise' – but also marked the routing of the IPP, which was reduced to just six seats. Curran was unforgiving in his characterisation of the failures of that party:

> [O]ne may regard the proud and scornful spirit of Parnell avenging itself on the party which exorcised it. But the bulk of the voters had little concern for past history or the working out of a political nemesis. It is true that, as many Liberals in England voted Labour, so in Ireland, many people voted Sinn Féin, regarding it as a necessary act of political hygiene to remove a degenerate and deliquescent party. But they were a minority, and so far as Sinn Féin propaganda was concerned an uncourted minority. It was the creed and positive programme of Sinn Féin that counted.[31]

This was somewhat exaggerated; there was still a fair degree of ambiguity about what Sinn Féin stood for, and its manifesto was open to different interpretations. Fr Michael O'Flanagan, the republican activist and priest in Roscommon who had been elected joint vice-president of the newly consolidated party, was put in charge of Sinn Féin publicity during the general election and at its conclusion allegedly said, 'The people have voted Sinn Féin. What we have to do now is explain to people what Sinn Féin is.'[32]

[30] Michael Gahan, 'From Our Irish Correspondent', *Nation*, 3 November 1917
[31] Ibid., 'The Return of the Native', *Nation*, 4 January 1919
[32] Patrick Maume, 'O'Flanagan, Michael, 1876–1942', in McGuire and Quinn (eds), *Dictionary of Irish Biography*, vol. 7, pp 474–6

PARLIAMENTARIANISM

IN A NUT SHELL.

For **THIRTY THREE YEARS** the English Parliament have been considering **Home Rule Bills.**

The English Parliament, though it had during all that time an Irish Party demanding and voting for Home Rule, **never gave us Self-Government.**

But **IN THREE WEEKS** the English Parliament passed **a Conscription Act for Ireland,** although the same Irish Party voted solidly against it!

Are YOU going to continue the Farce of sending Irishmen to this Treacherous Assembly, where they are powerless to do good, but where THEIR PRESENCE IS USED BY THE ENEMY AS THE SANCTION FOR ALL HIS EVIL ACTS?

I I 3/9

The theme of the supposed degeneracy of the IPP was reflected in the extent to which 'parliamentarianism' became a pejorative term and the views expressed by Curran mirrored the criticisms in such publications as Rev. J. Clancy's *The Failure of Parliamentarianism* (1917) and the Sinn Féin propaganda pamphlets *The Policy of Abstention* (1918) and *Parliamentarianism in a nut shell* (1918), all of which appear in the Curran collection in UCD, reflecting the range of ephemera and contemporary publications he amassed. That collection also includes the election literature of Patrick Little, editor of various Sinn Féin newspapers and a member the Sinn Féin executive 1917–22, who was elected as Sinn Féin MP for Dublin Rathmines. Little sneered at 'honest John Dillon', the IPP leader, in cahoots with the British government. There was also a determination to root up historic parliamentary contributions, such as Dillon's assertion in 1881 at Westminster that 'if you sent angels into parliament, unless they are controlled by a public body sitting in Dublin, they would betray the people.' IPP members were characterised as both 'conscriptionists' and 'corruptionists', and the targeting of the IPP at Westminster was also linked to economic arguments with particular leaflets and pamphlets aimed at businesspeople and farmers: 'Ireland, thanks to parliamentarianism, has lost half her wealth in man-power and her expenses have been increased seventeen times.'[33]

Curran's embrace of Sinn Féin tightened and he stated baldly that it 'has the right to speak on behalf of Ireland'.[34] He also proclaimed Sinn Féin's victory as 'the triumphant return of an exile with uproarious popularity'; that it was 'less of a party than of a people' and then stuck the knife in: 'Ireland has seen herself, the camp-follower of a political party, eating dog at Westminster. The diet revolted her. Sinn Féin may be over-sanguine and may, like Poland, starve awhile for its credulity. But it will not eat dog.' He also made much of the idea of 'self-determination', invoking the rhetoric of US president Woodrow Wilson.[35]

Anthony Tighe has identified the degree to which Curran's rhetorical ardour dimmed during the subsequent war of independence and his

contributions became more 'cold reporting of events in Ireland'.[36]
That is only partly true. He wrote at length about the RIC in October
1920: 'In modern conditions the indispensable instrument of English
control in Ireland' and how positive views of the force had turned since
'the delicate system which trained them is now brutalised by newcomers
and well-nigh swept away, and they themselves reduced by resignations
and submerged in a turbid flood of "black and tans".'[37] Curran was
well placed to elaborate on the broader context for how the RIC had
evolved – ' it may be well to set down here their place in regard to
their predecessors and supplanters' – and become part of the Irish
community. Unlike British police, the RIC had historically assisted with
collecting statistics and census returns, involving an 'intimacy which
made them indispensable to government'. It was a well-integrated
force, 'for the most part from the sons of "small" farmers'. He also
referred to 'the pogrom' in Belfast against Catholics – the RIC inspector-
general, referring to intense violence and house burnings, observed
that 'sectarian feeling had been raised to fever heat' – and the growing
marginalisation of the RIC there 'as the corrupt barony constable is
reborn'. This was a reference to the promised British financed Ulster
Special Constabulary established later that month which became
notorious, trigger-happy and self-regulatory. As for the Black and Tans,
'their record is becoming public, even in some degree in England. It is
also a record of murder and torturing, of arson and loot.'[38]

As editor of the Nation, Massingham was 'burning with rage' over the
Government of Ireland Act that year creating two parliaments for Ireland
and a partition of the country between the south and six Ulster counties.[39]
Curran also wrote scathingly about this development as 'the final triumph
of the allied oligarchies of Belfast and England' which would 'dismember
Ireland'.[40] What interested him too was 'the mentality which directs the
[Dublin] Castle administration'. As for partition, it was 'detested by all
Irishmen; to the Orangeman it is the lesser of two evils' and 'essential to
the British control of Ireland… we are now back to Henry VIII and a Pale of
six counties'.[41] He elaborated on this issue the following month: 'The Irish

[36] Ibid.
[37] Michael Gahan, 'The Story of the RIC', Nation, 2 October 1920
[38] Ibid.
[39] Havighurst, Radical Journalist, p. 284
[40] Michael Gahan, 'Back to the Pale', Nation, 6 March 1920
[41] Ibid.

well understand the necessity which compels [Ulster Unionist leader] Sir Edward Carson to gather in his catch-crops even though in his harvesting he must forswear his covenant [the solemn and binding oath sworn in 1912 that the nine counties of Ulster would resist and prevent home rule] and abandon his Southern friends among whom he was born.'[42]

Curran underestimated the robustness of unionist purpose and the divisions within nationalism in predicting that 'the erection of a parliament for Northern Ireland will lead to experience which will explode old prejudices; in spite of the most careful jerrymandering, the new confrontation of parties within it will overwhelm Carsonism and present England and not Ireland as the enemy.' He also identified an indifference in southern Ireland to debates at Westminster: 'The country has made up its mind for a long war in which the full forces of Sinn Féin are not yet engaged' and he reiterated the speeches from Sinn Féin about endurance. He referred to recent events like the assassinations of the Lord Mayor of Cork Tomás Mac Curtain and Alan Bell, the magistrate who was investigating the source of republican funds in Ireland: 'on the one hand we are apparently faced with lamentable reprisals for the brutalities and lawlessness of the executive, and on the other with a public charge and widespread suspicion that the friends of the executive, with or without its knowledge, have contrived murder'. Curran was also clear about what was needed:

> Stop the bullying and the illegalities. Stop the arrests without charge and the deportations without trial… call off the spies and the agents provocateurs… the government of Ireland against its will, in the long run, will be found impossible, and this course will not make an essentially impossible task less difficult. But the struggle will cease to be accompanied by some of its worst incidents.[43]

These lines were written at a time when David Lloyd George was captured by the hawks in cabinet and just after General Nevil Macready,

[42] Michael Gahan, 'The Bill and the Reckoning', *Nation*, 10 April 1920
[43] Ibid.

a man who hated Ireland and the Irish ('I loathe the country'), was appointed commander of the British forces in Ireland and when the weaknesses of Dublin Castle's administration in Ireland were being lambasted privately by the British establishment. The permanent secretary to the Treasury, Warren Fisher, investigated the workings of Dublin Castle and found them in a pitiful state.[44]

For all the urgency of the warnings in the Spring of 1920, that year only got worse as the violence intensified, eventually prompting a reassessment of the nature and long-term objectives of the conflict as neither side could inflict a decisive defeat; the war, however, continued until the summer of 1921. At the end of 1920 Massingham contacted 'Irish Catholic moderates' such as Timothy Healy, the former IPP MP who had channels of communication with Sinn Féin and also sought to use his wider contacts to urge greater restraint in British policy towards Ireland. Massingham was aware that the cabinet was seeking 'some intermediary force.'[45] Various people were being suggested for such a role, including writer George Russell and Winston Churchill's cousin Shane Leslie. Ultimately it was Clare-born Archbishop Patrick Clune of Perth who began a shuttle diplomacy with Lloyd George's approval; this could have resulted in a truce at the end of 1920 but it failed to materialise, partly because Lloyd George recoiled in the face of British Conservative opposition.[46]

As a result, the *Nation's* editorial hostility towards the government continued. A leader under the title 'The Outrage in Ireland' was published in March 1921; similar criticisms were reflected in headings such as 'The Proclamation of Anarchy' and 'The War on Ireland'.[47] Journalist J. L. Hammond 'devoted much of 1921 to Ireland' writing both for the *Manchester Guardian* and the *Nation* and his eight-page 'Irish supplements' in the *Nation* in January and April 1921 entitled a 'tragedy of errors' and 'the Terror in action' were also widely circulated in pamphlet form.[48]

The moves towards conciliation in the summer of 1921, however, including the speech of King George V in opening the new parliament

[44] Ronan Fanning, *Fatal Path: British Government and Irish Revolution, 1910–1922* (London, 2013), p. 223

[45] Havighurst, *Radical Journalist*, p. 285

[46] Michael Hopkinson, *The Irish War of Independence* (Dublin, 2000), pp 182–5

[47] Havighurst, *Radical Journalist*, p. 284

[48] Ibid.

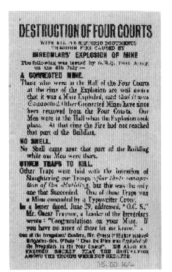

DESTRUCTION OF FOUR COURTS

Destruction of Four Courts with all its historic documents.' poster, 1922, 35.DD.16/4.[48]

[49] Michael Gahan, 'Prospects for an Irish Peace', *Nation*, 16 July 1921

[50] Michael Fewer, *Battle of the Four Courts: The first three days of the Irish Civil War* (Dublin, 2018), pp 78–9; Richard Ellmann, *James Joyce* (Oxford paperback, 1983), p. 247

[51] University College Dublin Archives, Papers of Hugh Kennedy, P4/283/2+3: Notes of C. P. Curran, Clerk of the Four Courts regarding Public Record Office, June and July 1922

[52] Diarmaid Ferriter, *Between Two Hells: The Irish Civil War* (London, 2021), p. 46

[53] Michael Gahan, 'Arthur Griffith', *Nation*, 19 August 1922

in Northern Ireland in June 1921, were welcomed by the *Nation*. As the possibility of dialogue opened up, Massingham's view of Lloyd George shifted and his Irish policy eventually won Massingham's approval.

During the run up to the Treaty negotiations (held in London from October to December 1921) Curran continued to insist that Sinn Féin had the moral authority to speak for Irish people; unlike some of his peers, he did not see Ulster unionist fears as unreasonable but argued that 'Belfast' could not ignore the 'wider imperial and international issues' that had produced Lloyd George's invitation to Sinn Féin negotiators.[49] Curran was pro-Treaty and welcomed the formation of the new Irish Free State, a self-governing dominion within the British empire for the 26 counties of Southern Ireland.

He was appalled by the destruction of the Public Record Office in the Four Courts complex at the beginning of the civil war in late June 1922, where republicans opposed to any compromise had taken up residence in April. As first-class clerk of the Courts (and soon to be appointed High Court Registrar), he reminded both sides of the Treaty divide of the importance and uniqueness of the archival documents; he even turned up at the Four Courts and was taken to see Rory O'Connor, one of the senior IRA occupiers. Curran warned him about the inexcusability of damaging the holdings: 'he left without receiving a satisfactory reply' and subsequently showed considerable courage in the aftermath of the explosions to do a survey when the scene was still live and dangerous; 'cautious Conn' it seemed, was not so reticent when it came to seeking to protect precious heritage.[50] His account of the carnage, sent to the provisional Irish government's Attorney General, Hugh Kennedy, made for bleak reading: 'nothing is recoverable . . . in complete ruin'.[51] Under the auspices of the Royal Society of Antiquaries, and with backing from the government, a call went out for papers that had scattered and floated, 'however fragmentary or damaged', to be returned.[52]

Following the death of Arthur Griffith in August 1922, Curran wrote glowingly of his friend who, as a negotiator and signatory of the Anglo-Irish Treaty, was 'dead with his work done'.[53] This accords with the assessment of historian of Sinn Féin, Michael Laffan, that Griffith 'among Irish nationalists who fought against British rule, was unusual, if not unique, in one respect: by the time of his death he had achieved most of his objectives'.[54] Curran returned to his 1917 arguments and placed Griffith firmly in the Irish constitutional tradition: 'he blazed the trail to political freedom as surely as O'Connell enfranchised the religious conscience and Parnell the land.' He also referred to the traits that 'made Arthur Griffith very dear to his friends' and 'the twenty years of my acquaintanceship with him'. He defined him as exhibiting greatness 'if vision and an unshaken will exercised successfully and without selflessness for the good of a people constitute greatness'.[55]

Curran also observed that Griffith had lived 'next door to penury. He cared nothing for money… he worked incessantly, without haste and without rest.'[56] This was in keeping with other contemporary eulogies: Griffith had, in effect, as W. B. Yeats put it, taken a 'vow of poverty' to prioritise his political work.[57] His champions insisted he was 'the prophet who gave his people a policy'; they also lamented that he was 'crushed by the ingratitude and the fury of the fratricidal maniacs'.[58] Curran did not vent such raw anger but he did pointedly refer to Griffith's 'tenacious and logical mind' that 'put up an uncompromising resistance to the action of the Irregulars' [the pejorative term used by the pro-Treaty provisional government about its IRA opponents to deny them legitimacy] and referred to 'a barren and naked idealism' that 'is never absent from Ireland', but that Griffith 'aerated idealism with common sense'. While noting that Griffith had 'a very definite dislike and distrust of Englishmen politically and indeed personally', he characterised him as of a 'conservative mind, which saw things first in their political aspect and for these two reasons was supposed to be cold towards Labour… but his whole manner of life was simple and democratic; by birth and upbringing he was close to the Dublin artisan.'[59] As regards the Treaty, 'to what he signed he remained almost pedantically loyal.'[60]

Those engaged in the politics of 1922 drank deep from its well for many years afterwards. It was often a silent imbibing, but even fifty years

[54] Michael Laffan, 'Arthur Griffith', in McGuire and Quinn (eds), *Dictionary of Irish Biography*, vol. 4, pp 277–86
[55] Michael Gahan, 'Arthur Griffith'
[56] Ibid.
[57] Donald R. Pearce, *The Senate Speeches of W. B. Yeats*, (London, 2001), pp 22–3, speech of 14 March 1923
[58] George A. Lyons, *Some Recollections of Arthur Griffith and His Times* (Dublin, 1923); preface UCDSC, 39 K/28
[59] Michael Gahan, 'Arthur Griffith'
[60] Ibid.

later, Griffith was still in Curran's thoughts. Just after he died in 1972, Niall Montgomery's appreciation of Curran in the *Irish Times* referred to a chat Montgomery had with Curran just a week earlier and 'something reminded Mr Curran of Arthur Griffith and of a journey to Drumgoff [County Wicklow] when Griffith's bicycle broke down and Mr Curran carried him for the rest of the way on his crossbar.'[61]

Given Curran's relative reticence about speaking or writing about his own contributions – his memoir was notable for its 'attentive portraits of his many friends and former teachers, and for its lack of self-revelation – Curran was throughout his life an observer'[62] – it is important that his writing for the *Nation* is acknowledged, capturing as it did the sense of possibilities, change, idealism, but also fatal divisions of that 1916–23 period, and the determination of key figures in the world of British journalism to try and add an edge to their coverage of Ireland not just from within their own ranks but through contributions from native observers. Massingham's editorship of the *Nation* ended in April 1923 and, with that, so did Curran's contributions, perhaps fittingly, as by that point, the Irish civil war was coming to an end.

[61] Niall Montgomery, 'Constantine P. Curran: An appreciation', *Irish Times*, 3 January 1972
[62] Dempsey and Hourican, 'Curran, Constantine', *Dictionary of Irish Biography*

C. P. Curran in a Personal Vein:
Ghost Photographer, Correspondent, Collector

Helen Solterer

The bookroom, as C. P. Curran, my grandfather, called the room looking out over the garden that my grandmother had planted, was his favorite at home. Every June, when my family returned to Dublin to spend summertime with him in the 1960s, he'd greet us at the hall door, and usher us straightaway into this room. Daddo, as we called him, was bereted, and often gruff at 10 a.m. Yet once inside the bookroom, he warmed up. He'd beckon to me, this Yank of a kid, just off a transatlantic flight. He'd open up one or more of his hundreds of books to show me over our cup of tea. Or he'd take down a piece of sculpture and place it in our hands to feel the cut of the stone. All these colorful things astounded me. Everywhere I turned in that room, another puzzling language appeared on the page, or another bust of a man or woman emerged from the mass of objects. Daddo had gathered there much of what he'd discovered in his life-long explorations and writing about literature, politics, architecture and art. He put out some of the artwork he and Helen Laird, my grandmother, had accumulated over some 40 years together on Garville Avenue. Daddo's bookroom awakened my curiosity; it stirred my first inkling of someone called Joyce. In those years, he had turned the bookroom into command central for his latest writing. Surrounded by floor-to-ceiling books, sheaves of engravings and his 'wireless', he enjoyed remembering his long-time friend in that place.

Making his book of memories about Joyce was a collective venture, starting with my mother, Elizabeth. No sooner was my family back in the bookroom again than the banter started up. I'd tune into her cajoling her father about 'the book', debating his turns of phrase or making a bet with him: who had consulted Dinneen's Irish English Dictionary or Thom's Directory more often for Joyce? My mother had her own experience with 'Jimmie Joyce'. She had grown up with him as a member of the extended family. She was the only child the writer knew who had begun reading *Ulysses* at the ripe age of nine.[1] Joyce had described in jest how his friend's daughter was found with the book, in bed, Christmas night, 1923 – living proof that his novel was not censored in Ireland at first. No doubt my grandparents had enjoyed telling him of Elizabeth checking the book out for herself. My mother was a mischievous free spirit from early on. Encouraged by all she had observed with her parents and the Joyces, after schooling in Irish at Scoil Bhríde and her own UCD years, she too headed out to the Continent – to work in art. Several decades later, when she returned to Garville Avenue, with my father and me in tow, she was brought back to her memories of Joyce in 1920/30s Paris. She too had been drawn into his *Work in Progress*, caught between his requests for Irish words, and her father's curiosity about the goings-on in France. Daddo did not hesitate to introduce her voice into his book; a witty one of her letters home from Paris.

During all those summers in the 60s, I watched a stream of people coming and going in Daddo's bookroom to talk writing with him. Several generations of allies showed up. Padraic Colum, who 'came home' to Garville Avenue, as he often said, kept after him to deliver *his* Joyce at last. The two men, with their wives Helen Laird and Mary Maguire, advocated for Joyce, as well as for other Irish writers. It was a life-long compulsion that Margaret Kelleher brings into clearer view. Niall Montgomery was another regular visitor. He loved trying out his latest pun on my grandfather, in Latin or French à la Joyce. Daddo would steer the architect and critic back to talk about their 'handmade city'; he relished discussing the eighteenth-century architectural fictions that were just as important to him as any Joycean stories they were considering.[2]

[1] Curran–Laird Collection, Special Collections, The James Joyce Library, University College, Dublin, CUR ms. 6. Letter from James Joyce to Paul Léon, 17 August 1934, National Library of Ireland (hereafter 'NLI'), *The James Joyce Paul Léon Papers in the National Library of Ireland*, compiled by Catherine Fahy (Dublin,1992), p. 15

[2] Niall Montgomery Papers, 'X. Constantine P. Curran's essays and notebooks, 1959 and 1963', NLI

And Daddo's women friends came round often in support: Sheila Murphy, fresh from her last diplomatic assignment in Paris, and Eilis MacNeill McDowell, my mother's intimate and confidant. Just as Eoin MacNeill, her father, did with my grandfather, she'd put heads together with Daddo over politics. She'd listen to his view on the 'ructions in Dublin following 1916' that Joyce did not fully take in, and draw Daddo out on the Troubles they were facing again, 50 years later. All the engaging talk with all these people made clear how he wrote with an eye to others. Their figure of Joyce came alive in the bookroom for me – one Dubliner among many.

In much the same years, Daddo was completing a series of portraits of various contemporaries: the pacifist–activist Francis Skeffington, the jurist and Chief Justice Hugh Kennedy, the Sinn Féin judge and essayist Arthur Clery, the historian and Cumann na nGaedhael minister John Marcus O'Sullivan, the chemist Felix Hackett. Daddo was placing Joyce in a cohort larger than the University College classmates of 1902 – one among many talented, young men. He was casting them as a group in action, citizens of a new capital city who, together with his two intimates, Padraic Colum and Tom Kettle, were inventing culture on their own terms.[3] The book he was mustering on Joyce at last was one part of this collective portrait he'd been detailing for years, in reviews, on the radio and in drawing room talk.

Reading Daddo's memories of Joyce with a fresh eye conjures up this circle of people surrounding the two men in the bookroom. Today it makes me curious again: who else stands out, side-by-side with Joyce? How does his book fit in all he did? I went back into the bookroom – what is now the Curran–Laird collection – to find out.[4] All along the way, I was keenly aware of another presence: my grandmother whom I never knew. Although she had died in 1957, her sense of play and colour continued to make the bookroom a welcoming place. She was on the tips of the tongues of Daddo and those who accompanied him during all those summers he was tussling with Joyce.

[3] C. P. Curran, *Under the Receding Wave* (Dublin, 1970), pp 111–34
[4] This collection is complemented by the C. P. Curran Collection at the Irish Architectural Archive, 77/6

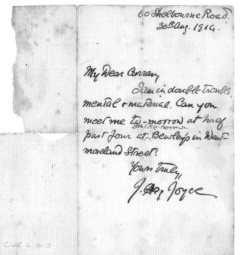

60 Shelbourne Road.
30ª Aug. 1904.

My Dear Curran
    I am in double trouble,
mental & material. Can you
meet me to-morrow at half
past four at Bewley's in Westmoreland Street?
        Yours truly,
        J. A. Joyce

CUR L 410

→ C.P. Curran, 1904, at home

← Inns Quay Four Courts Law Library,
  c. 1905. C.P. Curran Collection,
  Irish Architectural Archive

↑ Curran-Laird Collection,
  UCD CUR L 410

Ghost Photographer

Day 1 at College, 1899, was invariably Daddo's first memory of Joyce. Seeing 'his first poet', as he describes Joyce at the beginning of the book, is his epiphany of sorts. He recounted the scene with relish on several occasions, giving the writer his Irish literary title, and with a wink to Petrarch, his laurels too. This was one of several images of the writer that Daddo had been actively creating over many years, the original and most famous – the photograph he took of the rakish young buck. It's the summer of 1904 in his memory, and Joyce has called round to the Curran family home on Cumberland Terrace, on the North Circular Road. Daddo, the first college graduate in the family, imagined himself a man of letters.

Flush with his Arts degree and legal studies at the Kings' Inns, he took to experimenting with his father's photographic equipment. Patrick Curran, an amateur camera man, kept some of it at home, developing pictures in his workshop. The son had conferred with the father about doing the photograph of the graduating class of 1902 with a pneumatic camera. This time, did Daddo get the idea of setting up the pose in advance, calculating the time required to get the camera ready?

Or was it more spur-of-the-moment, decided upon when Joyce came by to Number 6, a picture he made catching his friend during a period when he was 'in double trouble', as he wrote Curran at the end of August?

Whichever choice it was, Curran and Joyce were co-conspirators in that instant. Curran was making a first iconic image of the writer as Joyce was drafting Stephen Hero. Looking at the glass plate of the photograph today, I peer at the shadowy profile through their eyes. The image comes into another focus, especially when I look at it with some of the books they shared around 1900.[5] These two twenty-somethings had discovered Rimbaud: the poet caught their fancy because he began revolutionising literature and art at a young age. Rimbaud had been photographed at seventeen by citizen photographer Étienne Carjat in 1871. This famous close-up of the young man, his eyes looking elsewhere, far ahead, created an aura around him. Carjat's Rimbaud helped the public see him as a boy genius; the photograph turning him into a visionary and rebel. Curran's Joyce began introducing him to interested viewers in Ireland and France, the photo turning him into an artist the public could picture. In that flash of a moment, when Joyce is a fledging writer, and Curran, an apprentice portrait maker of his Dubliners, I notice the young men's experiment. One captures the other in everyday life outdoors – among Mrs Curran's flowerpots. Far from a formal studio portrait, this photograph relays something of their canny, playful action. I can't say for sure that the two came up with a scheme of portraying Joyce, with Carjat's Rimbaud in their mind's eye. Yet Daddo was always attentive to what happened to the photo; I imagine him checking his memory – and books – one more time, chuckling at my hypothesis. *Se non è vero, è ben trovato.*

Daddo arranged several images of Joyce. Some 30 years after the 1904 photograph, when Joyce was ensconced in France, and deep into *Finnegans Wake*, he sent Seán O'Sullivan to sketch him.[6] This time, an Irish artist established in Dublin drew the internationally known artist in Paris. These drawings never had the impact of the photograph my grandfather made. Was the medium too traditional for a vanguard

[5] In particular, Paul Verlaine, *Poètes maudits*, initialed and dated 1902, Curran–Laird Collection

[6] C. P. Curran, *James Joyce Remembered*, p. 100. Letter from Seán O Sullivan to James Joyce, Easter 1935, NLI, *The James Joyce Paul Léon Papers*, p. 112

modernist? One thing is clear. Daddo liked photographing his intimates: Colum as they walked the countryside, and Kettle settling in for a chat in the back garden.[7] Whether he took shots or sketched or composed his portraits in words, he was working steadily at drawing the figures he wanted Dublin – and a wider world – to get to know over time.

Curran's Joyce from 1904 continues to lead a highly visible life. It condenses many layers of Dublin time and space, as Hugh Campbell reveals. It opens up to much more on the city's North Side that the Plattenbau drawing helps us to see. For many today, the photo my grandfather made before Joyce's first fiction was published became a signature portrait of the artist. The young man, rarely identified, and often judged for rejecting Joyce's Day of Rabblement for UCD's St Stephen's magazine, created an image for the writer that would go on to be consumed world-wide. You may have seen it on larger-than-life banners hanging from lampposts on O'Connell Street during the 2004 Centenary, or in last-century poster shops, online today. The image is so frequently reproduced that many people encounter this Joyce before reading a line of his writing. Back when the Celtic tiger was roaring, and the James Joyce pub opened round the corner from me in Durham, North Carolina, I went prospecting with my mother, and friends. A photocopy of Daddo's photo was emblazoned on the wall. The Clare man who had put it up was taken aback to meet the family of the ghost photographer. He'd never thought of a person actually taking that picture. We enjoyed introducing Daddo – making the photographer known with the photograph. 'Sure,' the bar owner said, 'they're powering on in the American South.'

Correspondent

Curran, Joyce and their generation were inveterate letter-writers. The packets tied in pink string that I found among the family papers gave me the sense of a habit that was vital. It became their lifeline. The scrawled letters felt different in the hand than the cleaned-up pages in archival folders at the UCD library. Yet they carry the same charge. When

[7] Curran–Laird Collection, CUR P 32, 33; CUR P 39, 40

both men were living in Dublin, they kept in close touch; they exchanged a flurry of notes to fix a rendezvous, or to pick up a conversation on a Moore's melody they had left off. Some exchanges hint at the confiding that happened when they met – just out of earshot for us. Others point to changes under way in the young men, in the storyteller Joyce, in the correspondent Curran entering the Crown legal service. During the early summer of 1904, they signed their letters with names that, in Joyce's case, have some readers running to the novels for a double-take on a fictional character. 'Daedalus' makes his appearance.[8] Joyce's persona is joined by another that my grandfather invents for himself. Several years later Michael Gahan emerged, introduced in a byline in one of the earliest essays Daddo had published on literary topics: his review of Colum's poetry, *Wild Earth*, in the *New Ireland Review*, 1908. This literary lark of a pen name would serve my grandfather as a necessary alias. It covered his later writing and protected him as he wrote in support of the Irish Republic.

When Joyce left Dublin for good in 1910, their letters became crucial for literary and personal reasons. Their desire to keep in contact by exchanging latest news bulletins was constant; as families grew and commingled, brothers and wives and daughters took to writing too. When Stanislaus, James' younger sibling, went out to Trieste in the summer of 1907, he wrote Curran quickly. In a note from July 8, he reported on his sibling's rheumatic fever, and an eye inflammation that took a toll on his writing.[9] Wars – European and Irish – complicated the Curran–Joyce exchanges, yet strengthened their wish to remain in touch. Since it was unlikely for them to meet in person, storyteller Joyce kept up the campaign of reporting on his writing; and correspondent Curran, a weathercock pointing steadily in one direction, plied his circuit of newspapermen to get the word out.

The first Curran–Joyce letters to and from my grandparents' house on Garville Avenue came under Crown surveillance. The large stamp, OPENED BY CENSOR., on Joyce's letter, March 15, 1917, makes clear how a letter posted to Dublin during wartime, even from neutral Switzerland, was subject to scrutiny. What did a British bureaucrat

[8] Stuart Gilbert (ed.), *Letters of James Joyce* (New York, 1957), vol. 1, p. 55
[9] Curran–Laird Collection, CUR L 42

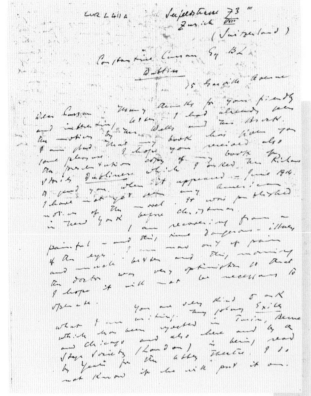

CUR L 411 A   Seefeldstrasse 73'''
                          Zurich VIII
                          (Switzerland)

Constantine Curran Esq BL
    Dublin
                    15 Garville Avenue

Dear Curran: Many thanks for your friendly
and interesting letter. I had already seen
the notices by MacWalls and "a Brook.
I am glad that my book has given you
some pleasure. I hope you received also
the presentation copy of my book "The Richard"
Which Dubliners which I ordered — June 1914.
I send you when it appeared — June 1914.
I have not yet seen any American
notice of the — vol. It was published
in New York before Christmas.

            I am recovering from a
painful — and this time dangerous — illness
of the eye. I am now out of pain
and much better and this morning
the doctor was very optimistic so that
I hope it will not be necessary to
operate.

            You are very kind to ask
what I am writing. My play Exiles
which has been rejected in Turin, Berne
and Chicago and also here and by a
Stage Society (London) is being read
by Yeats for the Abbey Theatre. I do
not know if he will put it on.

He would think this theatre should form
a right to stage it. In any case I
shall publish it in autumn. I finished
it in 1915. I am writing Ulysses which
I began six or seven years ago in Rome
and hope I shall be able to finish
it in 1918. The compositions you speak
of will then be made good as you
suppose. A few verses of — mine were
printed in Poetry (Chicago) last year.
I enclose. Most of them
I will send. I hope that you and
yours are well and beg you to give
my regards to any who remember
me.

            With all good wishes
                    sincerely yours
                    James Joyce

15 March 1917

make of Joyce's news about his writing; his inveterate promoting of
Dubliners; his complaining about the difficulty of staging *Exiles*? How
did he understand the report on the state of *Ulysses*, from its beginnings
in Rome to its wished-for end the next year, in 1918? As we read over
the censor's shoulder, as he did over Joyce's, do we imagine him as
one of the happy few who had already heard of the writer? For my
grandfather, the censor meant something very different. Discovering
his correspondence went through Crown security checks was a warning
to him, an employee in the Crown's Four Courts. It alerted him that
whatever Joyce and he wrote was always already caught up in the
struggle for Irish independence. His own position too was hardly safe.
A year later, Garville Avenue was under surveillance by the Crown. My
grandmother's friend, Mrs [Maud] Gonne McBride, was signalled to
Dublin Castle police.[10]

In Daddo's letter to Joyce, 26 February 1917, he makes mention
of his 'little work at present for the *Nation*'. His discretion may have
been politically motivated in this murky year following the Rising. Just
ten days earlier, the article he had published in the British weekly – his
first – reported on the Sinn Féin victory in Roscommon. He wrote under
the pseudonym Michael Gahan again. His choice of a family name
communicates a rich, radical journalistic heritage which he had learned
from his mother, a MacGahan. My grandfather placed his own political
writing in the line of J. A. MacGahan, a distant relation, born in America.
This freelance investigative reporter was one of the first to report in the
English-language press on an uprising in Bulgaria and massacres of the
freedom fighters at the hands of the Ottoman Turks in 1876.[11] Curran,
an 'Irish correspondent' in the *Nation*, 1917–22, takes his place among
other militants' writing during those revolutionary years, as Diarmaid
Ferriter outlines fully.

For Daddo, under Crown surveillance, getting his articles to Britain
during wartime was no mean feat. He got help from his own father. I
often heard my mother's accounts about Patrick Curran, her grandfather,
director of the Telegraph division of the G.P.O. He was instrumental in

[10] Constantine P. Curran,' Ireland,
Intelligence Profiles, 1914–1922
CO 904, Dublin Castle Records,
British National Archives
[11] J. A. MacGahan, Esq., *The Turkish
Atrocities in Bulgaria: Letters of the
Special Commissioner of the Daily
News, with an Introduction and
Mr. Schuyler's Preliminary Report*
(London, 1876)

helping transmit copy to the *Nation* offices in London to meet deadlines for printing and morning edition circulation. Daddo's father went back to the G.P.O. after hours to get the copy out. This life-long Home Ruler who also frequented *Freeman's Journal* newspapermen was committed to his son's political correspondence, ready to do his own discrete liaison work with him for an Irish Republic.

Did my grandfather ever fill in Joyce about his political writing on the War of Independence? I've often asked this question. I've imagined eavesdropping on their conversations, wanting to find out whether they talked about Daddo's close connections with the *Freeman's Journal* and journalists in English- and French-speaking circuits. Joyce, who was dubbed 'an Irish-Italian journalist' when writing for the *Evening Telegraph* from Trieste, did inquire whether he was still a correspondent in May 1919 – entirely for his own literary reasons. This remains a puzzle still. I don't see any sign that they discussed it years later in Paris. My grandfather does make his view clear: Joyce's self-absorption distorted the writer's understanding of the War in all its Black-and-Tan cruelty. While Joyce was single-mindedly occupied by his 'revolutionary' business in literature during 1917–22, he was short-sighted about the political revolution in Ireland to which Daddo committed with his writing.

Nor is it evident that there was any exchange between the two men about the outbreak of Civil War in late June, 1922. When the Four Courts was occupied by those opposing the Treaty signed with Britain, and the building blown up, Daddo was sent by the Irish Provisional Government to evaluate the destruction. Michael Collins authorised him to report on what could be rescued from the Public Record Office. My grandfather, in waders, picked his way through the rooms that held Ireland's centuries-long history of documents; they were flooded and still booby-trapped with live mines. 'Completely gutted,' he writes, 'land judge deeds and law tracts obliterated.'[12]

The handwritten report, signed Conn O Curraín, stunned me. In the year Joyce finally published *Ulysses*, here was Daddo working to salvage fragments of Irish written culture. He sought to safeguard what

[12] Hugh Kennedy Papers, UCD Archives, P 4 / 283/4

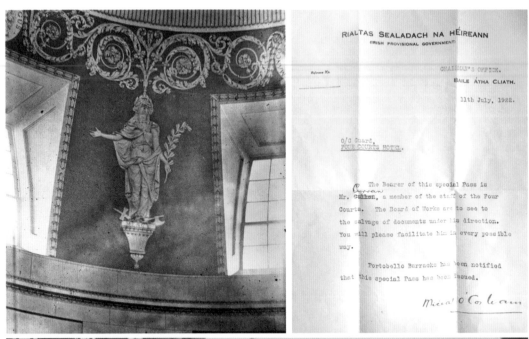

RIALTAS SEALADACH NA HÉIREANN
(IRISH PROVISIONAL GOVERNMENT)

CHAIRMAN'S OFFICE.

BAILE ÁTHA CLIATH.

11th July, 1922.

O/C Guard,
FOUR COURTS HOTEL.

The Bearer of this special Pass is
Mr. Cullen, a member of the staff of the Four
Courts. The Board of Works are to see to
the salvage of documents under his direction.
You will please facilitate him in every possible
way.

Portobello Barracks has been notified
that this special Pass has been issued.

← ← Four Courts plasterwork, Dome
Interior: Figure of Mercy
Undated photo, C.P. Curran, Curran
Collection, Irish Architectural Archive

← Public Record office, Four Courts,
Salvage Operation, family collection

✓ Four Courts, Destruction.
July 1922, Curran Collection,
Irish Architectural Archive

remained, and ensure transmitting it to future generations. I can no longer find out if he ever told Joyce of his reporting from the bombed-out Record Office, his rage at the wanton destruction, his sorrow at this loss. He regarded such manuscripts and books belonging to his people as precious, almost as precious as the men and women who made them. Almost as precious as the life of Rory O'Connor, who was summarily executed – a school chum, according to family stories, whom he tried to persuade not to detonate the mines.

Collector

In houses chock-a-block with books, like Garville Avenue, and ones like mine with less print and more screens, I have often wondered why people collect. For my grandfather, it began, at a young age. Buying books was alluring since there were few of them in his parents' home. Collecting them was stranger. Daddo's love of them took hold when he went down to the book barrows along the Liffey quays.[13] It was his favourite sport, and a growing habit he came to share with his college friends. He could not afford much. He recognised that he could easily collect what some of his closest friends had acquired. The small set of plays and poetry in French and Italian gives us glimpses of Daddo's steps in collecting Joyce.[14] This multilingual raw material that Joyce enjoyed using in *Portrait* and *Ulysses* entices still. Yet, above all, I see books that Joyce called his own, and which Curran took care to keep. Owning such books around 1900 was a significant sign that both chose to live with what others wrote.

While Daddo had the instinct to collect from early on, he needed space to do so. His marriage to Helen Laird, and their household set up on Garville Avenue in 1913, gave him that. Helen was glad that Conn had the means to collect at last. In those years, as he started making his bookroom, my grandmother began bringing people into it. She was known as very sociable, working with fellow militants in the Women's Franchise League, the Irish National Theatre Society, Cuala Press and Michael Collins' network of messenger-women at the height of the War

13 Curran, *Under the Receding Wave*, pp 42, 46
14 Maurice Maeterlinck, *Death of Tintagile*, dated 1899; Gabriele d'Annunzio, *La Gioconda*, signed and dated May 1900; Curran–Laird Collection

of Independence. She orchestrated their Wednesdays 'at home', inviting a political cross-section of locals and internationals. During their first War years, Chicago newspapermen reporting on the struggle arrived; Collins' and Mulcahy's gunmen on the run made it safely in the door too. Jane Addams, the American civil rights organiser and suffragette came; Micheál MacLiammóir, founder of the Gate Theatre, came too.

What my grandfather put up on shelves in Garville Avenue (now in UCD's James Joyce Library) extends beyond this writer and his family's writing. Daddo was collecting editions dedicated to him, alongside the books of many writers in Ireland, named and anonymous. Cultivating Joyce was part of his larger effort to assemble Dublin literature and the artwork of those working in stone, plaster, paint, glass. He was committed to the entire generation of creative people to which he and Joyce belonged; Anne Fogarty catches something of this particular zeal.

Daddo was equally intent on documenting the struggle for the first Irish Free State. The earliest manuscripts he amassed include Pádraic H. Pearse, 'A Song for Marie Magdalene' (1907), which likely comes from his and my grandmother's brief involvement in Pearse's school, Saint Enda's.[15] Witnessing the destruction of the Public Records Office and its bitter aftermath in his own circle changed him. The shock, I'm sure, made him redouble his efforts. He took the need to collect Irish books personally. Daddo was determined to amass as much of the writing of his people as he could. Those that were made long before his and Joyce's time were equally precious. If Brehan law tracts were lost, he could acquire works like Camden's *Hibernia* (1587).

Daddo was also focused on the next generation, and what they were up to in their writing. He enjoyed talking about their talent with Joyce. These fathers supported the experiments of daughters and sons. They revelled in the Joycean 'gene' pool, the writing of their adopted literary families. Niall Montgomery was among the first elect in Dublin. My mother copied the poem of her friend, 'Ave Aviary' [written in what I am pleased to call annoyed alexandrines], and sent it to Eilis MacNeill, studying in Germany, in December 1932: 'Niall has written or rather gotten a poem printed in "Motley" the Gate Theatre Mag. And we can't get over it. Some people think he was <u>serious</u> in imitating Jimmy Joyce – Michael Sayers an Irish-Jewish 19-year-old poet said to Mary Manning "he's written a great satire on Joyce if he only knew it."[16] Niall chuckled when he heard… and Mum split her sides laughing.' Niall Sheridan was another among the Dublin elect.[17] This 1930s UCD cohort was creative in its own right, active in the students rags of *Comhthrom Féinne* and *Blather* – beside Brían Ó Nualainn/Flann O'Brien. Quick to take up Joyce, they wrote their own poetry and fiction. Daddo was right there to collect it.

Joyce and Curran were yin and yang in their rapport to collecting. While Joyce's books in Trieste and Paris have been constituted retroactively as libraries by his circle of friends, aficionados and digital sleuths, Joyce did not take the step fully himself. Worrying about the fate of his own books, he left the work largely to others. My grandfather assembled Joyce's first library in Dublin. He collected his earliest letters and some works in manuscript, with first editions of each work that Joyce sent him. It was part of promoting the accomplished writer in their hometown. It substantiated what he would begin saying on Raidió Éireann, in a personal sketch broadcast for the writer's birthday in 1938. It was the ground for what he developed in writing after Joyce's sudden death in 1941, and the devastation of World War II. Post war, as Europeans, Americans and the Irish were regrouping, he collaborated with the photographer Lee Miller in a piece for *Vogue*, published in the States (1947).[18] He led this remarkable creator around his city; Miller who had accompanied American GIs liberating the Nazi camps, Auschwitz and Dachau, was this time, a year later, on assignment to photograph the townscape of *Ulysses*. Curran and Miller's montage participated in a post-war plan to brand Dublin for 'foreign' consumption, advertising its home-grown writer to a new class of middle-brow reader. Their work points to 'Curran's notable collection of Joyciana' for the first time.

Collecting – whatever the object or its time – created a personal presence for my grandfather with whom he and my grandmother and mother lived, day in and day out. The household copy of *Finnegans*

16 Elizabeth Curran-Eilis MacNeill correspondence, 1927–38, family collection. Niall Montgomery, *Dublin Man: Selected Writings*, ed. Christine O'Neill (Dublin, 2014)
17 Niall Sheridan and Donagh MacDonagh, *Twenty Poems*, Dublin, 1934. Letter from Niall Sheridan to James Joyce, 2 May 1939, NLI, *The James Joyce Paul Léon Papers*, p. 116
18 Constantine P. Curran, 'When James Joyce Lived in Dublin', photographs, Lee Miller, *Vogue*, 1 May 1947, pp 144–9

→ Constantine Curran and Paul Léon,
Fontainebleau, 1935, Curran-Laird
collection, CUR P 13

Wake sent by Joyce was just such a living, breathing companion.
'Presently,' Daddo wrote his friend in thanks, 'it will look very lordly on
my shelves but just now it wanders from room to room, living from hand
to mouth. This is the mere truth, the blamed thing lives when it is read
aloud and hovers near intelligibility…'[19] Daddo understood his growing
collection as a way to cultivate many diverse circles of his people who
shaped a cultural and artistic Dublin in the new Irish State. Collecting
what they created was his credo of civic activism.

In all this work, my grandfather found a kindred spirit in Paul Léon.
This Jewish savant, coming from the opposite end of Europe, had left
Bolshevik Russia for London and Paris. He too was trained as a lawyer
yet was far more committed to his own writing in political philosophy,
his love of books and languages.[20] The two men shared a similar
practical approach to their friend. My grandfather first met Léon through
correspondence around Joyce that mixed his books, as ever, with
intimate family affairs. In 1931 they were faced first with John Stanislaus
Joyce, the writer's father in decline. My mother – a teenager at the time

[19] Letter from C. P. Curran to James
Joyce, 15 May 1939, NLI; *The
James Joyce Paul Léon Papers*, p. 92
[20] Maria Jolas translates some
fragments of his work into
English early on in 'The Little
Known Paul Léon', *A James Joyce
Miscellany* Second Series, ed.
Marvin Magalaner (Carbondale,
1959), pp 228–33

– recounted the situation to her friend Eilis MacNeill: 'You see Jimmie Joyce who lives in Paris, his father was dying, and he phoned Dad to see after him and all that. The old man died today… God bless him – 85. It was quite exciting to hear Jimmie's voice again. You know he's about the best-known Irishman in the world next to Liam MacCosgair.'[21] My mother sensed what Daddo had been asked to do, and why. Curran took up the task and, with Léon, they handled father Joyce's funeral, will and personal effects. Their letters speak of their solidarity, and their shared modus operandi.[22] When Joyce obsesses about reclaiming the letters and books he had sent to his father, the two right-hand men go about saving – and collecting – their friend's work.

My grandfather and Léon worked more closely in tandem around Lucia Joyce and her artwork. Other family members rallied to back them up; my grandmother and mother, Lucie Léon, as well as other friends in the Joycean circle, Maria Jolas, translator and *transition* editor, as well as the Colums in Paris. In the spring of 1935, Joyce's beloved only daughter had travelled to Ireland for a change of scene, in search of a break from the psychological pain badgering her. She went missing. This Paris–Dublin team went into action again, together with Harriet Weaver in London. My grandparents accompanied Lucia on the mailboat to Holyhead where Weaver met them and whisked her off for care in London. As soon as Lucia's safety was ensured, it was – once more – a question of the fate of books – her books. In September, my grandmother wrote Joyce to reassure him. 'I went passporting to Bray yesterday… I saved some of Lucia's clothes and books… As to the copy of "Pomes Penyeach" they were not given to a policeman but are in the hands of Paddy Schaurek who seems to be really interested in his uncle's work.'[23] At the time, the distress over Lucia was doubled for my grandparents. They were grappling with deaths of their own: Conn's mother in the spring, and Helen and Conn's friend Æ – George Russell – in the same month they were looking after Lucia. How they responded to all these losses coming all at once amazes me still. In the midst of it all, they did not lose sight of Lucia's books. Conn had written

[21] Letter 12 December 1931, Elizabeth Curran-Eilis MacNeill correspondence, 1927–38, family collection.
[22] Curran–Laird Collection, CUR ms. 6; Exchange of Letters, Paul Léon, Constantine Curran, 5, 9 January; 2, 14 February 1932, NLI; *The James Joyce Paul Léon Papers*, pp 88–9
[23] Letter from Helen Curran to James Joyce, 10, 16 September 1935, NLI; *The James Joyce Paul Léon Papers*, p. 91

Léon in early May to thank Joyce for his copy of *Pomes*. 'No gift of his has touched me more…'[24] My grandfather was moved by Lucia's artistic independence, her own modern style. He made sure to keep this book with other pieces of her work, including a thank-you card she made for the Currans. 'Any news of Napoleon?'[25] Her 'French' sense of humour about her father had not left her.

The teamwork of my grandfather and Léon reached a critical point when another World War began scattering everyone. During the late summer, 1939, Conn and Helen who were in Paris to visit my mother apprenticing at the Jeanne Bucher art gallery, and the Joyces, were sent packing. All 'foreign nationals' were ordered to leave France in the grip of the 'phony war'. Joyce and his family were also compelled to leave; their exit to Switzerland delayed for many months until winter 1940. Paul Léon and his family faced a much more dangerous situation, once the anti-Jewish statutes of the collaborationist Vichy government went into effect, as his widow Lucie Léon would chronicle post war.[26]

This latest war necessitated the most far-reaching coordination of Léon with my grandfather in support of Joyce. During the fall of 1940, Léon took the intrepid step of returning to the Joyce apartment to gather up personal correspondence left behind. He brought this material, including Léon–Joyce–Curran letters, to the Irish delegation, a neutral site in Paris. He left it for Count O'Kelly with instructions that these letters be sent to Ireland; and in the event of Joyce's death and his own, that Curran should give direction to the next steps to be taken in Dublin.[27] As Léon foresaw all possibilities with a knowing eye, he turned to Curran.

My grandfather tells us in his working notebook on Joyce that he learned informally of this material making it to the Irish National Library in 1946.[28] It was not until years later, in August 1953, that the Library asked him to inspect it confidentially. By this time, his two friends were already dead: Joyce succumbing to poor health in Zurich in January 1941; and Léon, deported in one of the first convoys leaving France for Auschwitz, killed there in April 1942. At the Library that day, some

[24] Letter from Constantine Curran to Paul Léon, 7 May 1935, NLI; *The James Joyce Paul Léon Papers*, p. 90

[25] Curran–Laird Collection, CUR L 323; Helen Solterer, 'L for Lucia and her Lettrines: Opening UCD's Curran Collection', *Irish Times* 2 February 2020

[26] Lucie Léon, *James Joyce and Paul L. Léon: The Story of a Friendship* (New York, 1950), pp 36–41. Luca Crispi is preparing a new edition of this testimonial

[27] Curran–Laird Collection, CUR L 303 a–b, Patricia Donlon, *The James Joyce Paul Léon Papers*, p. v

[28] Curran–Laird Collection, CUR ms. 6. A year later, he was advocating for the National Library as 'the natural destination' for Joyce manuscripts. See *Dear Miss Weaver, Harriet Shaw Weaver 1876–1961*, Jane Lidderdale & Mary Nicholson (New York, 1970), p. 381

ten years after Léon had secured the papers with the Irish delegation in Paris, my grandfather saw a further Joyce collection in the making. I imagine him discovering Léon's projection of his own death at the hands of the Nazis, and wincing. Here was my grandfather who had been lucky enough to survive the violence in his war-torn town facing Léon who did not. Daddo was left bereft. The memory of their camaraderie a few years back, and their work together handling Joyce's intimate affairs may have offered some consolation. A bittersweet one.

In his notebook, my grandfather portrays Léon and something of his letter-collecting:

> The letters confirm what we know about the relations of Paul
> Léon with Joyce in remarkable, astonishing degree. There
> appear no limits to Paul Léon's unselfish devotion to Joyce
> as a man of genius and his letters to Miss Weaver show him
> to be a friend gifted not only with the most sympathetic
> understanding of Joyce's character, difficulties, and relations,
> but with a wise, penetrating and independent judgement. In
> business as in other matters, he shows himself to be tactful,
> diplomatic, and dexterous. At every moment and in every
> detail, he appears to have been at Joyce's service. Knowing
> all Nora Joyce's devotion to her husband, it is still difficult to
> see how Joyce could have managed his complicated affairs
> without the unselfish and undeviating work of Léon. To the
> outside world, he appeared Joyce's *conseiller juridique* or
> *homme d'affaires*, giving professional service for a fee.
> In fact he worked unpaid out of friendship.[29]

My grandfather knew what it meant for Léon to give his all to Joyce. He understood how Léon valued his writing to such a degree as to do everything he could to prevent it from falling into the wrong hands, to get it back to Ireland. While Joyce never returned there, it was Léon who enabled more of the writer's personal papers to 'come home'.

[29] Curran–Laird Collection, CUR ms. 6

While Daddo does not describe Léon retrieving Joyce's papers during the first autumn in Nazi-occupied Paris, 1940, he does tell us what happened to the man himself. Léon is 'last seen half-carried by his companions in misery in a wretched procession to a concentration camp'.[30] Daddo gives us a glimpse of Léon, ill and weak, leaving Royallieu, the camp in Compiègne, outside of Paris, and being deported to Auschwitz. His description bears something of the last look Lucie and Alexis Léon had of him as she recounts in her book. I see my grandfather's effort to honour Léon's absolute commitment to Joyce. To this day I still have a hard time with Léon's poignant dilemma, one that Daddo understood and Joyce never knew.

When I sought out Alexis Léon, to learn more of the unlikely trio of his father, my grandfather and Joyce, we met in Paris one May day, 2012, with his wife, Marielena. Over lunch in his family and Joyce's old neighbourhood where, by coincidence, I had lived during my student days, we talked about what was missing from accounts then. Alec spoke especially of his father's writing on Irish Home Rule; I told him of my grandfather's collecting Fauviste painting. We left much unsaid. His cautiousness, my discretion and our mutual respect reined in the talk. Still I came away from that one-time encounter with Alec with a keener sense that Joyce's *Ulysses* and *Finnegans Wake* are time-released happenings. When the Currans, the Léons, the Colums and others are put more fully in the picture, the novels appear now as collective events, rich with who was lost, and what is gained.

Durham, North Carolina, Dublin, Paris
March–October 2021

---

[30] C. P. Curran, *JJR*, p. 94

A Joycean Coda

Modernism, Memory and the Biographical Impulse

Anne Fogarty

C. P. Curran's *James Joyce Remembered* is a unique volume, an inimitable, evocative, fastidiously exact and sometimes unsparing portrait of Joyce as student, friend, and artist. Yet, simultaneously, it belongs to a distinctive sub-genre, a constellation of memoirs about Joyce and UCD written by friends, including J. F. Byrne's *Silent Years*, Eugene Sheehy's *May It Please the Court* and *Our Friend James Joyce* by Padraic and Mary Colum.[1] They have been little examined and taken for granted as an inevitable offshoot of Joyce studies, a collateral aspect of the myriad publications inspired by a revolutionary author who has become a celebrity and a universally acclaimed icon. In revisiting *James Joyce Remembered*, my purpose in this essay is threefold: to consider views of and debates about biography and the self within modernist studies, briefly to cross-compare Curran's portrait of Joyce with those of his friends and coevals, to pinpoint its peculiar features, and to identify the distinctive stylistic traits and structural and framing devices that make it such an enduring, individualistic and beguiling piece of writing.

The burden of my examination is that the Dublin memoirs of Joyce's friends, but most of all Curran's recollections, are born of competing impulses: they unite critique, biography, memory, self-writing, a generational story and artistic invention. Rather than being dismissed as historical curiosities or homages in a minor key to a literary genius, they should be seen as acts of co-creation as well as being an epi-phenomenon of modernism and a part of its unfurling aftermath. Joyce co-opted family,

[1] J. F. Byrne, *Silent Years: An Autobiography with Memoirs of James Joyce and Our Ireland* (New York, 1953); Eugene Sheehy, *May It Please the Court* (Dublin, 1951); Padraic and Mary Colum, *Our Friend James Joyce* (London, 1959). For excerpts from Sheehy and the Colums, see Ulick O'Connor (ed.), *The Joyce We Knew* (Dingle, 2004). For discussion of the Colums' relationship with Joyce, see Kelleher, pp 130-1, 135-7.

friends and patrons throughout his life to engage with his writing projects as amanuenses, agents, patrons, publicists, dynamically engaged readers and implicit co-authors. This process of collaborative creation began during his student days, even when all of his major literary works had still to be written.

Leopold Bloom in 'Lestrygonians' concludes his vividly sensory reminiscences about an all-consuming sexual assignation with Molly Bloom on Howth with the rueful afterthought: 'Me. And me now.'[2] He thereby points to the instability of the self and the way in which memory confounds the present and reveals identity to be discontinuous. Stephen Dedalus in a similar vein but with greater irony muses on a way out of his chronic indebtedness: 'Wait. Five months. Molecules all change. I am other I now. Other I got pound.'[3] The mutability of the body over time underscores the fluctuating nature of identity, cancelling out the obligation of the debtor who has become other.

Life writing was a vexed phenomenon in modernism precisely because of such apprehensions about the self as unfixed and a compound of non-cohering fragments and dispersed historical moments. Yet, modernism also aimed to encompass the quotidian and felt bodily experience into fiction in more all-encompassing ways. In 'Scylla and Charybdis', Stephen Dedalus apparently refutes as old-fashioned and regressive George Russell's claim that the only criterion by which to judge a literary work is 'out of how deep a life does it spring', but his theory of Shakespeare at once propounds a view of the playwright as unknowable and enigmatic and as incorporating the material world and his vexed psychosexual history into his art.[4]

Paradoxically, despite its reservations about the truth claims of traditional biography, our knowledge of modernism is centrally mediated by biographies and critical works that interweave life writing and artistic commentary, such as Frank Budgen's much-cited *James Joyce and the Making of 'Ulysses'*.[5] Richard Ellmann's detailed, lapidary and monumental biography, which first appeared in 1959, followed by a revised edition in 1982, has lastingly stamped our views of Joyce to the chagrin of Hugh Kenner who castigated it in a tetchy review for what he called the

[2] *Ulysses*, Hans Walter Gabler (ed.) (London 1986), 8.917
[3] Ibid., 9.205–6
[4] Ibid., 9.501
[5] Frank Budgen, *James Joyce and the Making of 'Ulysses'* (Oxford, 1972)

'impertinence of being definitive'.[6] In making a case for Joyce as a single-minded genius and family man, Ellmann's work confronts us with what Hermione Lee has described as the abiding conflict of all biographies, an internal tussle between 'forms of alteration or untruth' and 'the responsibility to likeness and the need for accuracy'.[7] For Lee, biographers are torn between a contradictory array of approaches. They make up their subjects by constructing them from piecemeal fragments and make them over by remodelling them, yet they also seek veracity and endeavour to convey a sense of 'a living person in a body'.[8] Lee's observations are instructive as they posit that biographical writings are predicated on opposing objectives and methods: they seek coherence, but are built around gaps and parts; they have fictional aspects but aim to have historical purchase; they set out to convey existence as it is lived, but cannot avoid rendering their subjects as abstractions or projected images at times.

Juxtaposing Curran's work with the memoirs of two of his UCD contemporaries, J. F. Byrne and Eugene Sheehy, underscores commonalities between them as well as divergences. Unlike Curran, both Byrne and Sheehy outline overviews of their own lives as well as giving an account of Joyce. In her unfinished memoir, *A Sketch of the Past*, Virginia Woolf argued that one can make little sense of the subjects of biographies without paying attention to the 'invisible presences' that surround them.[9] This apprehension that all biography hinges on the representation of the group and not the solitary individual is evident in all three of these memoirs about Joyce. Hence, he is described as part of a gifted cohort of students in UCD, including Felix Hackett, Tom Kettle and Francis Sheehy Skeffington, by Curran, Byrne, and Sheehy.[10] Further, the teachers whom he disparaged in real life or misrepresented in his fictional versions of UCD in *Stephen Hero* and *A Portrait of the Artist as a Young Man* are redrawn for the reader: Byrne is at pains to provide a more accurate and forgiving account of Father Darlington, the Dean of Studies, and Curran of Édouard Cadic, the Professor of French.[11] Both Sheehy and Byrne make Joyce over in the manner described by Hermione Lee. Sheehy, while stressing that Joyce was always in his

[6] Richard Ellmann, *James Joyce* (1959; Oxford, 1982). Hugh Kenner, 'The Impertinence of Being Definitive', in *Times Literary Supplement* (17 December 1982), pp 1383–4

[7] Hermione Lee, *Virginia Woolf's Nose* (New Jersey, 2005), pp 37, 38

[8] Ibid, p. 2

[9] Virginia Woolf, 'A Sketch of the Past', in Jeanne Schulkind (ed.), *Moments of Being* (New York, 1985), pp 61–160 (p. 80)

[10] For an account of UCD during Joyce's term as a student, see Donal McCartney, 'Joyce's UCD', in Anne Fogarty and Fran O'Rourke (ed.), *Voices on Joyce* (Dublin, 2015), pp 65–75

[11] Byrne, pp 33–40 and C. P. Curran, *James Joyce Remembered* (hereafter *JJR*) (Oxford, 1968), pp 22-3

Gaiety Theatre

SUNDAY THEATRE
presents
Exiles
by James Joyce

Sunday, 18th. January, 1948

Programme for a production of Exiles in
the Gaiety Theatre, Dublin, 18 January
1948, the first Irish performance of
this play which had been rejected by
W. B. Yeats in 1917 as unsuitable for
the Abbey theatre

eyes an incipient artist as a schoolboy and student, lays stress on the
lighter side of his character. Through his predilection for anecdote and
funny incidents, he fashions a benign view of Joyce as anarchic and an
entertaining mischief-maker.[12] Byrne makes Joyce over in a different
way, presenting him as a dependent and needy younger friend who was
endowed with 'an immanent and abiding simplicity', but yet served as an
intellectual sparring partner.[13] Moreover, he exercises the right to correct
the record and reclaims experiences that Joyce had commandeered,
such as Byrne's conversation with the Dean of Studies while he was
lighting the fire in the Physics Theatre that furnished material for the
well-known encounter in chapter 5 of *A Portrait*.[14] Overall, both Sheehy
and Byrne are at one in giving simultaneous importance to their own life
stories; their encounters with Joyce, though vital, are of episodic interest
only and widen out to accounts of their own development. To this
degree, they insinuate themselves as invisible presences into his story.

Curran's measured and layered reckoning with Joyce proceeds from
very different premises, which are at once aesthetic and forensic. He
registers his presence in far more oblique but nonetheless binding ways.
It is telling that he begins his preface with a vignette of Sarah Purser and
himself having a late-night conversation on the steps of Mespil House
in which they lament the way in which Dublin has been misrepresented.
This carefully chosen opening moment is redolent of everyday life
in Dublin, but also bears an artistic aspect. It echoes the scene in a
painting of Purser by Mary Swanzy, *Sarah Purser on the Steps of Mespil
House*, now held in the Dublin City Gallery, The Hugh Lane.[15] It hence
indirectly advertises Curran's interest in the visual and in the imbrication
of art and life. His design to represent Dublin anew, moreover, aligns
him with Joyce and allows him to cross-connect their artistic purposes.

Curran's text is composite, at once a memoir, an oblique
autobiography that decentres its subject, a series of meditations on
Dublin, a scholarly perusal of an artist and his influences and a summation
of a lifelong devotion to reading and book collecting. However, a forensic
intent is also evident; more thoroughly than his fellow memoirists he even-

[12] See Sheehy, pp 30–41
[13] Byrne, p. 37
[14] Ibid., pp 35–7
[15] See http://emuseum.pointblank.
ie/online_catalogue/work-detail.
php?objectid=1949

handedly dissects Joyce's personality, draws out its conflicting aspects, and also identifies negative traits such as his 'persecution mania'.[16] Moreover, despite Joyce's general eschewal of bookish conversation, Curran draws on his knowledge as bibliophile and scholar of European literature to isolate his sources and influences, thereby supplying gaps in their exchanges and glossing the complex webs of allusion in Joyce's texts from both a readerly and writerly point of view.

Virginia Woolf explains that the isolation of 'moments of being' and 'scene making' are the chief methods she used to set about recording memories from her past.[17] Curran deploys similar techniques to build up his account of Joyce. The figure he paints for us is layered, scattered temporally, and made concrete primarily through impactful visual images. Thus, the insouciant young Joyce on Blacquiere Bridge in Phibsboro in 1904 or showing up for a rendezvous at the Bull Wall is memorably cross-connected with the older, more urbane artist encountered on the Pont des Arts in Paris in 1921. Significantly, Curran presents us with these Leitmotifs and uses them to knit separate chapters together, but does not attempt to present us with a finished or cohesive view of Joyce. Rather, Joyce is situated in liminal spaces and made part of the surrounding urban streetscapes. Crucially, Curran as Joyce's co-creator presses visual and imaginative tropes and devices into service as well as placing his writings in a ramifying web of intertextual allusions.

In his preface, Curran declares he has 'written memories but not memoirs'.[18] His text, in fact, partakes of both modes. Memoirs are customarily defined as works that are selective and apply a particular lens to a shared historical experience.[19] Curran's book meets these criteria, as it furnishes us with a particularly inflected, generational view of Dublin and Joyce by a lifelong friend and advocate and fellow aesthete and scholar. In this regard, it returns us to what is often cursorily dubbed 'Joyce's Dublin', but shows us aspects of it that deviate from those we glean from the writer's works, in particular the panorama it proposes of the intellectually ambitious generation that attended UCD from the late 1890s onwards and their learned and unabashedly bookish

"Lucia Joyce A Chaucer A.B.C. : Being a Hymn to the Holy Virgin in an English version by Geoffrey Chaucer from the French of Guillaume de Deguilleville; initial letters designed and illuminated by Lucia Joyce; preface by Louis Gillet. Paris: Obelisk Press, 1936. The Q lettrine from a copy of this rare book, privately published by Joyce, in the Curran/Laird collection, The volume features 23 initials created by Lucia Joyce". Curran-Laird Collection, UCD 39.R.9

[16] C. P. Curran, *JJR* (London: Oxford University Press, 1968), p. 80.
[17] Woolf, 'A Sketch of the Past', pp 70–2 and p. 142. On Woolf and autobiography, see Elizabeth Abel, 'Spaces of Time: Virginia Woolf's Life-Writing', in Maria DiBattista and Emily O. Wittmann (eds), *Modernism and Autobiography* (Cambridge, 2014), pp 55–68
[18] *JJR*, n.p.
[19] For a discussion of the memoir as form, see Jerome Boyd Maunsell, *Portraits from Life: Modernist Novelists and Autobiography* (Oxford, 2018), pp 1–9

and clashing political viewpoints. Curran's text also peddles memories, Woolfian moments of being, which are fleeting, impressionistic, never fully recuperable, and resist narrativisation. Overall, he presents a knowing, often contrarian, but ultimately open-ended view of Joyce and evenly intertwines in-depth analysis of his artistic sources, such as Samuel Ferguson, Henrik Ibsen and Gabriele D'Annunzio, into an account of his everyday behaviour and dealings.

Curran avers with approval that Joyce was 'a serious artist'.[20] It is a seriousness that they both share and which lends weight and enduring power to this erudite and poised memoir. As we celebrate the centenary of *Ulysses* in 2022, this re-issue of *James Joyce Remembered* allows us to revisit, not only the shaping socio-historical and cultural contexts from which Joyce emerged, but also to appreciate anew the inter-animating aesthetic peculiar to his texts which allows the modernist author, scholars, friends and readers to work collaboratively and creatively together. To immerse oneself in Curran's text involves being returned to Dublin in the early decades of the twentieth century, but also reminds us of the revolutionary energy discerned in Joyce's works by those who knew the author as a young man and were his earliest readers. These initial contexts in Dublin were for Joyce perdurable and all-determining in ways we may never be able fully to fathom. But Curran's assembled essays help us to become time travellers and to appreciate the particular tenor and grain of the intellectual, political and artistic passions that animated a remarkable generation of students in Dublin, including Joyce, at the turn of the twentieth century.

Richard Ellmann pithily declared at the start of his biography that we are still learning to be Joyce's contemporaries.[21] In reading *James Joyce Remembered*, we encounter the informed, engaged and evolving reflections of someone with the unique vantage points of an unwavering and lifelong friend, a Dublin peer, and an early and astute exegete of Joyce, the man and his works. C. P. Curran's scrupulously reconstructed and contestatory memories, passionate advocacy and learned interpretations show us how we can carry forward the work of reading Joyce into the future and continue the process of becoming his contemporaries.

[20] *JJR*, p. 85
[21] Ellmann, p. 3

Annex

The Constantine Curran and Helen Laird Collection at University College Dublin's James Joyce Library

Eugene Roche and Evelyn Flanagan

Constantine Peter Curran first met James Augustine Joyce in 1899 in the First Arts class at University College, Stephen's Green, Dublin. It was that start of a friendship that would last up to Joyce's death in 1941. That the friendship endured is validated by an over 30-year exchange of letters and postcards and by gifts to Curran that varied from a signed first edition copy of *Ulysses* to a case of *Châteauneuf Clos San Patrice* wine.

On Curran's death in 1972, the bulk of the books, manuscripts, correspondence and photographs of Curran and his wife, Helen Laird, came to University College Dublin, and UCD Library Special Collections became the beneficiary of the Curran/Joyce long-distance relationship. A further three letters were acquired in 2021.

The collection is intimately connected to the city of Dublin where the Currans were part of a large social circle of writers, civic leaders and artists for more than 50 years. Curran's marriage in 1913 to Helen Laird ('Honor Lavelle') (1874–1957), an activist who was also an actress, costumier and science teacher, widened the circle to include many from the Dublin theatre world. In a letter to Curran written in November 1922, Padraic Colum signs off with the valedictory 'please remember me to all the Wednesday night folk' a reference to the Currans' regular Wednesday evening *soirées* that were attended by, among many others, Colum, Æ and Stephen McKenna.[1]

Among Curran's material in UCD Library involving James Joyce and his family are letters, photographs, manuscripts and books. The letters are

[1] Curran–Laird Collection, Special Collections, The James Joyce Library, University College, Dublin, CUR L 200

a mixture of intimate family matters including the health of his daughter, Lucia Joyce, and the funeral of his father, but also issues dealing with Joyce's writings and research on Dublin geography, history and its singular 'characters'.

The letters are not without import and shed much light on Joyce's writing. In July of 1904 Joyce mentions having finished the 'awful chapter' and says 'I am writing a series of epicleti... I call the series 'Dubliners'.[2] In a very significant exchange in 1933, Joyce wrote to Curran of 'two trying years' and the overturning of the *Ulysses* ban in the United States.[3]

From the letters acquired in 2021 a note from Joyce to Curran in August 1904 speaks of his 'double trouble, mental and material'.[4] His mental anxiety possibly relates to his developing relationship with Nora Barnacle; the material problem almost certainly refers to Joyce's usual lack of funds. Moving to literary matters, a later letter of this batch, dated March 1917, tells of the almost universal rejection of *Exiles* and also Joyce's wildly inaccurate prediction that he would finish *Ulysses* in 1918.

There are letters from Joyce's brother, Stanislaus, and Lucia Joyce, as well as members of the Joyce circle including Harriet Weaver, Sylvia Beach and Paul Léon. The list of other correspondents in the collection form a 'who's who' of the Irish literary scene: Padraic and Mary Colum, the Butler Yeats family (William, Jack, John and Susan), James Stephens, Lord Dunsany, Lennox Robinson, Tom Kettle, Daniel Corkery, Seán O'Faolain and Seumas O'Sullivan. One letter from Æ in which the letter's composer discusses his book *The Avatars* includes a wonderful ink and crayon drawing at the head of the letter.[5] The letters from Jack Yeats to Helen and Conn Curran, a number of which include sketches, span four decades and reveal a close friendship. In a letter from Padraic Colum addressed to Helen Laird, costumes designed by Æ and made by Helen Laird are discussed, as is his proposed visit to Maud Gonne and William Butler Yeats. These letters reveal the literary network of early twentieth-century Dublin within which the Currans moved. The 2021 additions bring the total count of letters in the collection to 412.

[2] Ibid., CUR L 178
[3] Ibid., CUR L 184
[4] Ibid., CUR L 410
[5] Ibid., CUR L 30

Curran was a keen photographer and fan of photography as evidenced by the approximately 70 examples of his work in the collection. Among the Joyce photos is the famous 'Glasshouse' image taken in Curran's family garden. The photo of Joyce's graduation class at University College in 1902 was set up by Curran, who appears in the front row, but the camera shutter was activated by a passing college porter. Lesser-known images would include a portrait of Joyce in a sailor-suit aged six and a print of the Belvedere College Solidarity ca. 1898 with Joyce as prefect. Joyce's brief interlude as a cinema manager in 1909 is reflected in the Volta cinema photo. Curran's original glass negatives of the Joycean photographs, including the 'Glasshouse', 'Sailor Suit' and the two graduation images, are also held.

The manuscripts, 38 in number, form a diverse sub-collection with transcriptions in Joyce's hand of two poems from *Chamber Music*. Manuscript number 6 is Curran's working notes for the original edition of *James Joyce Remembered*. This part of the Curran–Laird Collection also includes manuscript poems by P. H. Pearse and poems by Padraic Colum, including a draft of *Images of Departure* from 1961 and drafts of several essays and poems by Æ. One manuscript is the draft of a speech by Tom Kettle entitled 'The Royal University, a scene and some explanatory notes'. It also includes the minutes of the meetings of the Catholic Graduate Association, of which Curran was a member, dating from 1904 to 1907. The enduring friendship with Jack B. Yeats is demonstrated here too with a letter by Mary Cottenham Yeats, sent to the Currans by Jack B. Yeats in memory of his late wife.

Joyce looms again in the book collection, which includes eight titles owned by him when at University College. Most are signed and dated, and include works by Ibsen, Hauptmann and Gabriele d'Annunzio. Curran's friendship with Joyce is reflected in the numerous editions of Joyce's works contained therein including a copy of *Ulysses*, number 309, inscribed to Curran from Joyce. All of Joyce's own published works from *The Day of the Rabblement* (1901) onwards are represented in first editions and usually with the author's signature. Rare editions would include *Pomes Penyeach* (1932) with initial letters designed and illuminated by Lucia Joyce and two excerpts from *Work in Progress: Two Tales of Shem and Shaun* (1932) and *The Mime of Mick, Nick and the Maggies* (1934).

Many of Joyce's works were originally serialised in magazines and issues of the *Irish Homestead (Dubliners), The Little Review (Ulysses)* and *Transition /Le Navire d'Argent (Finnegans Wake)*; some with author's annotations, form part of the collection.

Like the correspondence, the full book collection is a reflection of the literary world of Dublin in the early 1900s of which Conn Curran and Helen Laird were part. It contains first editions (many signed) from the Irish revival period. This includes works by W. B. Yeats, George Russell, Padraic and Mary Colum, James Stephens, Douglas Hyde, Thomas MacDonagh, J. M. Synge, Lady Gregory, Eva Gore Booth, Dora Sigerson, Maud Gonne, Ella Young, as well as many other figures in early-to-mid-twentieth century Irish writing. The provenance of many of these books is clear from the presence of one of two Curran bookplates, designed for Curran by Jack B. Yeats in the early 1940s.

In addition, there is a marvellous collection of Dun Emer and Cuala press imprints, some with the original receipts enclosed, and a set of both series one and series two of the *Cuala Press Broadsides*, a very successful production that involved the efforts of the whole Yeats family. There are also very significant collections of Dublin theatre programmes and playbills. These aspects of the collection are, perhaps, a reflection of Helen Laird's work in the Abbey Theatre, as well as Curran's theatre criticism for the *Irish Statesman*. Conn Curran's links to those involved in the political upheaval of the early twentieth century, his role as registrar of the High Court and his work as a political commentator are represented by the large collection of ephemera relating to the revolutionary period. This includes a set of '1916 Postcards' showing Dublin in the immediate aftermath of the Easter Rising, souvenir albums of the rising and the Civil War, and a vast array of propaganda leaflets relating to the War of Independence and the Civil War.

In its full scale, the printed collection, including periodicals, pamphlets and ephemera, numbers in excess of 1500 items.

UCD is justifiably proud of the Curran–Laird Collection, not only because of its relevance to the history of UCD itself and its association with so many of its distinguished graduates; but also, because, with its many treasures, it is relevant to the study of so much of the literature and arts in Ireland during the first part of the twentieth century.

Letter from James Joyce to C. P. Curran (July 1904). First use of 'epicleti', Joyce's word for the stories that would form Dubliners (published as a collection in 1914) . "I call the series Dubliners to betray the soul of that hemiplegia or paralysis which many consider a city" Curran would not have wholly agreed with Joyce's estimation of Dublin. Curran-Laird Collection, UCD. CUR L 178

Frank J. Fay
Marie nic Shiubhlaigh
George Roberts.
Honor Lavelle
P. Mac Shiubhlaigh
Maire nic Shiubhlaigh
Dudley Digges

Geo. Russell

M. Gwendolin

Mary Price

Augusta Gregory

← On 27th December 1925, the Abbey Theatre, to celebrate the theatre's twenty-first birthday, held a special performance featuring one-act plays by W. B. Yeats, J.M. Synge and Lady Gregory. This anniversary programme is signed by members of the cast and Abbey associates. Helen Laird signed under her stage name 'Honor Lavelle'. Curran-Laird Collection, UCD. 1.I.1/28

Letter, dated 17 October 1933, with
→ ink and crayon drawing, to 'Con' Curran from Æ (George William Russell). Poet, painter, editor, novelist and mystic, Æ met Curran through Helen Laird, Curran's wife, and would remain friends with him until Æ's death in 1935. Correspondence from the collection shows that Curran was involved in the administration of Æ's estate. Curran-Laird Collection, UCD. CUR L 30

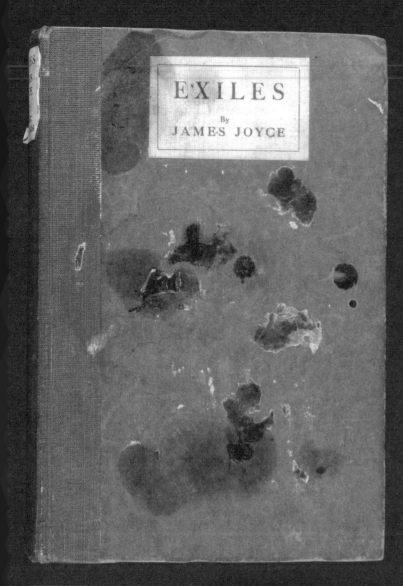

Cover of John Stanislaus Joyce's well worn copy of Exiles, with the original address label. It's appearance would indicate uses other than reading. Curran did much to help James Joyce during his father's fatal illness and after his death in December 1931. Curran-Laird Collection, UCD. 39.K.12

Henrik Ibsen was a major influence on the young James Joyce. Joyce's published review of Ibsen's 'When We Dead awaken' in 1900 elicited a letter of thanks from the playwright – much to Joyce's delight. Joyce's own copy of Ibsen's Little Eyolf. Signed and dated '1900' by Joyce. Curran-Laird Collection, UCD. (SR)

AVENUE EDITION

Little Eyolf

Jas Joyce

–1900–

A PLAY IN THREE ACTS

BY

HENRIK IBSEN

LONDON

WILLIAM HEINEMANN

1897

One Shilling and Sixpence.

First publication of James Joyce's story 'Eveline' in The Irish Homestead (September 10, 1904). Signed, 'Stephen Dædalus', a revised version of the story would later be included in Dubliners (1914). The Irish Homestead was a weekly journal promoting Irish agriculture and industry and was edited by Æ (George Russell) from 1905 onwards. Curran-Laird Collection, UCD. 1.L5/1-4

Tom Kettle helped found the Cui
Bono Club at University College in
1904. The club was a discussion
forum for recent graduates

(Standing) Vincent Clarke, Felix
Hackett (later Professor of Physics,
UCD), Tom Kettle (Professor of
National Economics, UCD, 1907.
Elected Member of Parliament (MP)
for East Tyrone in 1906. Killed in
action, Western Front, September 1916)

(Sitting) William Dawson, J. M.
O'Sullivan (later a member of the Dáil
(TD) and Minister for Education from
1926 to 1932. Hugh Kennedy (Chief
Justice of Ireland from 1924 to 1936)
, Charles McGarry, James Murnaghan
(Professor of Jurisprudence at UCD,
1911-1924. Appointed judge of the
Supreme Court in 1925). Constantine
Curran. Curran-Laird Collection,
UCD. CUR P 46

ACKNOWLEDGEMENTS

This book is the fruit of a remarkable virtual collaboration during the Covid days of 2020-21. My first thanks go to all the UCD colleagues who created this book, Zooming month after month with a newcomer in their midst. Your sense of intellectual adventure — intrepid and generous. Special thanks to Margaret Kelleher for imagining this group at the outset, and what we could do together; Hugh Campbell for his thoughtful way of seeing, and for bringing the next generation of architects on board, the plattenbau studio, Jennifer O'Donnell and Jonathan Janssens. Anne Fogarty gave her Joycean wisdom, and linked us to Alice Ryan whose research and editorial work was fundamental to giving the book its new shape. Evelyn Flanagan and Eugene Roche are committed representatives of the riches of Special Collections and fielded every inquiry with aplomb. Diarmaid Ferriter connected his work on the Civil War to the book.

Noelle Moran and Conor Graham have been canny stewards of this book from start to finish. I cannot imagine it without them and the UCD Press team, including Ryan. Daniel Morehead saw the heart of the book, and knew how to give it a new beat with his design. Colum O Riordan, Edward McParland, and Christine Casey have shared some of the riches of Dublin's architectural history. UCD's Research Council, and Duke University's Dean of Humanities, William A. Johnson, Vice-Dean for Faculty, Kevin Moore, and Chair of Romance Studies, Martin Eisner, gave invaluable support: they ensured the book would happen — across the international date line.

Maureen Murphy, Stateside, was an irreplaceable ally for this project, ever ready with another lead or tip. The McDowells, Michael, Antony, Nell, Louise, and Moore have welcomed me back to Dublin over years, and offered introductions, photographs, and confabs galore. Chris Krueger was my ace camera man. In the final stretch, Ann Rigney, Alice Kaplan, and Martha Stancill were there with their sharp eyes and sensitivity to the challenges of telling family history in my own voice.

This book is sent off in the spirit of my three "Es", who observed much, talked about what they saw, and then went to work.

INDEX

Hooper, John 65
Huneker, James Gibbon 108
Huysmans, Joris-Karl 29–30, 115–16
Hyde, Douglas vii, 17, 68, 200

Ibsen, Henrik viii, 3, 9, 12, 17, 30–1, 39, 76, 81–2, 107–8, 117–20, 196, 199
    Brand 25, 30
    Catilina 65–6
    John Gabriel Borkman 120
    Little Eyolf **205**
    The Master Builder 30
    Peer Gynt 30, 118
Ingram, John Kells 40
Irish Bulletin 156
Irish Civil War 165, 167, 179, 200
Irish Free State 165, 183
Irish Homestead 72–3, 78–9, 200, **207**
Irish Literary Theatre 9–10, 17–18, 31
Irish Monthly 3
Irish National Theatre Society 132, 181
Irish Parliamentary Party (IPP) 158–9, 161
Irish Republican Army (IRA) 156, 165–6
Irish Self-Determination League 156
Irish Statesman 200
Irish Times v, 145
Irish Volunteers 157
Irish War of Independence 153, 155–7, 161, 164, 179, 181–3, 200

Jacobsen, Jens Peter 18, 117–18
Jacopone da Todi 29, 87
James, Henry 31, 53–4, 110–12
    Portrait of a Lady 53
Jerrold, Douglas 31
Joachim di Flora 29
Johnson, Lionel 14, 18
Jolas, Eugène 90, 103